# Sex Roles in Literature

Longman English and Humanities Series
Series Editor: Lee A. Jacobus, University of
Connecticut, Storrs

# Sex Roles in
# Literature

Edited by

## Mary Beth Pringle

and

## Anne Stericker,

both of

*Wright State University*

## LONGMAN

NEW YORK AND LONDON

SEX ROLES IN LITERATURE

Longman Inc., New York
Associated companies, branches, and representatives
throughout the world.

Developmental Editor: Gordon T. R. Anderson
Interior Design: Pencils Portfolio Inc.
Cover Design: Dan Serrano
Manufacturing and Production Supervisor: Kris Becker
Composition: A & S Graphics
Printing and Binding: Fairfield Graphics

Manufactured in the United States of America

Library of Congress Cataloging in Publication Data
Main entry under title:

Sex Roles in Literature.

   (English and humanities series)
   1. Sex role—Fiction.   2. Sex role—Addresses,
essays, lectures.   I. Pringle, Mary Beth, 1943—
II. Stericker, Anne, 1944—   III. Series.
PN6071.S416S4        810'.8'0353        78-26710
ISBN 0-582-28103-2

9 8 7 6 5 4 3 2 1

We dedicate this book with love to our mothers,
Lucile Roxana Drake Pringle and Elinor
Crook Stericker, two people who gave us
choices.

# Contents

# Preface

The idea for this book arose from countless teaching and learning frustrations. In our university work, we frequently needed interdisciplinary material that would cast multiple lights on instructional topics, particularly on sex-role studies. One of the authors had been teaching courses in women's studies dealing with sex-role depictions in literature. Her students often came to the same conclusion: sex-role depictions are an important consideration in literary studies, and any thorough exploration of sex roles in literature is difficult without a scientific base of research evidence. Time and again, classes discovered that, across cultures and centuries, literature records the way in which people see themselves and others. As fiction depicts interactions between female and male characters, it presents the characters relating to one another in terms of gender. And when characters interact with others of their sex, they demonstrate how people feel they should behave when they are not with the opposite sex. Without systematic access to psychological studies on sex roles, the women's studies classes were often left with puzzling questions about the depiction of both sexes in the literature.

The second author was experiencing a related problem while teaching courses in the psychology of sex roles. Her classes examined research studies on sex roles, and students offered examples from their own lives to illustrate points in the findings. While the experiences that students shared in class sometimes illustrated published research, vivid well-written examples would have been especially useful in clarifying important concepts. Fiction sometimes can provide the epiphany that student accounts of personal moments cannot always communicate to the class.

From our common need grew the decision to create a book that would gather and systematize both empirical findings and literary and popular pieces about sex roles. Both our disciplines would be enriched. Several people have felt as we did and have helped in our book's preparation. We would like to thank them here.

Janine Plassard suggested many short stories that fit our book's theme. Leanne Smith provided superb organizational assistance and typing skills. We also thank Carol Chandler and Eileen Sestito for typing materials for the book. Robert Correale gave us administrative support and Nievis Leon secretarial help. A grant from the College of Liberal Arts Research Committee and its chairperson, Dean Eugene B. Cantelupe, was put to good use. The editorial guidance of Gordon Anderson and his assistant, Janet

Polster, is acknowledged with thanks. We appreciate the thorough copy-editing done by Irene Glynn and Dorothy Dean. Zachary Drake Spraggins helped as much as a nine-year-old could. Finally, Harvey Alan Siegal served as benchmark and beacon. His gentle strength and assertive tenderness set an example of freedom from rigid sex roles that nothing in literature or the popular press could possibly match.

# Introduction

Who am I? How have I become the person I am? We cannot answer either question adequately without considering gender. We know, of course, that being female or male affects personality development. What we don't know is to what extent or exactly how. As females, are we born submissive, or do we learn to behave that way? As males, are we intrinsically better at mathematical concepts than at verbal ones, or do we learn to excel in certain fields? At one time or another, many of us have asked ourselves such questions. And we have come up short of definite answers. Puzzling though it may be, scientists seem always to have invested more time and greater effort in learning about the natural world than they have in research that would lead to an understanding of human personality. When people did begin to study human personality a few decades ago, they studied men but seldom women. They typically made one of three assumptions: (1) males and females are alike (thus findings about males can be applied to females); (2) males and females are opposites (females are males in mirror image); or (3) females are incompletely developed males (and therefore would not provide the best examples of human personality).

More recently, however, the feminist movement pushed many of us to reexamine these assumptions and explore more systematically the effects of gender—both biological and learned—on personality development and human behavior. Feminists began to question why women generally were accorded fewer rights than men, why women were seen as less competent, less emotionally stable, and less rational than their male counterparts. Once the issues were brought to public attention, psychologists and investigators practicing other disciplines attempted to explore them and respond to the questions raised. Although some answers still elude us, some have come easily, and we are close to providing others.

Most investigators today agree that learning accounts for far more of the behavioral differences between women and men than do inherited biological factors. As very young children, we discover we are male or female, and thereafter we try to conduct ourselves as society tells us people of our sex should. Parents, teachers, guides, and friends, by their instruction and example, deepen our conviction that we should act in specific gender-related ways. This single fact—that we are taught so much of how to be women and men—is one important theme of our book.

Fiction, research articles, and material from popular culture all make important contributions to the understanding of sex roles. Fiction bestows on us a common personal history; we *become* the characters we read about and can make sense of their ordeals as if they were our own. Research articles provide us with scientific insights into the behavior of real people and fictional characters alike. Our popular culture daily bombards us with dogmatic definitions of acceptable behavior. Fiction addresses the personal and the specific, while research and popular culture treat issues in a more general way. The stories, the articles, and the cartoons in this book require equally close attention; all should help you recall your own sex-role education from years ago.

# Acknowledgments

"Petrified Man" by Eudora Welty. Copyright 1939, 1967 by Eudora Welty. Reprinted from her volume *A Curtain of Green and Other Stories* by permission of Harcourt Brace Jovanovich, Inc.

"Feminine Dependency" from *Fascinating Womanhood* by Helen Andelin. Copyright © 1963 by Helen B. Andelin. Reprinted by permission of Pacific Press Santa Barbara.

"The Fantasy of Dirt" by Lawrence S. Kubie. From *The Psychoanalytic Quarterly*, volume 6, pp. 388–425, copyright 1937 by *The Psychoanalytic Quarterly*. Reprinted by permission of the author and the publisher.

"Home" by James Thurber. Copr. © 1942 James Thurber. Copr. © 1970 Helen W. Thurber and Rosemary T. Sauers. From *Men, Women and Dogs*, published by Harcourt Brace Jovanovich, Inc. Originally printed in *The New Yorker*. Reprinted by permission of Helen W. Thurber.

"The Flight" by John Steinbeck. From *The Long Valley* by John Steinbeck. Copyright 1938 © renewed 1966 by John Steinbeck. All rights reserved. Reprinted by Permission of Viking Penguin, Inc.

"A Change of Air" by Ivan Gold. Copyright © 1963 by Ivan Gold. Originally published in *New World Writing* #4. Reprinted by permission of the author.

"Sorrow Acre" by Isak Dinesen. Copyright 1942 by Random House, Inc. and renewed 1970 by Johan Philip Thomas Ingerslev. Reprinted from *Winter's Tales*, by Isak Dinesen, by permission of Random House, Inc. and the Rungstedlund Foundation.

"Who's in Charge?" from *The Total Man: The Way to Confidence and Fulfillment* by Dan Benson. Copyright © 1977 by Tyndale House Publishers. Reprinted by permission of the publisher.

"The Male Sex Role" by Robert Brannon. Robert Brannon, "The Male Sex Role" from David/Brannon, *The 49 Percent Majority: The Male Sex Role*, © 1976, Addison-Wesley, Reading, Massachusetts. Pp. 11–36. Reprinted with permission.

"Manish Boy" by McKinley Morganfield, Ellas McDaniel, and Melvin London. Copyright © 1955 by Arc Music Corporation, 110 E. 59th Street, New York, NY 10022. All rights reserved. Intl copyright secured. Reprinted by permission of Arc Music.

"A Worn Path" by Eudora Welty. Copyright 1941, 1969 by Eudora Welty. Reprinted from her volume *A Curtain of Green and Other Stories* by permission of Harcourt Brace Jovanovich, Inc.

# PART I

# Development of Sex-Role Attitudes

It sometimes seems that very young children live in a world of exploration, discovery, and play. Yet we know that important and complex learning takes place in the first years of life, including learning how to be a girl or a boy. By age two or three most children know which sex they are, and by four or five years of age they have a fairly clear idea of traditional sex-role behaviors. For example, the typical child of four is generally aware that the roles of police officer, soldier, and firefighter are "men's roles," whereas the roles of mother, nurse, and secretary are "women's roles." In fact, such promptly acquired and firmly established knowledge sometimes amazes parents, especially those who believe their own lives provide unstereotyped sex-role modeling for their children. The little girl who insists that "only men can be doctors" although her own mother is a physician is not so unusual as one might suppose. She simply illustrates that there are more socializing agents impinging on young children's lives than the parental figures alone. The earliest influences on a child's life are usually the parents, or the caretakers charged with raising the child. But beyond these may be included other children, books and play materials, television, magazines, school, and social institutions. Young children are also well aware of which personality traits each sex is supposed to possess: females are emotional, helpful, and afraid to be alone; boys are blunt, rambunctious, and good at arithmetic. Girls express their feelings, and boys do not.

What can psychological research tell us about how children learn to be female or male? One popular assumption maintains that parents treat sons and daughters differently and that the difference in treatment contributes importantly to gender differences in behavior later in life. It is claimed, for instance, that parents encourage aggressiveness and discourage passivity in their sons, whereas the reverse is true with daughters. According to this view, little Jimmy's tale of settling a feud with a playmate by soundly thrashing him causes Daddy to puff out his chest, smile, and say, "Yes, sir, that's my boy." Little Janie, on the other hand, is expected to avoid fighting; if ever a disagreement should lead to blows, Mommy and Daddy react with disapproval and offer advice on how to preserve the peace through diplomacy, compromise, and, if necessary, passive retreat.

Unfortunately, research findings have not proved cooperative in illustrating this presumed difference in treatment of daughters and sons. To date the evidence is not clear, either from direct observation or from interviews with parents, that parents automatically reward aggressive behavior in sons and punish it in daughters. Fully half the studies that two psychologists, Maccoby and Jacklin, reviewed on this topic found no difference in the way parents respond to the aggressiveness in sons as opposed to daughters.[1] According to the other half, parents are somewhat more likely to punish aggressiveness in sons! In fact, one of the few consistent findings in child-rearing studies generally is that boys more frequently receive physical punishment for misbehavior than do girls.

Psychologists are beginning to view the socialization process boys go through in learning to be males as a good deal more restrictive and stressful than the process girls go through in learning to be females. For one thing, boys have few adult males to pattern themselves after. Many fathers work during the day and see their children only in the evenings and on weekends. Even in households where both parents have paid jobs, it is often the mother who spends more time with the children. In elementary schools, where most teachers are women, boys encounter few adult examples of how males are to behave and feel. Lacking a clear idea of what is required to be masculine, boys cling to one precept: avoid anything feminine. Ruth Hartley, another psychologist, describes this dilemma as socialization of boys by "prohibition" rather than "prescription."[2]

The prohibition comes from parents as well as from a boy's immediate conclusions drawn from his own scant data. Parents are far more concerned over cross-sex behavior or interests in their sons than in their daughters. Janie's interest in chemistry sets and baseball meets with affectionate good humor and even approval in parents, whereas Jimmy's eagerness to take dancing lessons or play with dolls may prompt his mother

---

1. E. E. Maccoby and C. N. Jacklin, *The Psychology of Sex Differences* (Stanford, Calif.: Stanford University Press, 1974).

2. Ruth Hartley, "Sex-Role Pressures and the Socialization of the Male," *Psychological Reports* 5 (1959): 457–68.

and father to take him to a psychologist. Thus, it seems that the range of behaviors permitted to boys is narrower than that for girls.

One way in which most parents clearly encourage sex-typed behavior in their children is by buying them "sex-appropriate" toys. Although quantitative research is unavailable, it seems obvious that parents buy more trucks and trains for their sons and more dolls and cooking stoves for their daughters. What we do not know is whether parents give toys that their children already prefer and ask for, or whether parents' selections influence their children's developing preferences.

Although studies of parents' treatment of girls and boys have yielded somewhat confusing results, school studies show clearer trends. They are beginning to indicate that teachers, unwittingly, encourage aggressive behavior in boys and dependent behavior in girls.[3] When boys are aggressive, teachers scold them more frequently and loudly. When girls misbehave, teachers are much more likely either to ignore the behavior or reprimand them softly and privately. By publicly drawing the class's attention to the boy's bad behavior, teachers reinforce the very action they wish to stop. When teachers ignore or react quietly to classroom disruptions, they practically disappear.

But teachers are not the sole influence on children's sex-role behavior in the classroom, as anyone who has ever read a few children's books can tell you. Little boy main characters outnumber little girl main characters by more than three to one in children's books. Even stories with animals as main characters are identified as "he" twice as often as "she."[4] Not only do girls figure much less frequently than do boys in the books children read today, but when they are portrayed, girls appear in a much less favorable light than boys. In the typical story, boys do exciting, interesting, imaginative things; girls watch, help, and admire the adventurous boys. Adult males are depicted in a variety of roles and occupations, while adult females are most often limited to such roles as housewife and mother. Regardless of their age, girls cook and clean and do helpful things for their brothers and fathers, fulfilling the traditional feminine role of passivity, dependency, and service. Boys climb trees, dig for treasure, track down criminals, play active physical games, and in general reflect the masculine stereotype of activity, independence, and competence.

Children apparently learn as much (or more) about sex roles by watching television as they do from reading books and being in the classroom.

3. L. A. Serbin, K. D. O'Leary, R. N. Kent, and I. J. Tonick, "A Comparison of Teacher Response to the Pre-Academic and Problem Behavior of Boys and Girls," *Child Development* 44 (1973): 796–804.

4. National Organization for Women Task Force of the Central New Jersey Chapter. *Dick and Jane as Victims: Sex Stereotyping in Children's Readers* (Princeton, N.J., 1972).

Research has shown that children who spend a great deal of time watching television acquire more strongly traditional sex-role attitudes than do children who watch less television.[5] This is not hard to understand when one surveys the content of both adult and juvenile programming, and commercial advertisements. As with children's books, most females in television shows and commercials appear in romantic, sexual, or family roles. Males outnumber females in major roles by more than two to one. As in books, the behaviors of the sexes on television are markedly different. Men are active, aggressive, and constructive, and their actions are likely to be recognized and rewarded. Women tend to be more passive and deferential. Those discouraged by the one-dimensional portrayal of women on television may have been gratified to witness a few unstereotyped women's roles in recent years: the Bionic Woman, Isis, Wonder Woman, Police Woman. Sex stereotypes are not wholly overcome even in these programs, however, since the Bionic Woman and Isis both teach school in their typical daily lives, Wonder Woman works as a secretary, and Police Woman often enough must be rescued by her male colleagues. Women in television commercials generally continue to be shown as bungling halfwits, whose only concerns are shiny floors and white laundry.

As these examples clearly show, teachers, books, television programs and commercials, and other influences provide powerful images of women and men that add to and even counteract the sex-role attitudes taught by parents. A letter to the editor of a leading feminist magazine illustrates the dilemma parents sometimes feel as they try to raise their children in non-sexist fashion. The letter reads: "I have some good news and some bad news. First the good news: My young daughter, aged two, has spent the morning playing with her Playskool workbench. Now the bad news: She's been using it as a stove."

The four fiction selections in Part I illustrate in different ways how children learn their proper sex roles. "The Baby Girl" by William Carlos Williams is taken from his novel *White Mule*. The story raises the question why through the centuries female infants have traditionally been less welcome than male infants. The story concerns the birth of a baby to a poor couple already burdened by several children. Her parents' reaction to her arrival illustrates a generally negative attitude toward female offspring. Considering how poor the parents are, one can perhaps understand why they feel as they do. They could reasonably expect a son to bring in more income to the family and, eventually, to carry on the family name. Besides,

5. T. Frueh and P. E. McGee, "Traditional Sex-Role Development and Amount of Time Spent Watching Television," *Developmental Psychology* 11 (1975): 109. Which is cause and which is effect here is not clear. It is possible that a heavy diet of television viewing contributes to traditional sex-role attitudes in children. Equally possible is that children with traditional attitudes actually prefer to watch more television than do children with less sex-typed attitudes.

another child, whether son or daughter, is an expensive undertaking. But how would this girl feel growing up and knowing she was not what her parents wanted? As she got older, she would realize that she was more of a liability than an asset to her family and in all likelihood would not keep or transmit the family name.

The second story, "Indian Camp," by Ernest Hemingway, portrays an important lesson about what it means to be a man. The story, told from the young boy's point of view, depicts a trip made by Nick Adams and his physician father to an Indian camp where an Indian woman is giving birth. Witnessing the birth is a very moving experience for Nick, who watches his father and the Indian husband attend the laboring woman. The lesson Nick learns from observing these two men is essentially the same: men do not show their feelings, no matter what the price may be.

"Her First Ball" by Katherine Mansfield illustrates the potent influence of social institutions and rituals on sex-role formation. In this case, the ball is the institution, serving well as a metaphor for the larger culture with its rigid sex roles. As Leila chats with her fat old dancing partner, she learns a depressing fact about her future, then promptly refuses to think further about it. Her first dance, the old man points out, is the beginning of her last. After the courtship rituals, the dancing, are finished, there will be little to dance about in Leila's future. Like the older women who sit watching on the stage, she will join the masses of women for whom youth, and therefore life, is over.

The story by Joan Didion, "When Did the Music Come This Way? Children Dear, Was It Yesterday?" concerns a memorable childhood event recalled by the narrator. That she remembers so clearly Christmas Day in 1945 confirms the importance of sex-role lessons learned in childhood. The memory is a glimpse of her Aunt Inez's marriage to a man named Ward. In a very short time the narrator gets an impression of what marriage is like. She sees Ward dominate and humiliate his wife. Now an adult, she reflects on that early experience and wonders whether all marriages, including her own, are like that one.

The research and popular culture pieces provide interesting commentary on the fictional selections. The research provides real-life examples of the important role that parents play in their children's developing sex-role identities. The excerpts from popular culture emphasize how subtle are the sex-role lessons that we learn and how resilient the stereotypes.

The psychologist authors of "The Eye of the Beholder: Parents' Views on Sex of Newborns" were curious to know whether parents of brand-new babies would describe their daughters and sons differently. Diapered boy and girl infants are usually indistinguishable either in physical characteristics or in behavior, as Jeffrey Rubin, Frank Provenzanzo, and Zella Luria determined objectively. Then they interviewed the parents, who were by no means in agreement. Although the parents' reactions are more positive than those in Williams' "The Baby Girl," both selections show us how early and how strongly parents react to a child solely in terms of gender.

In describing an unusual true case history, "Rearing of a Sex-Reassigned Normal Male Infant After Traumatic Loss of the Penis" takes scientific note of a virtually universal assumption concerning sexual identity: your sense of yourself as a male or female is determined first and foremost by the fact that you were born male or female, with the anatomical equipment distinctive to that sex. Nevertheless, John Money and Anke Ehrhardt here present fascinating evidence that biological sex is not nearly so powerful in this respect as is the gender "assigned" the child by the parents.

"Hats, Hats, and Hats" and "Boys Like to Play" are stories from an elementary school reader called Come With Me. The book was published in 1960 and shows girls doing "girlish" things and boys doing "boyish" things. In "Hats" for example, the girls are engaged in quiet play that involves primping and costuming themselves, both stereotypically feminine pastimes. At first the boys are excluded, but when a crisis develops, they are called to the rescue. "Boys Like to Play," shows boys about to play baseball, an active sport. The boys are depicted as energetic, responsible, and assertive. This careful separation in textbooks of boys' and girls' activities used to be much commoner than it is today. Over the past twenty years, the conviction has grown that children's behavior is limited by such narrow portrayals of male and female roles.

# Fiction

## THE BABY GIRL

### William Carlos Williams

She entered, as Venus from the sea, dripping. The air enclosed her, she felt it all over her, touching, waking her. If Venus did not cry aloud after release from the pressures of that seawomb, feeling the new and lighter flood springing in her chest, flinging out her arms—this one did. Screwing up her tiny smeared face, she let out three convulsive yells—and lay still.

Stop that crying, said Mrs. D, you should be glad to get outa that hole.

It's a girl. What? A girl. But I wanted a boy. Look again. It's a girl, Mam. No! Take it away. I don't want it. All this trouble for another girl.

What is it! said Joe, at the door. A little girl. That's too bad. Is it all right? Yes, a bit small though. That's all right then. Don't you think you'd better cover it up so it won't catch cold? Ah, you go on out of here now and let me manage, said Mrs. D. This appealed to him as proper so he went. Are you all right, Mama? Oh, leave me alone, what kind of a man are you? As he didn't exactly know what she meant he thought it better to close the door. So he did.

In prehistoric ooze it lay while Mrs. D wound the white twine about its pale blue stem with kindly clumsy knuckles and blunt fingers with black nails and with the wiped-off scissors from the cord at her waist cut it—while it was twisting and flinging up its toes and fingers into the way—free.

Alone it lay upon its back on the bed, sagging down in the middle, by the smeared triple mountain of its mother's disgusted thighs and toppled belly.

The clotted rags were gathered. Struggling blindly against the squeezing touches of the puffing Mrs. D, it was lifted into a nice woolen blanket and covered. It sucked its under lip and then let out two more yells.

Ah, the little love. Hear it, Mam, it's trying to talk.

La, la, la, la, la, la, la! it said with its tongue—in the black softness of the new pressures—and jerking up its hand, shoved its right thumb into its eye, starting with surprise and pain and yelling and rolling in its new agony. But finding the thumb again at random it sobbingly subsided into stillness.

Mrs. D lifted the cover and looked at it. It lay still. Her heart stopped. It's dead! She shook the . . .

With a violent start the little arms and legs flew up into a tightened knot, the face convulsed again—then as the nurse sighed, slowly the tautened limbs relaxed. It did not seem to breathe.

7

And now if you're all right I'll wash the baby. All right, said the new mother drowsily.

In that two ridges lap with wind cut off at the bend of the neck it lay, half dropping, regrasped—it was rubbed with warm oil that rested in a saucer on the stove while Mrs. D with her feet on the step of the oven rubbed and looked it all over, from the top of its head to the shiny soles of its little feet.

About five pounds is my guess. You poor little mite, to come into a world like this one. Roll over here and stop wriggling or you'll be on the floor. Open your legs now till I rub some of this oil in there. You'll open them glad enough one of these days—if you're not sorry for it. So, in all of them creases. How it sticks. It's like lard. I wonder what they have that on them for. It's a hard thing to be born a girl. There you are now. Soon you'll be in your little bed and I wish I was the same this minute.

She rubbed the oil under the arm pits and carefully round the scrawny folds of its little neck pushing the wobbly head back and front. In behind the ears there was still that white grease of pre-birth. The matted hair, larded to the head, on the brow it lay buttered heavily while the whole back was caked with it, a yellow-white curd.

In the folds of the groin, the crotch where the genitals all bulging and angry red seemed presages of some future growth, she rubbed the warm oil, carefully—for she was a good woman—and thoroughly, cleaning her fingers on her apron. She parted the little parts looking and wondering at their smallness and perfection and shaking her head forebodingly.

The baby lay back at ease with closed eyes—lolling about as it was, lifted by a leg, an arm, and turned.

Mrs. D looked at the toes, counted them, admired the little perfect nails—and then taking each little hand, clenched tight at her approach, she smoothed it out and carefully anointed its small folds.

Into the little sleeping face she stared. The nose was flattened and as-kew, the mouth was still, the slits of the eyes were swollen closed—it seemed.

You're a homely little runt, God pardon you, she said—rubbing the spot in the top of the head. Better to leave that—I've heard you'd kill them if you pressed on that too hard. They say a bad nurse will stop a baby crying by pressing there—a cruel thing to do.

She looked again where further back upon the head a soft round lump was sticking up like a jockey cap askew. That'll all go down, she said to herself wisely because it was not the first baby Mrs. D had tended, nor the fifth nor the tenth nor the twentieth even.

She got out the wash boiler and put warm water in it. In that she carefully laid the new-born child. It half floated, half asleep—opening its eyes a moment then closing them and resting on Mrs. D's left hand, spread out behind its neck.

She soaped it thoroughly. The father came into the kitchen where they were and asked her if she thought he could have a cup of coffee before he left for work—or should he go and get it at the corner. He shouldn't have asked her—suddenly it flashed upon his mind. It's getting close to six o'clock, he said. How is it? Is it all right?

He leaned to look. The little thing opened its eyes, blinked and closed them in the flare of the kerosene oil lamp close by in the gilded bracket on the wall. Then it smiled a crooked little smile—or so it seemed to him.

It's the light that hurts its eyes, he thought, and taking a dish towel he hung it on the cord that ran across the kitchen so as to cast a shadow on the baby's face.

Hold it, said Mrs. D, getting up to fill the kettle.

He held it gingerly in his two hands, looking curiously, shyly at that ancient little face of a baby. He sat down resting it on his knees, and covered its still wet body. That little female body. The baby rested. Squirming in the tender grip of his guarding hands, it sighed and opened its eyes wide.

He stared. The left eye was rolled deep in toward the nose; the other seemed to look straight at his own. There seemed to be a spot of blood upon it. He looked and a cold dread started through his arms. Cross eyed! Maybe blind. But as he looked—the eyes seemed straight. He was glad when Mrs. D relieved him—but he kept his peace. Somehow this bit of moving unwelcome life had won him to itself forever. It was so ugly and so lost.

The pains he had seemed to feel in his own body while the child was being born, now relieved—it seemed almost as if it had been he that had been the mother. It was his baby girl. That's a funny feeling, he thought.

He merely shook his head.

Coffee was cooking on the back of the stove. The room was hot. He went into the front room. He looked through the crack of the door into their bedroom where she lay. Then he sat on the edge of the disheveled sofa where, in a blanket, he had slept that night—and waited. He was a good waiter. Almost time to go to work.

Mrs. D got the cornstarch from a box in the pantry. She had to hunt for it among a disarray of pots and cooking things and made a mental note to put some order into the place before she left. Ah, these women with good husbands, they have no sense at all. They should thank God and get to work.

Now she took the baby once more on her lap, unwrapped it where it lay and powdered the shrivelling, gummy two inch stem of the gummy cord, fished a roll of Canton flannel from the basket at her feet and putting one end upon the little pad of cotton on the baby's middle wrapped the binder round it tightly, round and round, pinning the end in place across the back. The child was hard there as a board now—but did not wake.

She looked and saw a red spot grow upon the fabric. Tie it again. Once more she unwrapped the belly band. Out she took the stump of the cord and this time she wound it twenty times about with twine while the tiny creature heaved and vermiculated with joy at its relief from the too tight belly band.

Wrapping an end of cotton rag about her little finger, Mrs. D forced that in between the little lips and scrubbed those tender gums. The baby made a grimace and drew back from this assault, working its whole body to draw back.

Hold still, said Mrs. D, bruising the tiny mouth with sedulous care—until the mite began to cough and strain to vomit. She stopped at last.

Dried, diapered and dressed in elephantine clothes that hid it crinkily; stockinged, booted and capped, tied under the chin—now Mrs. D walked with her new creation from the sweaty kitchen into the double light of dawn and lamps, through the hallway to the front room where the father sat, to show him.

Where are you going? For a walk?, he said.

Look at it in its first clothes, she answered him.

Yes, he said, it looks fine. But he wondered why they put the cap and shoes on it.

Turning back again, Mrs. D held the baby in her left arm and with her right hand turned the knob and came once more into the smells of the birth chamber. There it was dark and the lamp burned low. The mother was asleep.

She put out the lamp, opened the inner shutters. There was a dim light in the room.

Waking with a start—What is it? the mother said. Where am I? Is it over? Is the baby here?

It is, said Mrs. D, and dressed and ready to be sucked. Are you flooding any?

Is it a boy? said the mother.

It's a girl, I told you before. You're half asleep.

Another girl. Agh, I don't want girls. Take it away and let me rest. God pardon you for saying that. Where is it? Let me see it, said the mother, sitting up so that her great breasts hung outside her undershirt. Lay down, said Mrs. D. I'm all right. I could get up and do a washing. Where is it?

She took the little thing and turned it around to look at it. Where is its face? Take off that cap. What are these shoes on for? She took them off with a jerk. You miserable scrawny little brat, she thought, and disgust and anger fought inside her chest, she was not one to cry—except in a fury.

The baby lay still, its mouth stinging from its scrub, its belly half strangled, its legs forced apart by the great diaper—and slept, grunting now and then.

Take it away and let me sleep. Look at your breasts, said Mrs. D. And with that they began to put the baby to the breast. It wouldn't wake.

The poor miserable thing, repeated the mother. This will fix it. It's its own mother's milk it needs to make a fine baby of it, said Mrs. D. Maybe it does, said the mother, but I don't believe it. You'll see, said Mrs. D.

As they forced the great nipple into its little mouth, the baby yawned. They waited. It slept again. They tried again. It squirmed its head away. Hold your breast back from its nose. They did.

Mrs. D squeezed the baby's cheeks together between her thumb and index finger. It drew back, opened its jaws and in they shoved the dripping nipple. The baby drew back. Then for a moment it sucked.

There she goes, said Mrs. D, and straightened up with a sigh, pressing her two hands against her hips and leaning back to ease the pain in her loins.

The mother stroked the silky hair, looked at the gently pulsing fontanelle, and holding her breast with the left hand to bring it to a point, straightened back upon the pillows and frowned.

The baby ceased to suck, squirming and twisting. The nipple lay idle in its mouth. It slept. Looking down, the mother noticed what had happened. It won't nurse, Mrs. D. Take it away. Mrs. D come here at once and take this thing, I'm in a dripping perspiration.

Mrs. D came. She insisted it should nurse. They tried. The baby waked with a start, gagging on the huge nipple. It pushed with its tongue. Mrs. D had it by the back of the neck pushing. She flattened out the nipple and pushed it in the mouth. Milk ran down the little throat, a watery kind of milk. The baby gagged purple and vomited.

Take it. Take it away. What's the matter with it? You're too rough with it.

If you'd hold it up properly, facing you and not away off at an angle as if—Mrs. D's professional pride was hurt. They tried again, earnestly, tense, uncomfortable, one cramped over where she sat with knees spread out, the other half kneeling, half on her elbows—till anger against the little rebellious spitting imp, anger and fatigue, overcame them.

Take it away, that's all, said the mother finally.

Reluctantly, red in the face, Mrs. D had no choice but to do what she was told. I'd like to spank it, she said, flicking its fingers with her own.

What! said the mother in such menacing tones that Mrs. D caught a fright and realized whom she was dealing with. She said no more.

But now, the baby began to rebel. First its face got red, its whole head suffused, it caught its breath and yelled in sobs and long shrill waves. It sobbed and forced its piercing little voice so small yet so disturbing in its penetrating puniness, mastering its whole surroundings till it seemed to madden them. It caught its breath and yelled in sobs and long shrill waves. It sobbed and squeezed its yell into their ears.

That's awful, said the mother, I can't have it in this room. I don't think it's any good. And she lay down upon her back exhausted.

Mrs. D with two red spots in her two cheeks and serious jaw and a headache took the yelling brat into the kitchen. Dose it up. What else?

She got the rancid castor oil and gave the baby some. It fought and spit. Letting it catch its breath, she fetched the fennel tea, already made upon the range, and sweetening it poured a portion into a bottle, sat down and rather roughly told the mite to take a drink. There, drat you. Sweet to unsweeten that unhappy belly. The baby sucked the fermentative warm stuff and liked it—and wet its diaper after.

Feeling the wet through her skirt and petticoat and drawers right on her thighs, Mrs. D leaped up and holding the thing out at arm's length, got fresh clothes and changed it.

Feeling the nice fresh diaper, cool and enticing, now the baby grew red all over. Its face swelled, suffused with color. Gripping its tiny strength together, it tightened its belly band even more.

The little devil, said Mrs. D, to wait till it's a new diaper on.

And with this final effort, the blessed little thing freed itself as best it could—and it did very well—of a quarter pound of tarrish, prenatal slime—some of which ran down one leg and got upon its stocking.

That's right, said Mrs. D.

# INDIAN CAMP

## Ernest Hemingway

At the lake shore there was another rowboat drawn up. The two Indians stood waiting.

Nick and his father got in the stern of the boat and the Indians shoved it off and one of them got in to row. Uncle George sat in the stern of the camp rowboat. The young Indian shoved the camp boat off and got in to row Uncle George.

The two boats started off in the dark. Nick heard the oar-locks of the other boat quite a way ahead of them in the mist. The Indians rowed with quick choppy strokes. Nick lay back with his father's arm around him. It was cold on the water. The Indian who was rowing them was working very hard, but the other boat moved further ahead in the mist all the time.

"Where are we going, Dad?" Nick asked.

"Over to the Indian camp. There is an Indian lady very sick."

"Oh," said Nick.

Across the bay they found the other boat beached. Uncle George was smoking a cigar in the dark. The young Indian pulled the boat way up the beach. Uncle George gave both the Indians cigars.

They walked up from the beach through a meadow that was soaking wet with dew, following the young Indian who carried a lantern. Then they went into the woods and followed a trail that led to the logging road that ran back into the hills. It was much lighter on the logging road as the timber was cut away on both sides. The young Indian stopped and blew out his lantern and they all walked on along the road.

They came around a bend and a dog came out barking. Ahead were the lights of the shanties where the Indian bark-peelers lived. More dogs rushed out at them. The two Indians sent them back to the shanties. In the shanty nearest the road there was a light in the window. An old woman stood in the doorway holding a lamp.

Inside on a wooden bunk lay a young Indian woman. She had been trying to have her baby for two days. All the old women in the camp had been helping her. The men had moved off up the road to sit in the dark and smoke out of range of the noise she made. She screamed just as Nick and the two Indians followed his father and Uncle George into the shanty. She lay in the lower bunk, very big under a quilt. Her head was turned to one side. In the upper bunk was her husband. He had cut his foot very badly with an ax three days before. He was smoking a pipe. The room smelled very bad.

Nick's father ordered some water to be put on the stove, and while it was heating he spoke to Nick.

"This lady is going to have a baby, Nick," he said.

"I know," said Nick.

"You don't know," said his father. "Listen to me. What she is going through is called being in labor. The baby wants to be born and she wants it to be born. All her muscles are trying to get the baby born. That is what is happening when she screams."

"I see," Nick said.

Just then the woman cried out.

"Oh, Daddy, can't you give her something to make her stop screaming?" asked Nick.

"No. I haven't any anaesthetic," his father said. "But her screams are not important. I don't hear them because they are not important."

The husband in the upper bunk rolled over against the wall.

The woman in the kitchen motioned to the doctor that the water was hot. Nick's father went into the kitchen and poured about half of the water out of the big kettle into a basin. Into the water left in the kettle he put several things he unwrapped from a handkerchief.

"Those must boil," he said, and began to scrub his hands in the basin of hot water with a cake of soap he had brought from the camp. Nick watched his father's hands scrubbing each other with the soap. While his father washed his hands very carefully and thoroughly, he talked.

"You see, Nick, babies are supposed to be born head first but sometimes they're not. When they're not they make a lot of trouble for everybody. Maybe I'll have to operate on this lady. We'll know in a little while."

When he was satisfied with his hands he went in and went to work.

"Pull back that quilt, will you, George?" he said. "I'd rather not touch it."

Later when he started to operate Uncle George and three Indian men held the woman still. She bit Uncle George on the arm and Uncle George said, "Damn squaw bitch!" and the young Indian who had rowed Uncle George over laughed at him. Nick held the basin for his father. It all took a long time.

His father picked the baby up and slapped it to make it breathe and handed it to the old woman.

"See, it's a boy, Nick," he said. "How do you like being an interne?"

Nick said, "All right." He was looking away so as not to see what his father was doing.

"There. That gets it," said his father and put something into the basin. Nick didn't look at it.

"Now," his father said, "there's some stitches to put in. You can watch this or not, Nick, just as you like. I'm going to sew up the incision I made."

Nick did not watch. His curiosity has been gone for a long time.

His father finished and stood up. Uncle George and the three Indian men stood up. Nick put the basin out in the kitchen.

Uncle George looked at his arm. The young Indian smiled reminiscently.

"I'll put some peroxide on that, George," the doctor said.

He bent over the Indian woman. She was quiet now and her eyes were closed. She looked very pale. She did not know what had become of the baby or anything.

"I'll be back in the morning," the doctor said, standing up. "The nurse should be here from St. Ignace by noon and she'll bring everything we need."

He was feeling exalted and talkative as football players are in the dressing room after a game.

"That's one for the medical journal, George," he said. "Doing a Caesarean with a jack-knife and sewing it up with nine-foot, tapered gut leaders."

Uncle George was standing against the wall, looking at his arm.

"Oh, you're a great man, all right," he said.

"Ought to have a look at the proud father. They're usually the worst sufferers in these little affairs," the doctor said. "I must say he took it all pretty quietly."

He pulled back the blanket from the Indian's head. His hand came away wet. He mounted on the edge of the lower bunk with the lamp in one hand and looked in. The Indian lay with his face toward the wall. His throat had been cut from ear to ear. The blood had flowed down into a pool where his body sagged the bunk. His head rested on his left arm. The open razor lay, edge up, in the blankets.

"Take Nick out of the shanty, George," the doctor said.

There was no need of that. Nick, standing in the door of the kitchen, had a good view of the upper bunk when his father, the lamp in one hand, tipped the Indian's head back.

It was just beginning to be daylight when they walked along the logging road back toward the lake.

"I'm terribly sorry I brought you along, Nickie," said his father, all his post-operative exhilaration gone. "It was an awful mess to put you through."

"Do ladies always have such a hard time having babies?" Nick asked.

"No, that was very, very exceptional."

"Why did he kill himself, Daddy?"

"I don't know, Nick. He couldn't stand things I guess."

"Do many men kill themselves, Daddy?"

"Not very many, Nick."

"Do many women?"

"Hardly ever."

"Don't they ever?"

"Oh, yes. They do sometimes."

"Daddy?"

"Yes."

"Where did Uncle George go?"

"He'll turn up all right."

"Is dying hard, Daddy?"

"No, I think it's pretty easy, Nick. It all depends."

They were seated in the boat, Nick in the stern, his father rowing. The sun was coming up over the hill. A bass jumped, making a circle in the water. Nick trailed his hand in the water. It felt warm in the sharp chill of the morning.

In the early morning on the lake sitting in the stern of the boat with his father rowing, he felt quite sure that he would never die.

# HER FIRST BALL

Katherine Mansfield

Exactly when the ball began Leila would have found it hard to say. Perhaps her first real partner was the cab. It did not matter that she shared the cab with the Sheridan girls and their brother. She sat back in her own little corner of it, and the bolster on which her hand rested felt like the sleeve of an unknown young man's dress suit; and away they bowled, past waltzing lamp-posts and houses and fences and trees.

"Have you really never been to a ball before, Leila? But, my child, how too weird—" cried the Sheridan girls.

"Our nearest neighbour was fifteen miles," said Leila softly, gently opening and shutting her fan.

Oh dear, how hard it was to be indifferent like the others! She tried not to smile too much; she tried not to care. But every single thing was so new and exciting. . . . Meg's tuberoses, Jose's long loop of amber, Laura's little dark head, pushing above her white fur like a flower through snow. She would remember for ever. It even gave her a pang to see her cousin Laurie throw away the wisps of tissue paper he pulled from the fastenings of his new gloves. She would like to have kept those wisps as a keepsake, as a remembrance. Laurie leaned forward and put his hand on Laura's knee.

"Look here, darling," he said. "The third and the ninth as usual. Twig?"

Oh, how marvellous to have a brother! In her excitement Leila felt that if there had been time, if it hadn't been impossible, she couldn't have helped crying because she was an only child, and no brother had ever said "Twig?" to her; no sister would ever say, as Meg said to Jose that moment, "I've never known your hair go up more successfully than it has to-night!"

But, of course, there was no time. They were at the drill hall already; there were cabs in front of them and cabs behind. The road was bright on either side with moving fan-like lights, and on the pavement gay couples seemed to float through the air; little satin shoes chased each other like birds.

"Hold on to me, Leila; you'll get lost," said Laurie.

"Come on, girls, let's make a dash for it," said Laurie.

Leila put two fingers on Laura's pink velvet cloak, and they were somehow lifted past the big golden lantern, carried along the passage, and pushed into the little room marked "Ladies." Here the crowd was so great there was hardly space to take off their things; the noise was deafening. Two benches on either side were stacked high with wraps. Two old women in white aprons ran up and down tossing fresh armfuls. And everybody was pressing forward trying to get at the little dressing-table and mirror at the far end.

A great quivering jet of gas lighted the ladies' room. It couldn't wait; it was dancing already. When the door opened again and there came a burst of tuning from the drill hall, it leaped almost to the ceiling.

Dark girls, fair girls were patting their hair, tying ribbons again, tucking handkerchiefs down the front of their bodices, smoothing marble-white gloves. And because they were all laughing it seemed to Leila that they were all lovely.

"Aren't there any invisible hair-pins?" cried a voice. "How most extraordinary! I can't see a single invisible hair-pin."

"Powder my back, there's a darling," cried some one else.

"But I must have a needle and cotton. I've torn simply miles and miles of the frill," wailed a third.

Then, "Pass them along, pass them along!" The straw basket of programmes was tossed from arm to arm. Darling little pink-and-silver programmes, with pink pencils and fluffy tassels. Leila's fingers shook as she took one out of the basket. She wanted to ask some one, "Am I meant to have one too?" but she had just time to read: "Waltz 3. *Two, Two in a Canoe.* Polka 4. *Making the Feathers Fly*," when Meg cried, "Ready, Leila?" and they pressed their way through the crush in the passage towards the big double doors of the drill hall.

Dancing had not begun yet, but the band had stopped tuning, and the noise was so great it seemed that when it did begin to play it would never be heard. Leila, pressing close to Meg, looking over Meg's shoulder, felt that even the little quivering coloured flags strung across the ceiling were talking. She quite forgot to be shy; she forgot how in the middle of dressing she had sat down on the bed with one shoe off and one shoe on and begged her mother to ring up her cousins and say she couldn't go after all. And the rush of longing she had had to be sitting on the veranda of their forsaken up-country home, listening to the baby owls crying "More pork" in the moonlight, was changed to a rush of joy so sweet that it was hard to bear alone. She clutched her fan, and, gazing at the gleaming, golden floor, the azaleas, the lanterns, the stage at one end with its red carpet and gilt chairs and the band in a corner, she thought breathlessly, "How heavenly; how simply heavenly!"

All the girls stood grouped together at one side of the doors, the men at the other, and the chaperones in dark dresses, smiling rather foolishly, walked with little careful steps over the polished floor towards the stage.

"This is my little country cousin Leila. Be nice to her. Find her partners; she's under my wing," said Meg, going up to one girl after another.

Strange faces smiled at Leila—sweetly, vaguely. Strange voices answered, "Of course, my dear." But Leila felt the girls didn't really see her. They were looking towards the men. Why didn't the men begin? What were they waiting for? There they stood, smoothing their gloves, patting their glossy hair and smiling among themselves. Then, quite suddenly, as if they had only just made up their minds that that was what they had to do, the men came gliding over the parquet. There was a joyful flutter among the girls. A tall, fair man flew up to Meg, seized her programme, scribbled something; Meg passed him on to Leila. "May I have the pleasure?" He ducked and smiled. There came a dark man wearing an eyeglass, then cousin Laurie with a friend, and Laura with a little freckled fellow whose tie was crooked. Then quite an old man—fat, with a big bald patch on his head—took her programme and murmured, "Let me see, let me see!" And he was a long time comparing his programme, which looked black with names, with hers. It seemed to give him so much trouble that Leila was ashamed. "Oh, please don't bother," she said eagerly. But instead of replying the fat man wrote something, glanced at her again. "Do I remember this bright little face?" he said softly. "Is it known to me of yore?" At that moment the band began playing; the fat man disappeared. He was tossed away on a great wave of music that came flying over the gleaming floor, breaking the groups up into couples, scattering them, sending them spinning. . . .

Leila had learned to dance at boarding school. Every Saturday afternoon the boarders were hurried off to a little corrugated iron mission hall where Miss Eccles (of London) held her "select" classes. But the difference between that dusty-smelling hall—with calico texts on the walls, the poor terrified little woman in a brown velvet toque with rabbit's ears thumping the cold piano, Miss Eccles poking the girls' feet with her long white wand—and this was so tremendous that Leila was sure if her partner didn't come and she had to listen to that marvellous music and to watch the others sliding, gliding over the golden floor, she would die at least, or faint, or lift her arms and fly out of one of those dark windows that showed the stars.

"Ours, I think—" Some one bowed, smiled, offered her his arm; she hadn't to die after all. Some one's hand pressed her waist and she floated away like a flower that is tossed into a pool.

"Quite a good floor, isn't it?" drawled a faint voice close to her ear.

"I think it's most beautifully slippery," said Leila.

"Pardon!" The faint voice sounded surprised. Leila said it again. And there was a tiny pause before the voice echoed, "Oh, quite!" and she was swung round again.

He steered so beautifully. That was the great difference between dancing with girls and men, Leila decided. Girls banged into each other, and stamped on each other's feet; the girl who was gentleman always clutched you so.

The azaleas were separate flowers no longer; they were pink and white flags streaming by.

"Were you at the Bells' last week?" the voice came again. It sounded tired. Leila wondered whether she ought to ask him if he would like to stop.

"No, this is my first dance," said she.

Her partner gave a little gasping laugh. "Oh, I say," he protested.

"Yes, it is really the first dance I've ever been to." Leila was most fervent. It was such a relief to be able to tell somebody. "You see, I've lived in the country all my life up until now. . . ."

At that moment the music stopped, and they went to sit on two chairs against the wall. Leila tucked her pink satin feet under and fanned herself, while she blissfully watched the other couples passing and disappearing through the swing doors.

"Enjoying yourself, Leila?" asked Jose, nodding her golden head.

Laura passed and gave her the faintest little wink; it made Leila wonder for a moment whether she was quite grown up after all. Certainly her partner did not say very much. He coughed, tucked his handkerchief away, pulled down his waistcoat, took a minute thread off his sleeve. But it didn't matter. Almost immediately the band started, and her second partner seemed to spring from the ceiling.

"Floor's not bad," said the new voice. Did one always begin with the floor? And then, "Were you at the Neaves' on Tuesday?" And again Leila explained. Perhaps it was a little strange that her partners were not more interested. For it was thrilling. Her first ball! She was only at the beginning of everything. It seemed to her that she had never known what the night was like before. Up till now it had been dark, silent, beautiful very often— oh, yes—but mournful somehow. Solemn. And now it would never be like that again—it had opened dazzling bright.

"Care for an ice?" said her partner. And they went through the swing doors, down the passage, to the supper room. Her cheeks burned, she was fearfully thirsty. How sweet the ices looked on little glass plates, and how cold the frosted spoon was, iced too! And when they came back to the hall there was the fat man waiting for her by the door. It gave her quite a shock again to see how old he was; he ought to have been on the stage with the fathers and mothers. And when Leila compared him with her other partners he looked shabby. His waistcoat was creased, there was a button off his gloves, his coat looked as if it was dusty with French chalk.

"Come along, little lady," said the fat man. He scarcely troubled to clasp her, and they moved away so gently, it was more like walking than dancing. But he said not a word about the floor. "Your first dance, isn't it?" he murmured.

"How *did* you know?"

"Ah," said the fat man, "that's what it is to be old!" He wheezed faintly as he steered her past an awkward couple. "You see, I've been doing this kind of thing for the last thirty years."

"Thirty years?" cried Leila. Twelve years before she was born!

"It hardly bears thinking about, does it?" said the fat man gloomily. Leila looked at his bald head, and she felt quite sorry for him.

"I think it's marvellous to be still going on," she said kindly.

"Kind little lady," said the fat man, and he pressed her a little closer, and hummed a bar of the waltz. "Of course," he said, "you can't hope to last anything like as long as that. No-o," said the fat man, "long before that you'll be sitting up there on the stage, looking on, in your nice black velvet. And these pretty arms will have turned into little short fat ones, and you'll beat time with such a different kind of fan—a black bony one." The fat man seemed to shudder. "And you'll smile away like the poor old dears up there, and point to your daughter, and tell the elderly lady next to you how some dreadful man tried to kiss her at the club ball. And your heart will ache, ache"—the fat man squeezed her closer still, as if he really was sorry for that poor heart—"because no one wants to kiss you now. And you'll say how unpleasant these polished floors are to walk on, how dangerous they are. Eh, Mademoiselle Twinkletoes?" said the fat man softly.

Leila gave a light little laugh, but she did not feel like laughing. Was it—could it all be true? It sounded terribly true. Was this first ball only the beginning of her last ball after all? At that the music seemed to change; it sounded sad, sad; it rose upon a great sigh. Oh, how quickly things changed! Why didn't happiness last for ever? For ever wasn't a bit too long.

"I want to stop," she said in a breathless voice. The fat man led her to the door.

"No," she said, "I won't go outside. I won't sit down. I'll just stand here, thank you." She leaned against the wall, tapping with her foot, pulling up her gloves and trying to smile. But deep inside her a little girl threw her pinafore over her head and sobbed. Why had he spoiled it all?

"I say, you know," said the fat man, "you mustn't take me seriously, little lady."

"As if I should!" said Leila, tossing her small dark head and sucking her underlip. . . .

Again the couples paraded. The swing doors opened and shut. Now new music was given out by the bandmaster. But Leila didn't want to dance any more. She wanted to be home, or sitting on the veranda listening to those baby owls. When she looked through the dark windows at the stars, they had long beams like wings. . . .

But presently a soft, melting, ravishing tune began, and a young man with curly hair bowed before her. She would have to dance, out of politeness, until she could find Meg. Very stiffly she walked into the middle; very haughtily she put her hand on his sleeve. But in one minute, in one turn, her feet glided, glided. The lights, the azaleas, the dresses, the pink faces, the velvet chairs, all became one beautiful flying wheel. And when her next partner bumped her into the fat man and he said, *"Pardon,"* she smiled at him more radiantly than ever. She didn't even recognize him again.

# WHEN DID THE MUSIC COME THIS WAY?
# CHILDREN DEAR, WAS IT YESTERDAY?

Joan Didion

I am now at that age, as is Cary, when two drinks before lunch can blur my looks. In fact I am careful about it: a Bloody Mary, I say, because I dislike tomato juice, or bouillon-and-vodka, because bouillon nourishes; I have watched too many women bungle an excess of nonchalance about one more vodka martini. Although there are afternoons (today was one) when I would myself prefer to have several vodka martinis and go home to bed, I remember in time that it is not much my style.

But I digress. I meant only to suggest that I am no longer so very young. You might say that thirty-three is not yet so very old, either, but it is old enough so that I will never now be photographed for the New York Sunday newspapers wearing a discothèque dress, old enough so that I no longer think optimistically about "changes." I could start over, but never fresh. Divorce would mean sadness. "Sadness" is a word I did not understand until recently.

I want to tell you about a Christmas. I wish that memory made no connections, for I would like to tell you about it straight, would like you to see it as finished and as self-contained as a painting on a gallery wall; would like *you* to interpret it to *me*. Here is the way I would like you to see it: *Christmas Day. 1945. A family gathers.* There's Cary, the snow princess by the Christmas tree, and there I am, a year younger, no snow princess but the homely cousin (in plainness lay all virtue, they hinted as solace, but perhaps I was not quite plain enough), and wasn't Aunt Inez the great beauty she was said to be and didn't we all live happily *ever* after? But nothing is ever finished, nothing self-contained. And because I am corrupt in the ways of making connections, you must walk through this gallery with an annotated catalogue.

The snow reminds me. It has been snowing here for three days now. My husband woke me at four this morning by throwing snow on the bed, and this afternoon I took the children to Carl Schurz Park to make angel wings in the drifted snow. That was a happy thing to do. In fact I did not want to leave the park, but a man came to lock the gate, and it was dark, and the children were hungry. Now. Just as it is snowing here tonight (drifting in the air shaft, sifting through the skylights, reminding me that the dining room window sash has been broken since summer and that the radiators need draining and that if I do not soon make the necessary telephone calls, the required small arrangements, our precarious shelter against the city will be lost), so it was snowing on that Christmas Day in 1945. Although Reno stands several thousand feet above sea level (4,490 feet, should you want the exact figure, and I will tell you right now that I am more and more interested in exact figures) we did not always have December snow; more often the dry wind would blow in from the desert and the Chamber of Commerce decorations along Virginia Street would tangle and whine with it and my mother would get sick headache from it and the boys in from the ranches would turn up the collars of their denim jackets and shove their knuckles deep into the pockets where the silver dollars were. They would hitch rides into town the afternoon before Christmas to buy presents and shoot craps and find some illuminated refuge from the wind.

*Obiter dictum:* It occurs to me that refuge was simpler then, to find and to maintain. Mere colored lights could do it. Last night I turned on all the lights still left on the Christmas tree they tell me has become a fire hazard, but nothing happened, except that more needles fell; in fact they have almost all fallen, and many of the ornaments are broken. I looked steadily at the lights and tried very hard to hold on, just as I am trying tonight, but nothing happened. Nothing warm. Instead I thought again of the jet that fell into the East River on a night very like this one the winter we bought this apartment; I think more and more about that jet, as well as about what would happen should a crack develop in the Queens-Midtown Tunnel. I mean exactly what would happen, precisely what volume of water would be involved, the actual facts. I have never seen a study on this, but think of it frequently; last night I thought of it until I had to lie down, on the floor in the children's room to be near something warm.

In any case. On that Christmas in 1945 we had not wind but snow, a dense fall of powder snow, so much snow that everyone who came to our house for dinner would have to stay the night. There was Cary, who arrived with snow on the shoulders of her new polo coat (we each had one, every Christmas, identical polo coats from our grandmother in San Francisco), with snow on her pale blonde hair and snow on the shopping bag of presents she thrust toward me when I opened the door. There was Aunt Inez, looking as she always looked, as if she were on the verge of something theatrical, some marriage or divorce or near-fatal accident. Whenever Aunt Inez took Cary and me to lunch at the Riverside Hotel, men would look up from the crap tables and stare as we walked through the lobby; I think now that they stared less because of her beauty (other people were beautiful, my own mother was beautiful, even I am not as homely as I once was, but men do not stare at me) than because of that air of moment, of imminent disaster. Men stared at Aunt Inez as we all stare at airplanes in flight.

And there was Ward. I try now to think of Ward and can call up only cartoon characters: Smilin' Jack, Steve Canyon, the nameless fliers in love with Lace. All I can say is that Ward was handsome, had flown a B-29, and did not, I think, like any of us. Presumably he liked Aunt Inez, since he had married her, but he did not like the rest of us. I do not mean that he disliked us; we simply failed to touch him. Very little touched him. Aunt Inez apparently had, and airplanes did, and there you were. Once, when my father observed that it was uncharacteristic of Aunt Inez to marry someone like Ward, who would have been a gas station attendant all his life had the war not happily intervened, my mother said sharply that it was quite in character. "She doesn't marry men," my mother added. "She married problems. All some problem has to do is come along and look at Inez as if to die, and Inez marries it."

I see that I have said "and there was Ward." That is inaccurate, an example of how we remember what should have been instead of what was. For the salient fact of the afternoon was that Ward did not come. When I asked where he was, Aunt Inez seemed startled, as if she had not before noticed his absence. "Ward?" she repeated after me. "Oh. *Ward.* He'll be along. He'll be along a little later. He's out at the airfield. That's *very* probably where he is."

We did, that afternoon, what we always did. We exchanged presents, a silver music box from Cary to me, an ivory bracelet from me to Cary; we lighted the Christmas candles and sang songs around the piano, and the snow fell outside and it seemed that we were safe and warm inside. Ward, Aunt Inez said a number of times, would be along any minute. Only when dessert was served did she stop saying it. "I can't understand what's keeping Ward," she said then, and in the silence which followed, Cary pushed back her chair and ran from the table. "Cary, for *heaven's* sake," Aunt Inez murmured helplessly, and then she followed Cary into the kitchen. When they reappeared Aunt Inez had two extra champagne glasses, one for me and one for Cary. We were both, she declared, old enough for a glass of champagne at Christmas; this moodiness, this downright *rudeness* of Cary's was just one more symptom of that. But all that was over now. We would toast our growing up.

"Never," Cary whispered later, sitting crosslegged on the floor while she wound long strands of hair around her finger and skewered each strand with a bobby pin. "I would *never* the longest day I ever lived marry somebody like Ward."

I sat up in bed. "How would you know?"

"How would I know what?"

"Know whether somebody was like Ward."

"I'd know," Cary said. "You can tell."

I lay back, and wondered what it was you could tell.

"Listen," Cary said, dipping her comb in a glass of water. "I'd have known before he even proposed. I'd have known the very first night he came to the house. You know what he did that night? He sat in front of the fire and drank an entire bottle of Jack Daniels bourbon. He sat there all night drinking Jack Daniels bourbon and when I came down for breakfast he was still there, just staring at Mama, and Mama staring at him."

"As if to die," I whispered.

"What's that supposed to mean?"

"Nothing."

"Jack Daniels is very expensive bourbon," she added. "Jack Daniels is one of the most expensive bourbons in the entire world. Bayard gave me a sip of it once and told me that. He used to buy it by the case."

"Bayard who?"

"You know perfectly well *Bayard who.* You're just trying to be smart and catty."

In fact I had forgotten Bayard, although I remembered as soon as I asked: he was married to Aunt Inez between Cary's father and Ward. It was difficult to keep Bayard in mind because he had spent only one Christmas with us. The rest of the time they were at Pensacola. All I remembered of that Christmas was that Bayard had taken a car into town on Christmas Eve and cracked it up.

"Anyway," Cary continued, "Bayard's not the point. Bayard was and is a *hero.* He was awarded the Purple Heart. He was wounded."

"In the Officers' Club at Pensacola." I had heard my father say it.

"All right. Just keep it up. You're not going to be the least bit popular, you keep on that way. Nobody likes a cat. *Anyway.* The point is, I would never make the mistake of marrying somebody like *Ward.*"

I watched Cary pinning up the last strands of her hair, and wished again that I had hair like hers. "Who you *plan*ning on marrying then?" I asked after a while. "Frank Sinatra? Audie Murphy? Dr. Albert Schweitzer?"

"Never you mind. He won't stay away three days at a time on *Christ*mas, you can be sure. I guess I can call that tune."

I cannot now tell you why I turned on Cary, for I loved her. Did we not share a grandmother, wear identical polo coats? Had we not spent Christmas together always? How could I have not loved her? In any case what I did was stupid, blunted, vicious only in tone. It is the kind of thing I still do. I did something very like it this morning, when Charlie came in and threw the snow on the bed. As he pointed out before he left, I did not even get her name right. I said everything that was ugly and nothing that hit the mark.

So it was with Cary. *You guess you can call that tune,* I chanted, *what tune is that, Cary, is this the tune?* And while I chanted I grabbed up the silver music box she had given me, wound it, jammed it against her ear. Frightened, she wrenched it from me and dropped it; neither of us moved as the box cracked and the works shattered and shot across the floor, under the dressing table, under the bed, into the open closet. Cary leaned back against the mirror then, sobbing, crying *I broke your present, I broke it, I picked it out myself and Mama said it was exactly right and now it's gone.*

"Never mind," I said. "It was my fault. We can have it fixed. You and I can take it into town and have—"

"Don't you even care? Didn't you even care about it?"

"It was my fault. We can get it fixed."

"Oh sweet God," Cary sobbed. "Sometimes I wish I could jump in the Truckee River."

"Why don't you," I whispered, but happily she had already run into the bathroom and locked the door—"happily" because what I had said was not in the spirit of Christmas, none of it was, and as my mother so often said, if we don't have our families, then who do we have—we have no one, no one at all.

It was not until it became clear that Cary would stay in the bathroom until I left that I went downstairs. And then it was not until I had been lying a long time on the sofa behind the Christmas tree, watching the shadows that the tree lights and dying fire threw on the ceiling, that I saw Aunt Inez and Ward. I could see them through the branches of the tree. Aunt Inez was wearing a robe of my mother's, but her hair was still up in a French twist, and she still wore her gold earrings and bracelets. Ward was slumped in a chair across from her, his arctic parka and a bottle of bourbon on the floor beside him. For a long time they said nothing, but finally they began talking. I do not remember all they said, not only because I was half asleep but because they repeated the same things over and over, words that meant nothing to me, fragments of sentences they seemed to have begun so many times before that there was no need to finish them. All I remember is that both their voices sounded sad, and wounded, and that every time Aunt Inez said that she could not go on, that she could not be made to look a fool up and down the state of Nevada, Ward would repeat *it has nothing to do with you, nothing, you're the one who's making a fool of yourself.* It has everything to do with me, she would say again. It has nothing, he would repeat.

I next remember Aunt Inez crying, and Ward leaning very close to her and saying: "Tell me, Inez. Tell me how much. Tell me what you'd do."

"Anything," Aunt Inez said again and again. "You know what I'd do. Anything."

"Tell me what you'd do for it."

"Don't. It's Christmas. Please."

"Say it."

"I'd do anything," she repeated.

"Say it out loud. Who would you betray."

"I can't tonight."

"*Say* it."

There was silence, and then Aunt Inez said, as if by rote, "I would betray my mother. I would betray my sister. I would betray Cary."

"OK," Ward said softly then, and sat back. "OK."

They said nothing for a long time, and when I woke there was a comforter over me and the lights were off and it was December 26, another Christmas gone, and when Cary came downstairs I could not look at her.

There it is. I have been trying hard tonight to remember exactly what Aunt Inez said, her precise words, not that it matters. We all say the same things. Here are some facts. Ward died in 1949, in an aerial show in South Dakota. Aunt Inez did not marry again, and is now on a cruise of the Balkans; I received a card today. "Happy landings," it closed. Cary has married, twice, and I saw her for lunch during the World's Fair. She had five vodka martinis, one in lieu of dessert. I see my mother and father once a year, in July, when I take the children out. They seem older, and to prefer talking to the children than to me. Charlie called a few hours ago to say that if the Christmas tree was not down by the time he came home he would call the Fire Department, that it would ignite one night soon and burn us in our beds. I pointed out that in any case it was unlikely to catch him. Those are the only facts. Now I have some questions. Was Aunt Inez as cold that night as I am tonight? When did Cary find out that she could not after all call the tune? Do we all marry Wards? If we are lucky? Was that Christmas warm only for me? How exactly did we get from there to here? As I told you, I am trying very hard tonight to hold on.

# Research and Popular Culture

## THE EYE OF THE BEHOLDER: PARENTS' VIEWS ON SEX OF NEWBORNS

Jeffrey Z. Rubin, Frank J. Provenzano, Zella Luria

As Schaffer (1971) has observed, the infant at birth is essentially an asocial, largely undifferentiated creature. It appears to be little more than a tiny ball of hair, fingers, toes, cries, gasps, and gurgles. However, while it may seem that "if you've seen one, you've seen them all," babies are *not* all alike—a fact that is of special importance to their parents, who want, and appear to need, to view their newborn child as a creature that is special. Hence, much of early parental interaction with the infant may be focused on a search for distinctive features. Once the fact that the baby is normal has been established, questions such as, "Who does the baby look like?" and "How much does it weigh?" are asked.

Of all the questions parents ask themselves and each other about their infant, one seems to have priority: "Is it a boy or a girl?" The reasons for and consequences of posing this simple question are by no means trivial. The answer, "boy" or "girl," may result in the parents' organizing their perception of the infant with respect to a wide variety of attributes— ranging from its size to its activity, attractiveness, even its future potential. It is the purpose of the present study to examine the kind of verbal picture parents form of the newborn infant, as a function both of their own and their infant's gender.

As Asch (1946) observed years ago, in forming our impressions of others, we each tend to develop a *Gestalt*—a global picture of what others are like, which permits us to organize our perceptions of the often discrepant, contradictory aspects of their behavior and manner into a unified whole. The awareness of another's status (Goodenough 1957), the belief that he is "warm" or "cold" (Asch 1946, Kelley 1950), "extroverted" or "introverted" (Luchins 1957), even the apparently trivial knowledge of another's name (Harari and McDavid, n.d.)—each of these cues predisposes us to develop a stereotypic view of that other, his underlying nature, and how he is likely to behave. How much more profound, then, may be the consequences of a cue as prominent in parents' minds as the gender of their own precious, newborn infant.

The study reported here is addressed to parental perceptions of their infants at the point when these infants first emerge into the world. If it can be demonstrated that parental sex-typing has already begun its course at this earliest of moments in the life of the child, it may be possible to understand better one of the important antecedents of the complex process by which the growing child comes to view itself as boy-ish or girl-ish.

Based on our review of the literature, two forms of parental sex-typing may be expected to occur at the time of the infant's birth. First, it appears likely that parents will view and label their newborn child differentially, as a simple function of the infant's gender. Aberle and Naegele (1952) and Tasch (1952), using only fathers as subjects, found that they had different expectations for sons and daughters: sons were expected to be aggressive and athletic, daughters were expected to be pretty, sweet, fragile, and delicate. Rebelsky and Hanks (1971) found that fathers spent more time talking to their daughters than their sons during the first three months of life. While the sample size was too small for the finding to be significant, they suggest that the role of father-of-daughter may be perceived as requiring greater nurturance. Similarly, Pedersen and Robson (1969) reported that the fathers of infant daughters exhibited more behavior labeled (by the authors) as "apprehension over well being" than did the fathers of sons.

A comparable pattern emerges in research using mothers as subjects. Sears, Maccoby, and Levin (1957), for example, found that the mothers of kindergartners reported tolerating more aggression from sons than daughters, when it was directed toward parents and peers. In addition, maternal nurturance was seen as more important for the daughter's than the son's development. Taken together, the findings in this body of research lead us to expect parents (regardless of their gender) to view their newborn infants differentially—labeling daughters as weaker, softer, and therefore in greater need of nurturance, than sons.

The second form of parental sex-typing we expect to occur at birth is a function both of the infant's gender *and* the parent's own gender. Goodenough (1957) interviewed the parents of nursery school children and found that mothers were less concerned with sex-typing their child's behavior than were fathers. More recently, Meyer and Sobieszek (1972) presented adults with videotapes of two seventeen-month-old children (each of whom was sometimes described as a boy and sometimes as a girl), and asked their subjects to describe and interpret the children's behavior. They found that male subjects, as well as those having little contact with small children, were more likely (although not always significantly so) to rate the children in sex-stereotypic fashion—attributing "male qualities" such as independence, aggressiveness, activity, and alertness to the child presented as a boy, and qualities such as cuddliness, passivity, and delicacy to the "girl." We expect, therefore, that sex of infant and sex of parent will interact, such that it is fathers, rather than mothers, who emerge as the greater sex-typers of their newborns.

In order to investigate parental sex-typing of their newborn infants, and in order, more specifically, to test the predictions that sex-typing is a function of the infant's gender, as well as the gender of both infant and parent, parents of newborn boys and girls were studied in the maternity ward of a hospital, within the first 24 hours postpartum, to uncover their perceptions of the characteristics of their newborn infants.

## Method

### Subjects

The subjects consisted of 30 pairs of primiparous parents, fifteen of whom had sons, and fifteen of whom had daughters. The subjects were drawn from the available population of expecting parents at a suburban Boston hospital serving local, predominantly lower-middle-class families. Using a list of primiparous expectant mothers obtained from the hospital, the experimenter made contact with families by mail several months prior to delivery, and requested the subjects' assistance in "a study of social relations among parents and their first child." Approximately one week after the initial contact by mail, the experimenter telephoned each family, in order to answer any questions the prospective parents might have about the study, and to obtain their consent. Of the 43 families reached by phone, 11 refused to take part in the study. In addition, one consenting mother subsequently gave birth to a low-birth-weight infant (a 74-ounce girl), while another delivered an unusually large son (166 ounces). Because these two infants were at the two ends of the distribution of birth weights, and because they might have biased the data in support of our hypotheses, the responses of their parents were eliminated from the sample.

All subjects participated in the study within the first 24 hours postpartum—the fathers almost immediately after delivery, and the mothers (who were often under sedation at the time of delivery) up to but not later than 24 hours later. The mothers typically had spoken with their husbands at least once during this 24-hour period.

There were no reports of medical problems during any of the pregnancies or deliveries, and all infants in the sample were full-term at time of birth. Deliveries were made under general anesthesia, and the fathers were not allowed in the delivery room. The fathers were not permitted to handle their babies during the first 24 hours, but could view them through display windows in the hospital nursery. The mothers, on the other hand, were allowed to hold and feed their infants. The subjects participated individually in the study. The fathers were met in a small, quiet waiting room used exclusively by the maternity ward, while the mothers were met in their hospital rooms. Every precaution was taken not to upset the parents or interfere with hospital procedure.

## Procedure

After introducing himself to the subjects, and after congratulatory amenities, the experimenter (FJP) asked the parents: "Describe your baby as you would to a close friend or relative." The responses were tape-recorded and subsequently coded.

The experimenter then asked the subjects to take a few minutes to complete a short questionnaire. The instructions for completion of the questionnaire were as follows:

> On the following page there are 18 pairs of opposite words. You are asked to rate your baby in relation to these words, placing an "x" or a checkmark in the space that best describes your baby. The more a word describes your baby, the closer your "x" should be to that word.
>
> Example: Imagine you were asked to rate Trees.
>
> Good :—:—:—:—:—:—:—:—:—:—:—:—:—:—:—:—:—:—: Bad
> Strong :—:—:—:—:—:—:—:—:—:—:—:—:—:—:—:—:—:—:Weak
>
> If you cannot decide or your feelings are mixed, place your "x" in the center space. Remember, the more you think a word is a good description of your baby, the closer you should place your "x" to that word. If there are no questions, please begin. Remember, you are rating your baby. Don't spend too much time thinking about your answers. First impressions are usually the best.

Having been presented with these instructions, the subjects then proceeded to rate their baby on each of the eighteen following, eleven-point, bipolar adjective scales: firm-soft; large featured-fine featured; big-little; relaxed-nervous; cuddly-not cuddly; easygoing-fussy; cheerful-cranky; good eater-poor eater; excitable-calm; active-inactive; beautiful-plain; sociable-unsociable; well coordinated-awkward; noisy-quiet; alert-inattentive; strong-weak; friendly-unfriendly; hardy-delicate.

Upon completion of the questionnaire, the subjects were thanked individually, and when both parents of an infant had completed their participation, the underlying purposes of the study were fully explained.

## Hospital Data

In order to acquire a more objective picture of the infants whose characteristics were being judged by the subjects, data were obtained from hospital records concerning each infant's birth weight, birth length, and Apgar scores. Apgar scores are typically assigned at five and ten minutes postpartum and represent the physician's ratings of the infant's color, muscle tonicity, reflex irritability, and heart and respiratory rates. No significant differences between the male and female infants were found for birth weight, birth length, or Apgar scores at five and ten minutes postpartum.[1]

## Results

In table 1, the subjects' mean ratings of their infant, by condition, for each of the eighteen bipolar adjective scales, are presented. The right-extreme column of table 1 shows means for each scale, which have been averaged across conditions. Infant stimuli, overall, were characterized closer to the scale anchors of soft, fine featured, little, relaxed, cuddly, easy going, cheerful, good eater, calm, active, beautiful, sociable, well coordinated, quiet, alert, strong, friendly, and hardy. Our parent-subjects, in other words, appear to have felt on Day 1 of their babies' lives that their newborn infants represented delightful, competent new additions to the world!

Analysis of variance of the subjects' questionnaire responses (1 and 56 degrees of freedom) yielded a number of interesting findings. There were no rating differences on the eighteen scales as a simple function of Sex of Parent: parents appear to agree with one another, on the average. As a function of Sex of Infant, however, several significant effects emerged: Daughters, in contrast to sons, were rated as significantly softer ($F = 10.67$, $p < .005$), finer featured ($F = 9.27$, $p < .005$), littler ($F = 28.83$, $p < .001$), and more inattentive ($F = 4.44$, $p < .05$). In addition, significant interaction effects emerged for seven of the eighteen scales: firm-soft ($F = 11.22$, $p < .005$), large featured-fine featured ($F = 6.78$, $p < .025$), cuddly-not cuddly ($F = 4.18$, $p < .05$), well coordinated-awkward ($F = 12.52$, $p < .001$), alert-inattentive ($F = 5.10$, $p < .05$), strong-weak ($F = 10.67$, $p < .005$), and hardy-delicate ($F = 5.32$, $p < .025$).

The meaning of these interactions becomes clear in table 1, in which it can be seen that six of these significant interactions display a comparable pattern: fathers were more extreme in their ratings of *both* sons and

1. Birth weight ($\bar{X}_{Sons}$ = 114.43 ounces, $\bar{X}_{Daughters}$ = 110.00, $t (28) = 1.04$); Birth length ($\bar{X}_{Sons}$ = 19.80 inches, $\bar{X}_{Daughters}$ = 19.96, $t (28) = 0.52$); 5-minute Apgar score ($\bar{X}_{Sons}$ = 9.07, $\bar{X}_{Daughters}$ = 9.33, $t (28) = 0.69$); and 10-minute Apgar score ($\bar{X}_{Sons}$ = 10.00, $\bar{X}_{Daughters}$ = 10.00).

daughters than were mothers. Thus, sons were rated as firmer, larger featured, better coordinated, more alert, stronger, and hardier—and daughters as softer, finer featured, more awkward, more inattentive, weaker, and more delicate—by their fathers than by their mothers. Finally, with respect to the other significant interaction effect (cuddly-not cuddly), a rather different pattern was found. In this case, mothers rated sons as cuddlier than daughters, while fathers rated daughters as cuddlier than sons—a finding we have dubbed the "oedipal" effect.

### Table 1
### MEAN RATINGS ON THE 18 ADJECTIVE SCALES, AS A FUNCTION OF SEX OF PARENT (Mother vs. Father) AND SEX OF INFANT (Son vs. Daughter)[a]

| SCALE | EXPERIMENTAL CONDITION | | | | |
|---|---|---|---|---|---|
| (I) — (II) | M–S | M–D | F–S | F–D | $\bar{X}$ |
| Firm–Soft | 7.47 | 7.40 | 3.60 | 8.93 | 6.85 |
| Large featured–Fine featured | 7.20 | 7.53 | 4.93 | 9.20 | 7.22 |
| Big–Little | 4.73 | 8.40 | 4.13 | 8.53 | 6.45 |
| Relaxed–Nervous | 3.20 | 4.07 | 3.80 | 4.47 | 3.88 |
| Cuddly–Not cuddly | 1.40 | 2.20 | 2.20 | 1.47 | 1.82 |
| Easygoing–Fussy | 3.20 | 4.13 | 3.73 | 4.60 | 3.92 |
| Cheerful–Cranky | 3.93 | 3.73 | 4.27 | 3.60 | 3.88 |
| Good eater–Poor eater | 3.73 | 3.80 | 4.60 | 4.53 | 4.16 |
| Excitable–Calm | 6.20 | 6.53 | 5.47 | 6.40 | 6.15 |
| Active–Inactive | 2.80 | 2.73 | 3.33 | 4.60 | 3.36 |
| Beautiful–Plain | 2.13 | 2.93 | 1.87 | 2.87 | 2.45 |
| Sociable–Unsociable | 4.80 | 3.80 | 3.73 | 4.07 | 4.10 |
| Well coordinated–Awkward | 3.27 | 2.27 | 2.07 | 4.27 | 2.97 |
| Noisy–Quiet | 6.87 | 7.00 | 5.67 | 7.73 | 6.82 |
| Alert–Inattentive | 2.47 | 2.40 | 1.47 | 3.40 | 2.44 |
| Strong–Weak | 3.13 | 2.20 | 1.73 | 4.20 | 2.82 |
| Friendly–Unfriendly | 3.33 | 3.40 | 3.67 | 3.73 | 3.53 |
| Hardy–Delicate | 5.20 | 4.67 | 3.27 | 6.93 | 5.02 |

[a] The larger the mean, the greater the rated presence of the attribute denoted by the second (right-hand) adjective in each pair.

Responses to the interview question were coded in terms of adjectives used and references to resemblance. Given the open-ended nature of the question, many adjectives were used—healthy, for example, being a high-frequency response cutting across sex of babies and parents. Parental responses were pooled, and recurrent adjectives were analyzed by $X^2$ analysis for sex of child. Sons were described as big more frequently than were daughters ($X^2 (1) = 4.26, p < .05$); daughters were called little more often than were sons ($X^2 (1) = 4.28, p < .05$). The "feminine" cluster—

beautiful, pretty, and cute—was used significantly more often to describe daughters than sons ($X^2$ (1) $= 5.40, p < .05$). Finally, daughters were said to resemble mothers more frequently than were sons ($X^2$ (1) $< 3.87, p < .05$).

## Discussion

The data indicate that parents—especially fathers—differentially label their infants, as a function of the infant's gender. These results are particularly striking in light of the fact that our sample of male and female infants did *not* differ in birth length, weight, or Apgar scores. Thus, the results appear to be a pure case of parental labeling—what a colleague has described as "nature's first projective test" (personal communication, Leon Eisenberg). Given the importance parents attach to the birth of their first child, it is not surprising that such ascriptions are made.

But why should posing the simple question "Is it a boy or a girl?" be so salient in parents' minds, and have such important consequences? For one thing, an infant's gender represents a truly *distinctive* characteristic. The baby is either a boy or a girl—there are no ifs, ands, or buts about it. A baby may be active sometimes, and quiet at others, for example, but it can always be assigned to one of two distinct classes: boy or girl. Secondly, an infant's gender tends to assume the properties of a *definitive* characteristic. It permits parents to organize their questions and answers about the infant's appearance and behavior into an integrated *Gestalt*. Finally, an infant's gender is often a *normative* characteristic. It is a property that seems to be of special importance not only to the infant's parents, but to relatives, friends, neighbors, and even casual passersby in the street. For each of these reasons, an infant's gender is a property of considerable importance to its parents, and is therefore one that is likely to lead to labeling and the investment of surplus meaning.

The results of the present study are, of course, not unequivocal. Although it was found, as expected, that the sex-typing of infants varied as a function of the infant's gender, as well as the gender of both infant and parent, significant differences did not emege for all eighteen of the adjective scales employed. Two explanations for this suggest themselves. First, it may simply be that we have overestimated the importance of sex-typing at birth. A second possibility, however, is that sex-typing is more likely to emerge with respect to certain classes of attributes—namely, those which denote physical or constitutional, rather than "internal," dispositional, factors. Of the eight different adjective pairs for which significant main or interaction effects emerged, six (75%) clearly refer to external attributes of the infant. Conversely, of the ten adjective pairs for which no significant differences were found, only three (30%) clearly denote external attributes. This suggests that it is physical and constitutional factors that specially lend themselves to sex-typing at birth, at least in our culture.

Another finding of interest is the lack of significant effects, as a simple function of sex of parent. Although we predicted no such effects, and were therefore not particularly surprised by the emergence of "non-findings," the implication of these results is by no means trivial. If we had omitted the sex of the infant as a factor in the present study, we might have been led to conclude (on the basis of simply varying the sex of the parent) that *no* differences exist in parental descriptions of newborn infants—a patently erroneous conclusion! It is only when the infant's and the parent's gender are considered together, in interaction, that the lack of differences between overall parental mean ratings can be seen to reflect the true differences between the parents. Mothers rate both sexes closer together on the adjective pairs than do fathers (who are the stronger sex-typers), but *both* parents agree on the direction of sex differences.

An issue of considerable concern, in interpreting the findings of the present study appropriately, stems from the fact that fathers were not permitted to handle their babies, while mothers were. The question then becomes: Is it possible that the greater sex-typing by fathers is simply attributable to their lesser exposure to their infants? This, indeed, may have been the case. However, it seems worthwhile to consider some of the alternative possibilites. Might not the lesser exposure of fathers to their infants have led not to greater sex-typing, but to a data "wash-out"—with no differences emerging in paternal ratings? After all, given no opportunity to handle their babies, and therefore deprived of the opportunity to obtain certain first-hand information about them, the fathers might have been expected to make a series of neutral ratings—hovering around the middle of each adjective scale. The fact that they did not do this suggests that they brought with them a variety of sex stereotypes that they then imposed upon their infant. Moreover, the fact that mothers, who were allowed to hold and feed their babies, made distinctions between males and females that were in keeping with cultural sex-stereotypes (see table 1), suggests that even if fathers had had the opportunity of holding their infants, similar results might have been obtained. We should also not lose sight of the fact that father-mother differences in exposure to infants continue well into later years. Finally, one must question the very importance of the subjects' differential exposure on the grounds that none of the typical "exposure" effects reported in the social psychological literature (Zajonc 1968) were observed. In particular, one might have expected mothers to have come to rate their infants more favorably than fathers, simply as a result of greater exposure. Yet such was not the case.

The central implication of the study, then, is that sex-typing and sex-role socialization appear to have already begun their course at the time of the infant's birth, when information about the infant is minimal. The *Gestalt* parents develop, and the labels they ascribe to their newborn infant, may well affect subsequent expectations about the manner in which their infant ought to behave, as well as parental behavior itself. This parental behavior, moreover, when considered in conjunction with the rapid unfolding of the infant's own behavioral repertoire, may well lead to a modification of the very labeling that affected parental behavior in the first place. What began as a one-way street now bears traffic in two directions. In order to understand the full importance and implications of our findings, therefore, research clearly needs to be conducted in which delivery room stereotypes are traced in the family during the first several months after birth, and their impact upon parental behavior is considered. In addition, further research is clearly in order if we are to understand fully the importance of early paternal sex-typing in the socialization of sex-roles.

# References

ABERLE, D. AND NAEGELE, K. 1952. Middle-class fathers' occupational role and attitudes toward children. *Amer. J. Orthopsychiat,* 22(2):366–378.

ASCH, S. 1946. Forming impressions of personality. *J. Abnorm. Soc. Psychol.* 41:258–290.

GOODENOUGH. E. 1957. Interest in persons as an aspect of sex differences in the early years. *Genet. Psychol. Monogr.* 55:287–323.

HARARI, H. AND MC DAVID, J. Name stereotypes and teachers' expectations. *J. Educ. Psychol.* (in press).

KELLEY, H. 1950. The warm-cold variable in first impressions of persons. *J. Pers.* 18:431–439.

LUCHINS, A. 1957. Experimental attempts to minimize the impact of first impressions. In *The Order of Presentation in Persuasion.* C. Hovland, ed. Yale University Press, New Haven, Conn.

MEYER, J. AND SOBIESZEK, B. 1972. Effect of a child's sex on adult interpretations of its behavior. *Develpm. Psychol.* 6:42–48.

PEDERSEN, F. AND ROBSON, K. 1969. Father participation in infancy. *Amer. J. Orthopsychiat.* 39(3):466–472.

REBELSKY, F. AND HANKS, C. 1971. Fathers' verbal interaction with infants in the first three months of life. *Child Develpm.* 42:63–68.

SCHAFFER, H. 1971. *The Growth of Sociability.* Penguin Books, Baltimore.

SEARS, R., MACCOBY, E. AND LEVIN, H. 1957. *Patterns of Child Rearing.* Row, Peterson, Evanston, Ill.

TASCH, R. 1952. The role of the father in the family. *J. Exper. Ed.* 20:319–361.

WILSON, P. 1968. The perceptual distortion of height as a function of ascribed academic status. *J. Soc. Psychol.* 74:79–102.

ZAJONC, R. 1968. Attitudinal effects of mere exposure. *J. Pers. Soc. Psychol. Monogr.* Supplement 9:1–27.

# REARING OF A SEX-REASSIGNED NORMAL MALE INFANT AFTER TRAUMATIC LOSS OF THE PENIS

John Money and Anke A. Ehrhardt

The extreme unusualness of this case of sex-reassignment in infancy lies in the fact that the child was born a normal male and an identical twin, without genital malformation or sexual ambiguity. The idea of sex-reassignment would never have been entertained were it not for a surgical mishap at the age of seven months in which the penis was ablated flush with the abdominal wall. The mishap occurred when a circumcision was being performed by means of electrocautery. The electrical current was too powerful and burned the entire tissue of the penis which necrosed and sloughed off.

The parents were young people of rural background and grade-school education. They were understandably desperate to know what could be done and suffered through a rather long saga of finding no answer. Then a consultant plastic surgeon, familiar with the principles of sex-reassignment, recommended reassignment as a girl. The parents agonized their way to a decision, implementing it with a change of name, clothing and hair style when the baby was seventeen months old. Four months later, the surgical first step of genital reconstruction as a female was undertaken, the second step, vaginoplasty, being delayed until the body is full grown. Pubertal growth and feminization will be regulated by means of hormonal replacement therapy with estrogen.

At the time of surgery, when we saw the parents in person for the first time in the psychohormonal research unit at Johns Hopkins, we gave them advice and counseling on the future prognosis and management of their new daughter, based on experience with similar reassignments in herma-phroditic babies. In particular, they were given confidence that their child can be expected to differentiate a female gender identity, in agreement with her sex of rearing. They were broadly informed about the future medical program for their child and how to integrate it with her sex educa-tion as she grows older. They were guided in how to give the child informa-tion about herself to the extent that the need arises in the future; and they were helped with what to explain to friends and relatives, including their other child. Eventually, they would inform their daughter that she would become a mother by adoption, one day, when she married and wanted to have a family.

During the follow-up time of nearly six years since surgery, the parents have kept in close contact with us, making visits on an annual basis to get psychological support and guidance. The mother's observations and reports have provided us with an insight into changes in her rearing practices toward the sex-reassigned child, and into the different way that she rears this child as compared with the twin brother.

The first items of change were clothes and hairdo. The mother reported: "I started dressing her not in dresses but, you know, in little pink slacks and frilly blouses . . . and letting her hair grow." A year and six months later, the mother wrote that she had made a special effort at keeping her girl in dresses, almost exclusively, changing any item of clothes into something that was clearly feminine. "I even made all her nightwear into granny gowns and she wears bracelets and hair ribbons." The effects of emphasizing feminine clothing became clearly noticeable in the girl's attitude toward clothes and hairdo another year later, when she was observed to have a clear preference for dresses over slacks and to take pride in her long hair.

Related to being dressed nicely is the sense of neatness. The mother stated that her daughter by four and a half years of age was much neater than her brother, and, in contrast with him, disliked to be dirty: "She likes for me to wipe her face. She doesn't like to be dirty, and yet my son is quite different. I can't wash his face for anything. . . . She seems to be daintier. Maybe it's because I encourage it." Elsewhere in this same recorded interview, the mother said: "One thing that really amazes me is that she is so feminine. I've never seen a little girl so neat and tidy as she can be when she wants to be. . . . She is very proud of herself, when she puts on a new dress, or I set her hair. She just loves to have her hair set; she could sit under the drier all day long to have her hair set. She just loves it."

There is a whole pattern of dimorphism of rearing girls and boys with respect to genitalia, sex and reproduction. Boys and girls learn differently how to urinate—boys to stand up and girls to sit down. This child had not, of course, been able to stand when the penis was ablated at age seven months. When, at the age of two, she tried standing up, as many girls do, her mother made a special point of teaching her how little girls go to the bathroom. In this case it needed perhaps more training than usual, because after surgery the girl's urethral opening was so positioned that the urine sometimes would overshoot the seat of the toilet. At the last follow-up, when the girl was five years and nine months old, her mother reported that she had learned to sit down and, with slight pressure from the fingers direct the urinary stream downward. Sometimes she still tried copying her brother, usually making "an awful mess," according to her mother.

The family was relatively open in regard to matters of sex and reproduction, so that one can study particularly well the differences in treating a girl and boy regarding sex and their future adult reproductive role. When the twins were four and a half years old, the mother gave a good example of how parents react to boys' versus girls' genital play. Talking about the boy, the mother reported: ". . . in the summer time, one time I caught him—he went out and took a leak in my flower garden in the front yard, you know. He was quite happy with himself. And I just didn't say anything. I just couldn't. I started laughing and I told daddy about it. . . ." The corresponding comment about the girl ran thus: "I've never had a problem with her. She did once when she was little, she took off her panties and threw them over the fence. And she didn't have no panties on. But I just gave her a little swat on the rear, and I told her that nice little girls didn't do that and she should keep her pants on. . . . And she didn't take them off after that."

Once the children asked what their mother's breasts were for. She explained that when mommies have babies, they give milk. The boy answered that he wanted to be a mommy. His mother explained that he could only be a daddy—"and grow muscles so he could take care of mommy and baby, and just go to work in a car like daddy does. I finally convinced him he might have just as much fun as mommy does. . . . I've explained to each what their function will be as a grown-up, where babies grow, and that a daddy has to have a wife to have a baby and vice versa."

When the girl came across one of her mother's supply of sanitary pads, she was given an appropriate explanation about menstrual care and the fact that it is part of the female's role.

The mother of these two children was particularly good in pointing out the specifics of the female and male adult reproductive roles to her daughter and her son. When an incident happened that could be interpreted as penis envy in the girl and baby or pregnancy envy in the boy, she successfully offered explanations geared to the specific advantage of being female on the one hand, and male on the other. The incident happened some time when the children were five years of age. Both children were taking a bath together and the boy was bragging about his penis which was erect. The mother described the situation as follows: ". . . he managed to get a hard on, and he was standing there and saying, look what I got, look what I got, proud as a peacock and she (his sister) got so mad she slapped him—she didn't like it—right on his little penis. I think, she was a little jealous. So then I went and told her you wait and see, women can have babies and boys can't." When the girl had been reassured about the advantage of being female and having babies, the boy was disappointed and jealous. His mother hastened to reassure him that "little boys could have babies too" and she explained that the father was the one who had to provide the sperm or "seed" as she put it.

Of course, girls and boys are not only prepared differently for their future reproductive role as mother and father but also for their other different roles, such as wife and husband or financial supporter of the family and caretaker of children and house. The mother of these two children gave a good example of how her children were copying aspects of the wife and husband role. The parents were quite open in showing affection to each other in the presence of their children. The mother observed how her son would copy some of his father's behavior: "Like he'll bend over and give her a kiss on the cheek or he'll give her a hug . . . and if he (my husband) gives me a swat on the fanny, he'll go and give her a swat on her fanny, too." The boy was clearly the initiator of affection, copying what he saw in his father's behavior. The girl copied some of her mother's responses—"If she's in an affectionate mood, she'll like it; but very often she'll say, don't do that. . . . If he's been playing some place and comes in the house to where she is helping me . . . then she'll give him a little hug like she's glad to see him."

Regarding domestic activities, such as work in the kitchen and house traditionally seen as part of the female's role, the mother reported that her daughter copies her in trying to help her tidying and cleaning up the kitchen, while the boy could not care less about it. She encourages her daughter when she helps her in the housework.

Rehearsal of future roles can also be seen in girls' and boys' toy preferences. The girl in this case wanted and received for Christmas dolls, a doll house, and a doll carriage, clearly related to the maternal aspect of the female adult role, while the boy wanted and obtained a garage with cars and gas pumps and tools, part of the rehearsal of the male role. His father, like many men, was very interested in cars and mechanical activities.

According to today's standards, not only boys, but also girls often pursue a career. Regarding school and future plans, the mother formulated her own hopes, when the children were a year and ten months old, by saying: "Oh well . . . I am leaving it up to them, but I would like for both of them to go to college and university, and have some kind of career. That's what I would like for both of them. . . . As long as they get their high school, at least my daughter. My son, it's almost essential, since he will be earning a living for the rest of his life." This standpoint represents the opinion of many parents who encourage education and career plans to a stronger degree for boys than for girls. By the time the twins were five years and nine months of age, they expressed clearly different goals for the future. According to their mother's report:

"I found that my son, he chose very masculine things like a fireman or a policeman or something like that. He wanted to do what daddy does, work where daddy does, and carry a lunch kit, and drive a car. And she didn't want any of those things. I asked her, and she said she wanted to be a doctor or a teacher. And I asked her, well, did she have plans that maybe some day she'd get married, like mommy? She'll get married some day— she wasn't too worried about that. She didn't think about that too much, but she wants to be a doctor. But none of the things that she ever wanted to be were like a policeman or a fireman, and that sort of thing never appealed to her. So I felt that in a way that's a good sign . . . I think, it's nice if your boy wants to be a policeman or a fireman or something and the girl things like a doctor, or teaching, or something like that, and I've tried to show them that it's very good. . . ."

The girl had many tomboyish traits, such as abundant physical energy, a high level of activity, stubbornness, and being often the dominant one in a girls' group. Her mother had tried to modify her tomboyishness: ". . . of course, I've tried to teach her not to be rough . . . she doesn't seem to be as rough as him . . . of course, I discouraged that. I teach her more to be polite and quiet. I always wanted those virtues. I never did manage, but I'm going to try to manage them to—my daughter—to be more quiet and lady-like." From the beginning the girl had been the dominant twin. By the age of three, her dominance over her brother was, as her mother described it, that of a mother hen. The boy in turn took up for his sister, if anyone threatened her.

The examples of different rearing practices towards girls and boys here presented, are by no means a complete sample of the cues and reinforcements parents offer to their children. Most parents give them without conscious effort, routinely. It is unusual to have a mother to be as observant, and as good a reporter as this woman. Her husband, by contrast, was less alert in observing and reporting his own actions and behavior towards his daughter and his son, although he also was reinforcing different behavior in each one of his children. He is more typical than his wife in being relatively inarticulate regarding sex differences in rearing. He was more inclined to stress the idea of lack of favoritism in his responses to both children.

# from COME WITH ME

Russell G. Stauffer, Alvina Trent Burrows,
Mary Elisabeth Coleman, Miriam Mason Swain

*Illustrated by Joyce Hewitt*

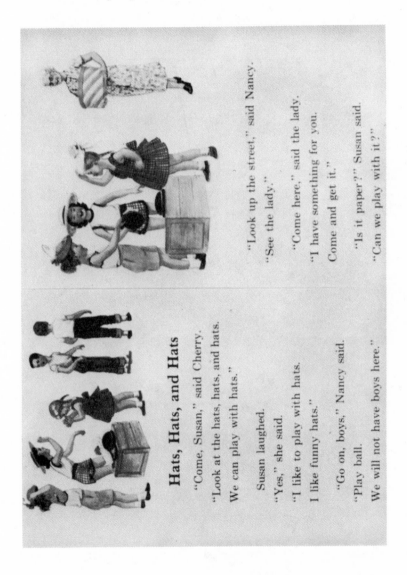

## Hats, Hats, and Hats

"Come, Susan," said Cherry.
"Look at the hats, hats, and hats.
We can play with hats."

Susan laughed.
"Yes," she said.
"I like to play with hats.
I like funny hats."

"Go on, boys," Nancy said.
"Play ball.
We will not have boys here."

"Look up the street," said Nancy.
"See the lady."

"Come here," said the lady.
"I have something for you.
Come and get it."

"Is it paper?" Susan said.
"Can we play with it?"

"Hats and hats," said Nancy.
"Look at the pretty hats.
See the umbrella hat."

The girls put on the hats.
Susan laughed and laughed.
Nancy and Cherry laughed.

"Here comes Red," said Cherry.
"Put a hat on Red.
Here is one with a green cherry.
Red likes green."

"My! My!" said Cherry.
"You look funny."

"Look at the cherry," Nancy said.
"Something is on it.
Something is on Susan."

"No! No!" Susan said.
"Get out! Get out!
You look hungry.
You will eat me."

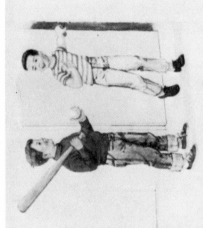

"Help! Help!" said Cherry.

"Come and help.

One is on me."

"Bill! Cooky!" said Nancy.

"Come here.

Come and help Cherry.

We will play with you."

The boys laughed.

"Get down, Cherry," Cooky said.

"Bill and I will help you.

We like to play with hats."

## Boys Like to Play

Cooky went to Bill's house.

"Good morning, Bill," said Cooky.

"Will you play ball with me?"

"I want to," said Bill.

"I will have to see my mother.

Help me look for her."

The boys looked for Bill's mother.

"Mother," said Bill.
"Cooky and I want to play ball.
I will go after I get something
for Red to eat."

"Good," said Mother.
"This is a good morning to play.
You cannot play in the street.
Cars can hurt you.
Play in the field down the street."

"I have my ball," said Cooky.
"I will go to the field.
You can come after you help Red."

Bill looked after Red
and went to the ball field.

"We cannot play," said Cooky.
"A man will put up a new house
on the field."

"I want to see this," said Bill.
"The field is big.
Will the man put up
a big new house?"

The man looked up.
"Good morning, boys," the man said.

"This is Cooky," Bill said.

"My name is Bill.
We play ball here.
We cannot play in a little field."

"This is not good," said the man.
"Boys like to play ball.
You help me this morning, and
I will help you."

"Look," said the man.
"Paint will have to go on here.
Will you put it on?"

"I will do it," said Cooky.
"I help my dad paint."

"I will help here," said Bill.
"I do work for my dad."

"After this, we will look
for a new field," said the man.

# STUDY QUESTIONS

1. Survey twenty males and twenty females, asking them whether they plan to have children and, if so, how many they would like, what sexes in what order, and what sex they would want if they were to have only one child. Summarize the results of your survey. How do they compare to Williams' point in "The Baby Girl"?

2. Recall an experience from your own early sex-role socialization, which taught you something about how each sex expresses its feelings. Compare your experience to Nick Adams's in "Indian Camp."

3. Leila's first dance in Mansfield's "Her First Ball" is perhaps a different initiation into adulthood from ones you have experienced. What similar rituals does our society provide for its young people? How do these rituals differ for the two sexes?

4. "When Did the Music Come this Way? Children Dear, Was It Yesterday?" is a story about disillusionment. To what extent are sex roles a part of this disillusionment?

5. Parents stereotype their children without realizing it, as "The Eye of the Beholder" points out. Most of us do this in spite of ourselves. Describe some of the gender stereotypical assumptions you have made about people you have encountered.

6. After reading "Rearing of a Sex-Reassured Normal Male Infant After Traumatic Loss of the Penis," discuss your attitudes about people who have undergone sex-change operations. Would you accept such a person as a member of the sex to which she or he had changed?

7. Although textbooks today seldom contain such stereotyped portrayals of male and female roles as those in Come With Me, other media persist in sex-typed depictions. Examine and discuss one magazine or several television programs that are especially stereotypical in their presentation of each gender.

# PART II

## Examining Sex-Role Stereotypes

When psychologists seek to define *masculine and feminine,* they study what is known from scientific research about behavioral differences between the sexes and examine what people *believe* to be the differences. This latter area of study is that of sex-role stereotypes.

Over and over, investigators find that men are viewed in positive terms, whereas women are described in less favorable ways. The typical study of sex-role stereotypes gives college students a list of personality traits and asks them to say which traits describe the average male and which the average female. Men are generally described as *active, competent, rational, independent,* and *adventurous.* Women are described as *passive, less competent, irrational, dependent,* and *unadventurous.* The few exceptions to this pattern are when women are seen in terms having to do with emotional sensitivity, sociability, and nurturing—*warm, comforting*—and men are described as lacking these qualities.

You may think that only men hold stereotyped views, but women often do too. You may say, "Yes, I am aware what the stereotypes are. But I don't prejudge people based on their sex. I judge them as individuals." One psychologist tested this assumption by asking a group of college women to read several scholarly papers and judge their merit. The women did not know that, although they had read identical articles, some had read copies attributed to a male author and some to a female author. With remarkable consistency, when an article was believed to be written by a man, it was judged more favorably than when the same article was thought to be the work of a woman.[1] The fact is we simply may not be aware that we stereotype.

1. Phillip A. Goldberg, "Are Women Prejudiced Against Women?" *Transaction,* April 1968, pp. 28–30.

Scientific research examining the actual behaviors of women and men produces results that are much less clear than those of studies examining beliefs about how women and men differ. In some areas of functioning, certain differences have been found consistently. For example, women usually score somewhat higher than men on tests of verbal skills, while men usually score somewhat higher on tests of mathematical skills and visual-spatial ability. Men demonstrate greater aggressiveness in a variety of situations, both physical and verbal. For example, men fight more and make more slighting and critical remarks than women do.

Often a discussion of gender differences in human behavior will lead students to say, "But that difference is learned; it's not innate! Boys and girls are raised differently and therefore learn to behave differently." Almost any claim that a behavioral difference exists between males and females seems to them to imply that the difference is inborn, inevitable, and irrevocable. This is a misunderstanding of the concept of gender differences. That such differences have been shown to exist in some areas of behavior does not imply that they are necessarily either innate or socially conditioned. In most cases, the causal factors are still imperfectly understood.

Researchers have collected abundant evidence suggesting that learning factors contribute to virtually every psychological behavior difference between women and men. Research investigating the effects of biological factors on behavioral differences between the sexes indicates that aggression is in part biologically caused. The difference between women and men in visual-spatial ability also seems to have a genetic component. However, evidence for biological influences on other behavioral gender differences remains weak. Many of the attributes characterizing masculine and feminine stereotypes are not so easily measured as, for instance, math and verbal ability, and studies exploring these attributes have yielded mixed results.

In 1974 Eleanor Maccoby and Carol Nagy Jacklin published *The Psychology of Sex Differences,* a report on more than two thousand research studies published, for the most part, between 1966 and 1973. They concluded that of the many stereotypical assumptions about gender differences in behavior, only four are clearly supported by research findings: the previously mentioned disparities in aggressiveness, and in verbal, mathematical, and visual-spatial abilities. Many others proved to be unfounded, what Maccoby and Jacklin described as "myths." More recently, other experts have concluded that a few more gender differences probably exist: dominance, self-esteem, and problem solving, among others.

Without any overwhelming empirical evidence that would support stereotyped views of males and females, the attitudes persist. The typical adult male, as depicted in popular culture, can balance the checkbook and fix things around the house. He prefers sports, politics, and beer to soap operas, domestic concerns, or wine. This typical male enjoys women more for their beauty than their accomplishments. He can watch a violent movie without flinching. The typical adult female, on the other hand, automatically knows how to comfort a crying baby and senses when her neighbor is not feeling well. She loves romantic movies, is concerned about how white her wash is, and spends hours making herself beautiful for the man who values her appearance more than her brains. When the traditional male and female become a couple, the stereotypes extend to their relationship. He drives the car when they go somewhere together, picks up the tab in a restaurant, and makes the first sexual advance. She more carefully selects the clothes she will wear, draws him out in conversation, and responds to his every amorous move. When men get together as a group, they drink, become rowdy, and discuss their recent sexual adventures. When women get together, they gossip, giggle, and count calories.

Of course, the stereotypes have positive and negative consequences for both women and men. On the positive side, the traditional woman can see the results of having comforted someone, is sheltered from the stresses of a competitive career, can express her emotions freely, can take pleasure in decorating and costuming her body, and can enjoy the thrill of sexual surrender. Conversely, there is a price one must pay for any pattern of behavior. For the traditional woman, the price may be surpressing her spontaneity, yielding her opinions, and nurturing others and encouraging their pursuits rather than her own. If she emulates the examples of beauty promoted by advertising, she must spend considerable time tending to her physical appearance.

On the positive side for men, the traditional male role allows considerable freedom of movement and choice. Society encourages him to test himself, to achieve competence in any field without the encumbrance of tending home and minding children. Social codes make it much easier for him to participate in social events alone, whereas the traditional female usually feels uncomfortable unless accompanied by a friend. His job daily takes him away from home and, frequently, on business trips that make him more cosmopolitan. In relationships with women, his accustomed role of guide and protector heightens his self-esteem. For him, the thrill in sexual relationships comes from mastery. The myth—the popularly held assumption—is that he can handle himself in any situation. But men also pay a price for strict adherence to a traditional role. The traditional man does not express his feelings openly; some men confess that because on so many occasions they have withheld tears, they are literally unable to cry. A further price the male pays for his constricted emotional expression is that his relationship with his children is somewhat distant. Typically, he is awkward in playing with them and finds it difficult to show them affection. Because he is so frequently away at work, he misses the pleasure of watching his children's day-to-day accomplishments.

Some may wonder what difference all this makes. If society can function smoothly when men and women observe their traditional roles, might we not be asking for trouble when we question the wisdom of these roles? Some behavioral scientists say no. They point to studies showing that men and women who adhere closely to traditional roles may not be as well adjusted psychologically as less sex-typed people. On the other hand, well-defined sex roles do provide a guide for behavior. They tell us not only what to do but also what to expect from others. For many people, that may be very reassuring.

Recently, a number of investigators working in psychology and literature have argued that individuals with a combination of strong "masculine" and strong "feminine" traits may represent an ideal in personality. These psychologically "androgynous" people can more freely adapt their behavior to the demands of many situations. We shall explore the concept of androgyny more fully in Part III.

The selections in Part II present the female and male stereotypes in four sections. In the women's fiction section the first and second stories depict woman as mother and wife. The third selection portrays a stereotyped "women's world." Sherwood Anderson's story "Mother," from his *Winesburg, Ohio* collection, concerns a woman's relationship with her son. George Willard's mother has lost all hope of personal happiness except as she achieves it through him. Her marriage has long since foundered. Anderson describes her as gaunt, a ghostly figure, with a face "marked with smallpox scars." Her husband is slender, graceful, and has a quick military step. Although he too is lonely, he can offer her no comfort: "As he went spruce and business-like through the streets of Winesburg, he sometimes stopped and turned quickly about as though fearing that the spirit of the hotel and of the woman would follow him even into the streets." All of the mother's energies are directed toward her son. Through him, through his sensitivity, through his plan to leave Winesburg, she hopes to re-create herself. In the son's presence, however, George's mother is timid and reserved. George does not yet understand his mother's profound investment in his life.

"Nikolai Vassilevitch's wife was not a woman" is Tommaso Landolfi's way of introducing "Gogol's Wife." "Nor was she," he adds, "any sort of human being, nor any sort of living creature at all, whether animal or vegetable." So begins Landolfi's surrealistic depiction of a woman who has lost all personal identity. Landolfi uses the husband's fantasy of a perfect wife—one who is utterly adaptable in response to her husband's whims—exaggerating it to absurd proportions. But even in the most freely imagined fantasy, something seems always to go awry. The author allows us to look in on the marriage with special attention given to its final stages. Perhaps you are thinking that a marriage such as Landolfi depicts is peculiar and unrealistic. After all, marriages take place between human beings. Still, do you see any similarities between this relationship and others you have known?

Although Eudora Welty's story is entitled "Petrified Man," it is set in a distinctly female world, the beauty shop. Leota and her ten o'clock shampoo-and-set customer, Mrs. Fletcher, conform to our stereotyped notion of women as gossips. They chat incessantly about trivial things: how one of Leota's friends gets along with her husband, what Mrs. Fletcher should wear to disguise her pregnancy, who told Leota in the first place that Mrs. Fletcher was pregnant. The story also illustrates the importance to women of their physical appearance. Even a woman on her way to the hospital to give birth stops to have her hair done. In this women's world, the men come off rather poorly. The women speak of them either disparagingly or condescendingly. And who is the petrified man?

The research and popular culture section for women presents three diverse views of women's roles. Helen Andelin's "Feminine Dependency" may seem at first to be something of an anachronism. At a time when many are encouraging women to strengthen their confidence in their own abilities, to exercise their natural competence, and to take an equal role with men both in personal relationships and in the business world, Andelin sounds a dissenting note. Her book, *Fascinating Womanhood,* was first published in 1965, was then reissued in the 1970s, and is reported still to be selling well. Her belief is that by suppressing all "masculine" characteristics and giving up all duties traditionally thought of as "masculine," women have the best chance of attracting, delighting, and holding the men they care about.

"The Fantasy of Dirt" by Lawrence S. Kubie explores one possible source of our negative views about women. The focus of Kubie's article is the attitude that women are dirtier than men. But what is dirt? Kubie argues that it has little to do with germs or a "bad smell." Rather, dirt is whatever issues from the body through its apertures (feces, sweat, mucus, spit) or whatever reminds us of such matter. The inside of the body, therefore, is unconsciously seen as filthy and is viewed with disgust. And since women have one more aperture than men have, and that one hidden and enfolded, Kubie says that both sexes are necessarily left with the unconscious conviction that women are dirtier than men.

James Thurber's well-known cartoon "Home" is a wry portrait of one possible effect of traditional sex roles: women and home seem to go together, and men are in some way excluded. The feeling of the cartoon is almost sinister. The wife, accepting her role as keeper of the house, lurks as if to ambush the husband who is returning meekly home. For his part, the man, as family provider, is uncomfortable approaching the very home he supports. Note how similar Thurber's message is to the thoughts of the husband in Sherwood Anderson's "Mother."

The male stereotyping section contains fictional and nonfictional accounts of the traditional male role. John Steinbeck's "Flight," the first of the three stories illustrating male stereotypes, portrays a youth who learns abruptly how to behave as a man. He discovers, first, courage and, second, the ability to endure physical hardship without complaining. Note that it is the boy's mother who ushers him into manhood; she tells him the practical things: to conserve his food and ammunition and not to stop when he feels like resting. Thus the story illustrates that men *and* women can be familiar, even comfortable, with the traditional male role. As researchers have shown in laboratory studies, each sex knows the other's role as well as its own.

Just as Eudora Welty's "Petrified Man" depicts a stereotypical women's world, "A Change of Air" by Ivan Gold describes a similarly stereotyped world of young men. Set in New York City, the story concerns a group of men in their early twenties who hang around Gelber's Chess Club. Their lives embody some of the most positive and negative male values. Although some of the men are talented at the difficult game of chess, they allow the competitive spirit of the game to dominate other aspects of their lives. One young man, for example, accepts and pays for a foolish dare as a result of the group's competitiveness. Their relationships with women are at best superficial, partly because of their own close camaraderie.

The third story, "Sorrow-Acre", by Isak Dinesen is an allegory on several levels. In a mythic milieu, characters act out the recurring struggle between peasant and landowner, youth and age, and women and men. Of primary concern to our examination of sex roles is the conflict between Adam's uncle and the aged mother, between "male" rationality and "female" emotion. Acting out of principle, the uncle offers the woman a chance to redeem her son. Acting out of a powerful emotion, love, the mother accepts the challenge. Some people might argue that class, age, and gender issues are connected, that power is the factor that links them all.

Dan Benson's "Who's in Charge?" is the first of the male Research and Popular Culture selections, and is a contemporary defense of the traditional male role. In some ways Benson's article parallels Helen Andelin's piece on traditional femininity. Benson argues from fundamental Christian teaching: God ordains that the husband is the head of the house. Not that the husband is to be a despot; rather he should be a kind and understanding leader of his wife and children. Both husband and wife should submit to each other, but someone—the husband—must make the important decisions.

"The Male Sex Role: Our Culture's Blueprint of Manhood and What It's Done For Us Lately" is a chapter from *The Forty-Nine Percent Majority: The Male Sex Role* by Deborah David and Robert Brannon. In this selection, the authors present an analysis of the traditional role that males learn in our society. Using examples from both research and popular culture, the authors discuss four striking characteristics of the commonly accepted male role. First, males must avoid "feminine" qualities such as openness and vulnerability. Second, they must strive to be successful. Third, they must be tough, confident, and self-reliant. And last, they need not shun violent activities. David and Brannon's concern is the effects of these attitudes on the culture.

What is a "manish boy"? In the song of that title sung by Muddy Waters on The Band's album *The Last Waltz,* we see who he is. Such a man is a boy at heart, even though he is "way past twenty-one." He likes a good time, he is irresistible to women, and he wants to be forever young. Although our culture glorifies youthfulness in both sexes, in men it perhaps promotes a special reluctance to growing up and growing old. The song's title itself illustrates the issue. Why is it "Manish Boy" and not "Boyish Man"?

## MOTHER

Sherwood Anderson

Elizabeth Willard, the mother of George Willard, was tall and gaunt and her face was marked with smallpox scars. Although she was but forty-five, some obscure disease had taken the fire out of her figure. Listlessly she went about the disorderly old hotel looking at the faded wall-paper and the ragged carpets and, when she was able to be about, doing the work of a chambermaid among beds soiled by the slumbers of fat traveling men. Her husband, Tom Willard, a slender, graceful man with square shoulders, a quick military step, and a black mustache trained to turn sharply up at the ends, tried to put the wife out of his mind. The presence of the tall ghostly figure, moving slowly through the halls, he took as a reproach to himself. When he thought of her he grew angry and swore. The hotel was unprofitable and forever on the edge of failure and he wished himself out of it. He thought of the old house and the woman who lived there with him as things defeated and done for. The hotel in which he had begun life so hopefully was now a mere ghost of what a hotel should be. As he went spruce and business-like through the streets of Winesburg, he sometimes stopped and turned quickly about as though fearing that the spirit of the hotel and the woman would follow him even into the streets. "Damn such a life, damn it!" he sputtered aimlessly.

Tom Willard had a passion for village politics and for years had been the leading Democrat in a strongly Republican community. Some day, he told himself, the tide of things political will turn in my favor and the years of ineffectual service count big in the bestowal of rewards. He dreamed of going to Congress and even of becoming governor. Once when a younger member of the party arose at a political conference and began to boast of his faithful service, Tom Willard grew white with fury. "Shut up, you," he

roared, glaring about. "What do you know of service? What are you but a
boy? Look at what I've done here! I was a Democrat here in Winesburg
when it was a crime to be a Democrat. In the old days they fairly hunted us
with guns."

Between Elizabeth and her one son George there was a deep unexpressed bond of sympathy, based on a girlhood dream that had long ago
died. In the son's presence she was timid and reserved, but sometimes
while he hurried about town intent upon his duties as a reporter, she went
into his room and closing the door knelt by a little desk, made of a kitchen
table, that sat near a window. In the room by the desk she went through a
ceremony that was half a prayer, half a demand, addressed to the skies. In
the boyish figure she yearned to see something half forgotten that had
once been a part of herself re-created. The prayer concerned that. "Even
though I die, I will in some way keep defeat from you," she cried, and so
deep was her determination that her whole body shook. Her eyes glowed
and she clenched her fists. "If I am dead and see him becoming a meaningless drab figure like myself, I will come back," she declared. "I ask God
now to give me that privilege. I demand it. I will pay for it. God may beat
me with his fists. I will take any blow that may befall if but this my boy be
allowed to express something for us both." Pausing uncertainly, the
woman stared about the boy's room. "And do not let him become smart
and successful either," she added vaguely.

The communion between George Willard and his mother was outwardly
a formal thing without meaning. When she was ill and sat by the window in
her room he sometimes went in the evening to make her a visit. They sat
by a window that looked over the roof of a small frame building into Main
Street. By turning their heads they could see through another window,
along an alleyway that ran behind the Main Street stores and into the back
door of Abner Groff's bakery. Sometimes as they sat thus a picture of
village life presented itself to them. At the back door of his shop appeared
Abner Groff with a stick or an empty milk bottle in his hand. For a long
time there was a feud between the baker and a gray cat that belonged to
Sylvester West, the druggist. The boy and his mother saw the cat creep
into the door of the bakery and presently emerge followed by the baker,
who swore and waved his arms about. The baker's eyes were small and
red and his black hair and beard were filled with flour dust. Sometimes he
was so angry that, although the cat had disappeared, he hurled sticks, bits
of broken glass, and even some of the tools of his trade about. Once he
broke a window at the back of Sinning's Hardward Store. In the alley the
gray cat crouched behind barrels filled with torn paper and broken bottles
above which flew a black swarm of flies. Once when she was alone, and
after watching a prolonged and ineffectual outburst on the part of the
baker, Elizabeth Willard put her head down on her long white hands and

wept. After that she did not look along the alleyway anymore, but tried to forget the contest between the bearded man and the cat. It seemed like a rehearsal of her own life, terrible in its vividness.

In the evening when the son sat in the room with his mother, the silence made them both feel awkward. Darkness came on and the evening train came in at the station. In the street below feet tramped up and down upon a board sidewalk. In the station yard, after the evening train had gone, there was a heavy silence. Perhaps Skinner Leason, the express agent, moved a truck the length of the station platform. Over on Main Street sounded a man's voice, laughing. The door of the express office banged. George Willard arose and crossing the room fumbled for the doorknob. Sometimes he knocked against a chair, making it scrape along the floor. By the window sat the sick woman, perfectly still, listless. Her long hands, white and bloodless, could be seen drooping over the ends of the arms of the chair. "I think you had better be out among the boys. You are too much indoors," she said, striving to relieve the embarrassment of the departure. "I thought I would take a walk," replied George Willard, who felt awkward and confused.

One evening in July, when the transient guests who made the New Willard House their temporary home had become scarce, and the hallways, lighted only by kerosene lamps turned low, were plunged in gloom, Elizabeth Willard had an adventure. She had been ill in bed for several days and her son had not come to visit her. She was alarmed. The feeble blaze of life that remained in her body was blown into a flame by her anxiety and she crept out of bed, dressed, and hurried along the hallway toward her son's room, shaking with exaggerated fears. As she went along she steadied herself with her hand, slipped along the papered walls of the hall, and breathed with difficulty. The air whistled through her teeth. As she hurried forward she thought how foolish she was. "He is concerned with boyish affairs," she told herself. "Perhaps he has now begun to walk about in the evening with girls."

Elizabeth Willard had a dread of being seen by guests in the hotel that had once belonged to her father and the ownership of which still stood recorded in her name in the county courthouse. The hotel was continually losing patronage because of its shabbiness and she thought of herself as also shabby. Her own room was in an obscure corner and when she felt able to work she voluntarily worked among the beds, preferring the labor that could be done when the guests were abroad seeking trade among the merchants of Winesburg.

By the door of her son's room the mother knelt upon the floor and listened for some sound from within. When she heard the boy moving about and talking in low tones a smile came to her lips. George Willard had a habit of talking aloud to himself and to hear him doing so had always given his mother a peculiar pleasure. The habit in him, she felt, strengthened the secret bond that existed between them. A thousand times she had whispered to herself of the matter. "He is groping about, trying to find himself," she thought. "He is not a dull clod, all words and smartness. Within him there is a secret something that is striving to grow. It is the thing I let be killed in myself."

In the darkness in the hallway by the door the sick woman arose and started again toward her own room. She was afraid that the door would open and the boy come upon her. When she had reached a safe distance and was about to turn a corner into a second hallway she stopped and bracing herself with her hands waited, thinking to shake off a trembling fit of weakness that had come upon her. The presence of the boy in the room had made her happy. In her bed, during the long hours alone, the little fears that had visited her had become giants. Now they were all gone. "When I get back to my room I shall sleep," she murmured gratefully.

But Elizabeth Willard was not to return to her bed to sleep. As she stood trembling in the darkness the door of her son's room opened and the boy's father, Tom Willard, stepped out. In the light that streamed out at the door he stood with the knob in his hand and talked. What he said infuriated the woman.

Tom Willard was ambitious for his son. He had always thought of himself as a successful man, although nothing he had ever done had turned out successfully. However, when he was out of sight of the New Willard House and had no fear of coming upon his wife, he swaggered and began to dramatize himself as one of the chief men of the town. He wanted his son to succeed. He it was who had secured for the boy the position on the *Winesburg Eagle*. Now, with a ring of earnestness in his voice, he was advising concerning some course of conduct. "I tell you what, George, you've got to wake up," he said sharply. "Will Henderson has spoken to me three times concerning the matter. He says you go along for hours not hearing when you are spoken to and acting like a gawky girl. What ails you?" Tom Willard laughed good-naturedly. "Well, I guess you'll get over it," he said. "I told Will that. You're not a fool and you're not a woman. You're Tom Willard's son and you'll wake up. I'm not afraid. What you say clears things up. If being a newspaper man had put the notion of becoming a writer into your mind that's all right. Only I guess you'll have to wake up to do that too, eh?"

Tom Willard went briskly along the hallway and down a flight of stairs to the office. The woman in the darkness could hear him laughing and talking with a guest who was striving to wear away a dull evening by dozing in a chair by the office door. She returned to the door of her son's room. The weakness had passed from her body as by a miracle and she stepped boldly along. A thousand ideas raced through her head. When she heard the scraping of a chair and the sound of a pen scratching upon paper, she again turned and went back along the hallway to her own room.

A definite determination had come into the mind of the defeated wife of the Winesburg hotel keeper. The determination was the result of long years of quiet and rather ineffectual thinking. "Now," she told herself, "I will act. There is something threatening my boy and I will ward it off." The fact that the conversation between Tom Willard and his son had been rather quiet and natural, as though an understanding existed between them, maddened her. Although for years she had hated her husband, her hatred had always before been a quite impersonal thing. He had been merely a part of something else that she hated. Now, and by the few words at the door, he had become the thing personified. In the darkness of her own room she clenched her fists and glared about. Going to a cloth bag that hung on a nail by the wall she took out a long pair of sewing scissors and held them in her hand like a dagger. "I will stab him," she said aloud. "He has chosen to be the voice of evil and I will kill him. When I have killed him something will snap within myself and I will die also. It will be a release for all of us."

In her girlhood and before her marriage with Tom Willard, Elizabeth had borne a somewhat shaky reputation in Winesburg. For years she had been what is called "stage-struck" and had paraded through the streets with traveling men guests at her father's hotel, wearing loud clothes and urging them to tell her of life in the cities out of which they had come. Once she startled the town by putting on men's clothes and riding a bicycle down Main Street.

In her own mind the tall dark girl had been in those days much confused. A great restlessness was in her and it expressed itself in two ways. First there was an uneasy desire for change, for some big definite movement to her life. It was this feeling that had turned her mind to the stage. She dreamed of joining some company and wandering over the world, seeing always new faces and giving something out of herself to all people. Sometimes at night she was quite beside herself with the thought, but when she tried to talk of the matter to the members of the theatrical companies that came to Winesburg and stopped at her father's hotel, she got nowhere. They did not seem to know what she meant, or if she did get something of her passion expressed, they only laughed. "It's not like that," they said. "It's as dull and uninteresting as this here. Nothing comes of it."

With the traveling men when she walked about with them, and later with Tom Willard, it was quite different. Always they seemed to understand and sympathize with her. On the side streets of the village, in the darkness under the trees, they took hold of her hand and she thought that something unexpressed in herself came forth and became a part of an unexpressed something in them.

And then there was the second expression of her restlessness. When that came she felt for a time released and happy. She did not blame the men who walked with her and later she did not blame Tom Willard. It was always the same, beginning with kisses and ending, after strange wild emotions, with peace and then sobbing repentance. When she sobbed she put her hand upon the face of the man and had always the same thought. Even though he were large and bearded she thought he had become suddenly a little boy. She wondered why he did not sob also.

In her room, tucked away in a corner of the old Willard House, Elizabeth Willard lighted a lamp and put it on a dressing table that stood by the door. A thought had come into her mind and she went to a closet and brought out a small square box and set it on the table. The box contained material for makeup and had been left with other things by a theatrical company that had once been stranded in Winesburg. Elizabeth Willard had decided that she would be beautiful. Her hair was still black and there was a great mass of it braided and coiled about her head. The scene that was to take place in the office below began to grow in her mind. No ghostly worn-out figure should confront Tom Willard, but something quite unexpected and startling. Tall and dusky cheeks and hair that fell in a mass from her shoulders, a figure should come striding down the stairway before the startled loungers in the hotel office. The figure would be silent—it would be swift and terrible. As a tigress whose cub had been threatened would she appear, coming out of the shadows, stealing noiselessly along and holding the long wicked scissors in her hand.

With a little broken sob in her throat, Elizabeth Willard blew out the light that stood upon the table and stood weak and trembling in the darkness. The strength that had been as a miracle in her body left and she half reeled across the floor, clutching at the back of the chair in which she had spent so many long days staring out over the tin roofs into the main street of Winesburg. In the hallway there was the sound of footsteps and George Willard came in at the door. Sitting in a chair beside his mother he began to talk. "I'm going to get out of here," he said. "I don't know where I shall go or what I shall do but I am going away."

The woman in the chair waited and trembled. An impulse came to her. "I suppose you had better wake up," she said. "You think that? You will go to the city and make money, eh? It will be better for you, you think, to be a businessman, to be brisk and smart and alive?" She waited and trembled.

The son shook his head. "I suppose I can't make you understand, but oh, I wish I could," he said earnestly. "I can't even talk to father about it. I don't try. There isn't any use. I don't know what I shall do. I just want to go away and look at people and think."

Silence fell upon the room where the boy and woman sat together. Again, as on the other evenings, they were embarrassed. After a time the boy tried again to talk. "I suppose it won't be for a year or two but I've been thinking about it," he said, rising and going toward the door. "Something father said makes it sure that I shall have to go away." He fumbled with the doorknob. In the room the silence became unbearable to the woman. She wanted to cry out with joy because of the words that had come from the lips of her son, but the expressions of joy had become impossible to her. "I think you had better go out among the boys. You are too much indoors," she said. "I thought I would go for a little walk," replied the son stepping awkwardly out of the room and closing the door.

# GOGOL'S WIFE

Tommaso Landolfi

At this point, confronted with the whole complicated affair of Nikolai Vassilevitch's wife, I am overcome by hesitation. Have I any right to disclose something which is unknown to the whole world, which my unforgettable friend himself kept hidden from the world (and he had his reasons), and which I am sure will give rise to all sorts of malicious and stupid misunderstandings? Something, moreover, which will very probably offend the sensibilities of all sorts of base, hypocritical people, and possibly of some honest people too, if there are any left? And finally, have I any right to disclose something before which my own spirit recoils, and even tends toward a more or less open disapproval?

But the fact remains that, as a biographer, I have certain firm obligations. Believing as I do that every bit of information about so lofty a genius will turn out to be of value to us and to future generations, I cannot conceal something which in any case has no hope of being judged fairly and wisely until the end of time. Moreover, what right have we to condemn? Is it given to us to know, not only what intimate needs, but even what higher and wider ends may have been served by those very deeds of a lofty genius which perchance may appear to us vile? No indeed, for we understand so little of these privileged natures. "It is true," a great man once said, "that I also have to pee, but for quite different reasons."

But without more ado I will come to what I know beyond doubt, and can prove beyond question, about this controversial matter, which will now—I dare to hope—no longer be so. I will not trouble to recapitulate what is already known of it since I do not think this should be necessary at the present stage of development of Gogol studies.

Let me say it at once: Nikolai Vassilevitch's wife was not a woman. Nor was she any sort of human being, nor any sort of living creature at all, whether animal or vegetable (although something of the sort has sometimes been hinted). She was quite simply a balloon. Yes, a balloon; and this will explain the perplexity, or even indignation, of certain biographers who were also the personal friends of the Master, and who complained that, although they often went to his house, they never saw her and "never even heard her voice." From this they deduced all sorts of dark and disgraceful complications—yes and criminal ones too. No, gentlemen, everything is always simpler than it appears. You did not hear her voice simply because she could not speak, or to be more exact, she could only speak in certain conditions, as we shall see. And it was always, except once, in tête-à-tête with Nikolai Vassilevitch. So let us not waste time with any cheap or empty refutations but come at once to as exact and complete a description as possible of the being or object in question.

Gogol's so-called wife was an ordinary dummy made of thick rubber, naked at all seasons, buff in tint, or as is more commonly said, flesh-colored. But since women's skins are not all of the same color, I should specify that hers was a light-colored, polished skin, like that of certain brunettes. It, or she, was, it is hardly necessary to add, of feminine sex. Perhaps I should say at once that she was capable of very wide alterations of her attributes without, of course, being able to alter her sex itself. She could sometimes appear to be thin, with hardly any breasts and with narrow hips more like a young lad than a woman, and at other times to be excessively well-endowed or—let us not mince matters—fat. And she often changed the color of her hair, both on her head and elsewhere on her body, though not necessarily at the same time. She could also seem to change in all sorts of other tiny particulars, such as the position of moles, the vitality of the mucous membranes and so forth. She could even to a certain extent change the very color of her skin. One is faced with the necessity of asking oneself who she really was, or whether it would be proper to speak of a single "person"—and in fact we shall see that it would be imprudent to press this point.

The cause of these changes, as my readers will already have understood, was nothing else but the will of Nikolai Vassilevitch himself. He would inflate her to a greater or lesser degree, would change her wig and her other tufts of hair, would grease her with ointments and touch her up in various ways so as to obtain more or less the type of woman which suited him at that moment. Following the natural inclinations of his fancy, he even amused himself sometimes by producing grotesque or monstrous forms; as will be readily understood, she became deformed when inflated beyond a certain point or if she remained below a certain pressure.

But Gogol soon tired of these experiments, which he held to be "after all, not very respectful" to his wife, whom he loved in his own way—however inscrutable it may remain to us. He loved her, but which of these incarnations, we may ask ouselves, did he love? Alas, I have already indicated that the end of the present account will furnish some sort of an answer. And how can I have stated above that it was Nikolai Vassilevitch's will which ruled that woman? In a certain sense, yes, it is true; but it is equally certain that she soon became no longer his slave but his tyrant. And here yawns the abyss, or if you prefer it, the Jaws of Tartarus. But let us not anticipate.

I have said that Gogol obtained with his manipulations *more or less* the type of woman which he needed from time to time. I should add that when, in rare cases, the form he obtained perfectly incarnated his desire,

Nikolai Vassilevitch fell in love with it "exclusively," as he said in his own words, and that this was enough to render "her" stable for a certain time—until he fell out of love with "her." I counted no more than three or four of these violent passions—or, as I suppose they would be called today, infatuations—in the life (dare I say in the conjugal life?) of the great writer. It will be convenient to add here that a few years after what one may call his marriage, Gogol had even given a name to his wife. It was Caracas, which is, unless I am mistaken, the capital of Venezuela. I have never been able to discover the reason for this choice: great minds are so capricious!

Speaking only of her normal appearance, Caracas was what is called a fine woman—well built and proportioned in every part. She had every smallest attribute of her sex properly disposed in the proper location. Particularly worthy of attention were her genital organs (if the adjective is permissible in such a context). They were formed by means of ingenious folds in the rubber. Nothing was forgotten, and their operation was rendered easy by various devices, as well as by the internal pressure of the air.

Caracas also had a skeleton, even though a rudimentary one. Perhaps it was made of whalebone. Special care had been devoted to the construction of the thoracic cage, of the pelvic basin and of the cranium. The first two systems were more or less visible in accordance with the thickness of the fatty layer, if I may so describe it, which covered them. It is a great pity that Gogol never let me know the name of the creator of such a fine piece of work. There was an obstinacy in his refusal which was never quite clear to me.

Nikolai Vassilevitch blew his wife up through the anal sphincter with a pump of his own inventions, rather like those which you hold down with your two feet and which are used today in all sorts of mechanical workshops. Situated in the anus was a little one-way valve, or whatever the correct technical description would be, like the mitral valve of the heart, which, once the body was inflated, allowed more air to come in but none to go out. To deflate, one unscrewed a stopper in the mouth, at the back of the throat.

And that, I think, exhausts the description of the most noteworthy peculiarities of this being. Unless perhaps I should mention the splendid rows of white teeth which adorned her mouth and the dark eyes which, in spite of their immobility, perfectly simulated life. Did I say simulate? Good heavens, simulate is not the word! Nothing seems to be the word, when one is speaking of Caracas! Even these eyes could undergo a change of color, by means of a special process to which, since it was long and tiresome, Gogol seldom had recourse. Finally, I should speak of her voice, which it was only once given to me to hear. But I cannot do that without going more fully into the relationship between husband and wife, and in this I shall no longer be able to answer to the truth of everything with absolute certitude. On my conscience I could not—so confused, both in itself and in my memory, is that which I now have to tell.

Here, then, as they occur to me, are some of my memories.

The first and, as I said, the last time I ever heard Caracas speak to Nikolai Vassilevitch was one evening when we were absolutely alone. We were in the room where the woman, if I may be allowed the expression, lived. Entrance to this room was strictly forbidden to everybody. It was furnished more or less in the Oriental manner, had no windows and was situated in the most inaccessible part of the house. I did know that she could talk, but Gogol had never explained to me the circumstances under which this happened. There were only the two of us, or three, in there. Nikolai Vassilevitch and I were drinking vodka and discussing Butkov's novel. I remember that we left this topic, and he was maintaining the necessity for radical reforms in the laws of inheritance. We had almost forgotten her. It was then that, with a husky and submissive voice, like Venus on the nuptial couch, she said point-blank: "I want to go poo poo."

I jumped, thinking I had misheard, and looked across at her. She was sitting on a pile of cushions against the wall; that evening she was a soft, blonde beauty, rather well-covered. Her expression seemed commingled of shrewdness and slyness, childishness and irresponsibility. As for Gogol, he blushed violently and, leaping on her, stuck two fingers down her throat. She immediately began to shrink and to turn pale; she took on once again that lost and astonished air which was especially hers, and was in the end reduced to no more than a flabby skin on a perfunctory bony armature. Since, for practical reasons which will readily be divined, she had an extraordinarily flexible backbone, she folded up almost in two, and for the rest of the evening she looked up at us from where she had slithered to the floor, in utter abjection.

All Gogol said was: "She only does it for a joke, or to annoy me, because as a matter of fact she does not have such needs." In the presence of other people, that is to say of me, he generally made a point of treating her with a certain disdain.

We went on drinking and talking, but Nikolai Vassilevitch seemed very much disturbed and absent in spirit. Once he suddenly interrupted what he was saying, seized my hand in his and burst into tears. "What can I do now?" he explained. "You understand, Foma Paskalovitch, that I loved her?"

It is necessary to point out that it was impossible, except by a miracle, ever to repeat any of Caracas' forms. She was a fresh creation every time, and it would have been wasted effort to seek to find again the exact proportions, the exact pressure, and so forth, of a former Caracas. Therefore the plumpish blonde of that evening was lost to Gogol from that time forth forever; this was in fact the tragic end of one of those few loves of Nikolai Vassilevitch, which I described above. He gave me no explanation, he sadly rejected my proffered comfort, and that evening we parted early. But his heart had been laid bare to me in that outburst. He was no longer so reticent with me, and soon had hardly any secrets left. And this, I may say in parenthesis, caused me very great pride.

It seems that things had gone well for the "couple" at the beginning of their life together. Nikolai Vassilevitch had been content with Caracas and slept regularly with her in the same bed. He continued to observe this custom till the end, saying with a timid smile that no companion could be quieter or less importunate than she. But I soon began to doubt this, especially judging by the state he was sometimes in when he woke up. Then, after several years, their relationship began strangely to deteriorate.

All this, let it be said once and for all, is no more than a schematic attempt at an explanation. About that time the woman actually began to show signs of independence or, as one might say, of autonomy. Nikolai Vassilevitch had the extraordinary impression that she was acquiring a personality of her own, indecipherable perhaps, but still distinct from his, and one which slipped through his fingers. It is certain that some sort of continuity was established between each of her appearances—between all those brunettes, those blondes, those redheads and auburn-headed girls, between those plump, those slim, those dusky or snowy or golden beauties, there was a certain something in common. At the beginning of this chapter I cast some doubt on the propriety of considering Caracas as a unitary personality; nevertheless I myself could not quite, whenever I saw her, free myself of the impression that, however unheard of it may seem, this was fundamentally the same woman. And it may be that this was why Gogol felt he had to give her a name.

An attempt to establish in what precisely subsisted the common attributes of the different forms would be quite another thing. Perhaps it was no more and no less than the creative afflatus of Nikolai Vassilevitch himself. But no, it would have been too singular and strange if he had been so much divided off from himself, so much averse to himself. Because whoever she was, Caracas was a disturbing presence and even—it is better to be quite clear—a hostile one. Yet neither Gogol nor I ever succeeded in formulating a remotely tenable hypothesis as to her true nature; when I say formulate, I mean in terms which would be at once rational and accessible to all. But I cannot pass over an extraordinary event which took place at this time.

Caracas fell ill of a shameful disease—or rather Gogol did—though he was not then having, nor had he ever had, any contact with other women.

I will not even try to describe how this happened, or where the filthy complaint came from; all I know is that it happened. And that my great, unhappy friend would say to me: "So, Foma Paskalovitch, you see what lay at the heart of Caracas; it was the spirit of syphilis."

Sometimes he would even blame himself in a quite absurd manner; he was always prone to self-accusation. This incident was a real catastrophe as far as the already obscure relationship between husband and wife, and the hostile feelings of Nikolai Vassilevitch himself, were concerned. He was compelled to undergo long-drawn-out and painful treatment—the treatment of those days—and the situation was aggravated by the fact that the disease in the woman did not seem to be easily curable. Gogol deluded himself for some time that, by blowing his wife up and down and furnishing her with the most widely divergent aspects, he could obtain a woman immune from the contagion, but he was forced to desist when no results were forthcoming.

I shall be brief, seeking not to tire my readers, and also because what I remember seems to become more and more confused. I shall therefore hasten to the tragic conclusion. As to this last, however, let there be no mistake. I must once again make it clear that I am very sure of my ground. I was an eyewitness. Would that I had not been!

The years went by. Nikolai Vassilevitch's distaste for his wife became stronger, though his love for her did not show any signs of diminishing. Toward the end, aversion and attachment struggled so fiercely with each other in his heart that he became quite stricken, almost broken up. His restless eyes, which habitually assumed so many different expressions and sometimes spoke so sweetly to the heart of his interlocutor, now almost always shone with a fevered light, as if he were under the effect of a drug. The strangest impulses arose in him, accompanied by the most senseless fears. He spoke to me of Caracas more and more often, accusing her of unthinkable and amazing things. In these regions I could not follow him, since I had but a sketchy acquaintance with his wife, and hardly any intimacy—and above all since my sensibility was so limited compared with his. I shall accordingly restrict myself to reporting some of his accusations, without reference to my personal impressions.

"Believe it or not, Foma Paskalovitch," he would, for example, often say to me: "Believe it or not, *she's aging!*" Then, unspeakably moved, he would, as was his way, take my hands in his. He also accused Caracas of giving herself up to solitary pleasures, which he had expressly forbidden. He even went so far as to charge her with betraying him, but the things he said became so extremely obscure that I must excuse myself from any further account of them.

One thing that appears certain is that toward the end Caracas, whether aged or not, had turned into a bitter creature, querulous, hypocritical and subject to religious excess. I do not exclude the possibility that she may have had an influence on Gogol's moral position during the last period of his life, a position which is sufficiently well known. The tragic climax came one night quite unexpectedly when Nikolai Vassilevitch and I were celebrating his silver wedding—one of the last evenings we were to spend together. I neither can nor should attempt to set down what it was that led to his decision, at a time when to all appearances he was resigned to tolerating his consort. I know not what new events had taken place that day. I shall confine myself to the facts; my readers must make what they can of them.

That evening Nikolai Vassilevitch was unusually agitated. His distaste for Caracas seemed to have reached an unprecedented intensity. The famous "pyre of vanities"—the burning of his manuscripts—had already taken place; I should not like to say whether or not at the instigation of his wife. His state of mind had been further inflamed by other causes. As to his physical condition, this was ever more pitiful, and strengthened my impression that he took drugs. All the same, he began to talk in a more or less normal way about Belinsky, who was giving him some trouble with his attacks on the *Selected Correspondence*. Then suddenly, tears rising to his eyes, he interrupted himself and cried out: "No. No. It's too much, too much. I can't go on any longer," as well as other obscure and disconnected phrases which he would not clarify. He seemed to be talking to himself. He wrung his hands, shook his head, got up and sat down again after having taken four or five anxious steps round the room. When Caracas appeared, or rather when we went in to her later in the evening in her Oriental chamber, he controlled himself no longer and began to behave like an old man, if I may so express myself, in his second childhood, quite giving way to his absurd impulses. For instance, he kept nudging me and winking and senselessly repeating: "There she is, Foma Paskalovitch; there she is!" Meanwhile she seemed to look up at us with a disdainful attention. But behind these "mannerisms" one could feel in him a real repugnance, a repugnance which had, I suppose, now reached the limits of the endurable. Indeed . . .

After a certain time Nikolai Vassilevitch seemed to pluck up courage. He burst into tears, but somehow they were more manly tears. He wrung his hands again, seized mine in his, and walked up and down, muttering: "That's enough! We can't have any more of this. This is an unheard of thing. How can such a thing be happening to me? How can a man be expected to put up with *this?*"

He then leapt furiously upon the pump, the existence of which he seemed just to have remembered, and, with it in his hand, dashed like a whirlwind to Caracas. He inserted the tube in her anus and began to inflate her. . . . Weeping the while, he shouted like one possessed: "Oh, how I love her, how I love her, my poor, poor darling! . . . But she's going to burst! Unhappy Caracas, most pitiable of God's creatures! But die she must!"

Caracas was swelling up. Nikolai Vassilevitch sweated, wept and pumped. I wished to stop him but, I know not why, I had not the courage. She began to become deformed and shortly assumed the most monstrous aspect; and yet she had not given any signs of alarm—she was used to these jokes. But when she began to feel unbearably full, or perhaps when Nikolai Vissilevitch's intentions became plain to her, she took on an expression of bestial amazement, even a little beseeching, but still without losing that disdainful look. She was afraid, she was even committing herself to his mercy, but still she could not believe in the immediate approach of her fate; she could not believe in the frightful audacity of her husband. He could not see her face because he was behind her. But I looked at her with fascination, and did not move a finger.

At last the internal pressure came through the fragile bones at the base of her skull, and printed on her face an indescribable rictus. Her belly, her thighs, her lips, her breasts and what I could see of her buttocks had swollen to incredible proportions. All of a sudden she belched, and gave a long hissing groan; both these phenomena one could explain by the increase in pressure, which had suddenly forced a way out through the valve in her throat. Then her eyes bulged frantically, threatening to jump out of their sockets. Her ribs flared wide apart and were no longer attached to the sternum, and she resembled a python digesting a donkey. A donkey, did I say? An ox! An elephant! At this point I believed her already dead, but Nikolai Vassilevitch, sweating, weeping and repeating: "My dearest! My beloved! My best!" continued to pump.

She went off unexpectedly and, as it were, all of a piece. It was not one part of her skin which gave way and the rest which followed, but her whole surface at the same instant. She scattered in the air. The pieces fell more or less slowly, according to their size, which was in no case above a very restricted one. I distinctly remember a piece of her cheek, with some lip attached, hanging on the corner of the mantlepiece. Nikolai Vassilevitch stared at me like a madman. Then he pulled himself together and, once more with furious determination, he began carefully to collect those poor rags which once had been the shining skin of Caracas, and all of her.

"Good-by, Caracas," I thought I heard him murmur, "Good-by! You were too pitiable!" And then suddenly and quite audibly: "The fire! The fire! She too must end up in the fire." He crossed himself—with his left hand, of course. Then, when he had picked up all those shriveled rags, even climbing on the furniture so as not to miss any, he threw them straight on the fire in the hearth, where they began to burn slowly and with an excessively unpleasant smell! Nikolai Vassilevitch, like all Russians, had a passion for throwing important things in the fire.

Red in the face, with an inexpressible look of despair, and yet of sinister triumph too, he gazed on the pyre of those miserable remains. He had seized my arm and was squeezing it convulsively. But those traces of what had once been a being were hardly well alight when he seemed yet again to pull himself together, as if he were suddenly remembering something or taking a painful decision. In one bound he was out of the room.

A few seconds later I heard him speaking to me through the door in a broken, plaintive voice: "Foma Paskalovitch, I want you to promise not to look. *Golubchik,* promise not to look at me when I come in."

I don't know what I answered, or whether I tried to reassure him in any way. But he insisted, and I had to promise him, as if he were a child, to hide my face against the wall and only turn round when he said I might. The door then opened violently and Nikolai Vassilevitch burst into the room and ran to the fireplace.

And here I must confess my weakness, though I consider it justified by the extraordinary circumstances. I looked round before Nikolai Vassilevitch told me I could; it was stronger than me. I was just in time to see him carrying something in his arms, something which he threw on the fire with all the rest, so that it suddenly flared up. At that, since the desire to see had entirely mastered every other thought in me, I dashed to the fireplace. But Nikolai Vassilevitch placed himself between me and it and pushed me back with a strength of which I had not believed him capable. Meanwhile the object was burning and giving off clouds of smoke. And before he showed any sign of calming down there was nothing left but a heap of silent ashes.

The true reason why I wished to see was because I had already glimpsed. But it was only a glimpse, and perhaps I should not allow myself to introduce even the slightest element of uncertainty into this true story. And yet, an eyewitness account is not complete without a mention of that which the witness knows with less than complete certainty. To cut a long story short, that something was a baby. Not a flesh and blood baby, of course, but more something in the line of a rubber doll or a model. Something, which, to judge by its appearance, could have been called *Caracas' son.*

Was I mad too? That I do not know, but I do know that this was what I saw, not clearly, but with my own eyes. And I wonder why it was that when I was writing this just now I didn't mention that when Nikolai Vassilevitch came back into the room he was muttering between his clenched teeth: "Him too! Him too!"

And that is the sum of my knowledge of Nikolai Vassilevitch's wife. In the next chapter I shall tell what happened to him afterwards, and that will be the last chapter of his life. But to give an interpretation of his feelings for his wife, or indeed for anything, is quite another and more difficult matter, though I have attempted it elsewhere in this volume, and refer the reader to that modest effort. I hope I have thrown sufficient light on a most controversial question and that I have unveiled the mystery, if not of Gogol, then at least of his wife. In the course of this I have implicitly given the lie to the insensate accusation that he ill-treated or even beat his wife, as well as other like absurdities. And what else can be the goal of a humble biographer such as the present writer but to serve the memory of that lofty genius who is the object of his study?

# PETRIFIED MAN

Eudora Welty


"Reach in my purse and git me a cigarette without no powder in it if you kin, Mrs. Fletcher, honey," said Leota to her ten o'clock shampoo-and-set customer. "I don't like no perfumed cigarettes."

Mrs. Fletcher gladly reached over to the lavender shelf under the lavender-framed mirror, shook a hair net loose from the clasp of the patent-leather bag, and slapped her hand down quickly on a powder puff which burst out when the purse was opened.

"Why, look at the peanuts, Leota!" said Mrs. Fletcher in her marveling voice.

"Honey, them goobers has been in my purse a week if they's been in it a day. Mrs. Pike bought them peanuts."

"Who's Mrs. Pike?" asked Mrs. Fletcher, settling back. Hidden in this den of curling fluid and henna packs, separated by a lavender swing-door from the other customers, who were being gratified in other booths, she could give her curiosity its freedom. She looked expectantly at the black part in Leota's yellow curls as she bent to light the cigarette.

"Mrs. Pike is this lady from New Orleans," said Leota, puffing, and pressing into Mrs. Fletcher's scalp with strong red-nailed fingers. "A friend, not a customer. You see, like maybe I told you last time, me and Fred and Sal and Joe all had us a fuss, so Sal and Joe up and moved out, so we didn't do a thing but rent out their room. So we rented it to Mrs. Pike. And Mr. Pike." She flicked an ash into the basket of dirty towels. "Mrs. Pike is a very decided blonde. *She* bought me the peanuts."

"She must be cute," said Mrs. Fletcher.

"Honey, 'cute' ain't the word for what she is. I'm tellin' you, Mrs. Pike is attractive. She has her a good time. She's got a sharp eye out, Mrs. Pike has."

She dashed the comb through the air, and paused dramatically as a cloud of Mrs. Fletcher's hennaed hair floated out of the lavender teeth like a small storm-cloud.

"Hair fallin'."

"Aw, Leota."

"Uh-huh, commencin' to fall out," said Leota, combing again, and letting fall another cloud.

"Is it any dandruff in it?" Mrs. Fletcher was frowning, her hair-line eyebrows diving down toward her nose, and her wrinkled, beady-lashed eyelids batting with concentration.

"Nope." She combed again. "Just fallin' out."

"Bet it was that last perm'nent you gave me that did it." Mrs. Fletcher said cruelly. "Remember you cooked me fourteen minutes."

"You had fourteen minutes comin' to you," said Leota with finality.

"Bound to be somethin'," persisted Mrs. Fletcher. "Dandruff, dandruff. I couldn't of caught a thing like that from Mr. Fletcher, could I?"

"Well," Leota answered at last, "you know what I heard in here yestiddy, one of Thelma's ladies was settin' over yonder in Thelma's booth gittin' a machineless, and I don't mean to insist or insinuate or anything, Mrs. Fletcher, but Thelma's lady just happ'med to throw out—I forgotten what she was talkin' about at the time—that you was p-r-e-g, and lots of times that'll make your hair do awful funny, fall out and God knows what all. It just ain't our fault is the way I look at it."

There was a pause. The women stared at each other in the mirror.

"Who was it?" demanded Mrs. Fletcher.

"Honey, I really couldn't say." said Leota. "Not that you look it."

"Where's Thelma? I'll get it out of her," said Mrs. Fletcher.

"Now, honey I wouldn't go and git mad over a little thing like that," Leota said, combing hastily, as though to hold Mrs. Fletcher down by the hair. "I'm sure it was somebody didn't mean no harm in the world. How far gone are you?"

"Just wait," said Mrs. Fletcher, and shrieked for Thelma, who came in and took a drag from Leota's cigarette.

"Thelma, honey, throw your mind back to yestiddy if you kin," said Leota, drenching Mrs. Fletcher's hair with a thick fluid and catching the overflow in a cold wet towel at her neck.

"Well, I got my lady half wound for a spiral," said Thelma doubtfully.

"This won't take but a minute," said Leota. "Who is it you got in there, old Horse Face? Just cast your mind back and try to remember who your lady was yestiddy who happ'm to mention that my customer was pregnant, that's all. She's dead to know."

Thelma drooped her blood-red lips and looked over Mrs. Fletcher's head into the mirror. "Why, honey, I ain't got the faintest," she breathed. "I really don't recollect the faintest. But I'm sure she meant no harm. I declare, I forgot my hair finally got combed and thought it was a stranger behind me."

"Was it that Mrs. Hutchinson?" Mrs. Fletcher was tensely polite.

"Mrs. Hutchinson? Oh, Mrs. Hutchinson." Thelma batted her eyes. "Naw, precious, she come on Thursday and didn't ev'm mention your name. I doubt if she ev'm knows you're on the way."

"Thelma!" cried Leota stanchly.

"All I know is, whoever it is'll be sorry someday. Why, I just barely knew it myself!" cried Mrs. Fletcher. "Just let her wait!"

"Why? What're you gonna do to her?"

It was a child's voice, and the women looked down. A little boy was making tents with aluminum wave pinchers on the floor under the sink.

"Billy Boy, hon, mustn't bother nice ladies," Leota smiled. She slapped him brightly and behind her back waved Thelma out of the booth. "Ain't Billy Boy a sight? Only three years old and already just nuts about the beauty-parlor business."

"I never saw him here before," said Mrs. Fletcher, still unmollified.

"He ain't been here before, that's how come," said Leota. "He belongs to Mrs. Pike. She got her a job but it was Fay's Millinery. He oughtn't to try on those ladies' hats, they come down over his eyes like I don't know what. They just git to look ridiculous, that's what, an' of course he's gonna put 'em on: hats. They tole Mrs. Pike they didn't appreciate him hangin' around there. Here, he couldn't hurt a thing."

"Well! I don't like children that much," said Mrs. Fletcher.

"Well!" said Leota moodily.

"Well! I'm almost tempted not to have this one," said Mrs. Fletcher. "That Mrs. Hutchinson! Just looks straight through you when she sees you on the street and then spits at you behind your back."

"Mr. Fletcher would beat you on the head if you didn't have it now," said Leota reasonably. "After going this far."

Mrs. Fletcher sat up straight. "Mr. Fletcher can't do a thing with me."

"He can't!" Leota winked at herself in the mirror.

"No siree, he can't. If he so much as raises his voice against me, he knows good and well I'll have one of my sick headaches, and then I'm just not fit to live with. And if I really look that pregnant already—"

"Well, now, honey, I just want you to know—I habm't told any of my ladies and I ain't goin' to tell 'em—even that you're losin' your hair. You just get you one of those Stork-a-Lure dresses and stop worryin'. What people don't know don't hurt nobody, as Mrs. Pike says."

"Did you tell Mrs. Pike?" asked Mrs. Fletcher sulkily.

"Well, Mrs. Fletcher, look, you ain't ever goin' to lay eyes on Mrs. Pike or her lay eyes on you, so what diffunce does it make in the long run?"

"I knew it!" Mrs. Fletcher deliberately nodded her head so as to destroy a ringlet Leota was working on behind her ear. "Mrs. Pike!"

Leota sighed. "I reckon I might as well tell you. It wasn't any more Thelma's lady tole me you was pregnant than a bat."

"Not Mrs. Hutchinson?"

"Naw, Lord! It was Mrs. Pike."

"Mrs. Pike!" Mrs. Fletcher could only sputter and let curling fluid roll into her ear. "How could Mrs. Pike possibly know I was pregnant or otherwise, when she doesn't even know me? The nerve of some people!"

"Well, here's how it was. Remember Sunday?"

"Yes," said Mrs. Fletcher.

"Sunday, Mrs. Pike an' me was all by ourself. Mr. Pike and Fred had gone over to Eagle Lake, sayin' they was goin' to catch 'em some fish, but they didn't, a course. So we was settin' in Mrs. Pike's car, is a 1939 Dodge—"

"1939, eh," said Mrs. Fletcher.

"—An' we was gettin' us a Jax beer apiece—that's the beer that Mrs. Pike says is made right in N.O., so she won't drink no other kind. So I seen you drive up to the drugstore an' run in for just a secont, leavin' I reckon Mr. Fletcher in the car, an' come runnin' out with what looked like a perscription. So I says to Mrs. Pike, just to be makin' talk, 'Right yonder's Mrs. Fletcher, and I reckon that's Mr. Fletcher—she's one of my regular customers,' I says."

"I had on a figured print," said Mrs. Fletcher tentatively.

"You sure did," agreed Leota. "So Mrs. Pike, she give you a good look—she's very observant, a good judge of character, cute as a minute, you know—and she says, 'I bet you another Jax that lady's three months on the way.' "

"What gall!" said Mrs. Fletcher. "Mrs. Pike!"

"Mrs. Pike ain't goin' to bite you," said Leota. "Mrs. Pike is a lovely girl, you'd be crazy about her, Mrs. Fletcher. But she can't sit still a minute. We went to the travelin' freak show yestiddy after work. I got through early— nine o'clock. In the vacant store next door? What, you ain't been?"

"No, I despise freaks," declared Mrs. Fletcher.

"Aw. Well, honey, talkin' about bein' pregnant an' all, you ought to see those twins in a bottle, you really owe it to yourself."

"What twins?" asked Mrs. Fletcher out of the side of her mouth.

"Well, honey, they got these two twins in a bottle, see? Born joined plumb together—dead of course." Leota dropped her voice into a soft lyrical hum. "They was about this long—pardon—must of been full time, all right, wouldn't you say? —an' they had these two heads an' two faces an' four arms an' four legs, all kind of joined *here*. See, this face looked this-a-way, and the other face looked that-a-way, over their shoulder, see. Kinda pathetic."

"Glah!" said Mrs. Fletcher disapprovingly.

"Well, ugly? Honey, I mean to tell you—their parents was first cousins and all like that. Billy Boy, git me a fresh towel from off Teeny's stack—this 'n's wringin' wet—an' quit ticklin' my ankles with that curler. I declare! He don't miss nothin'."

"Me and Mr. Fletcher aren't one speck of kin, or he could never of had me," said Mrs. Fletcher placidly.

"Of course not!" protested Leota. "Neither is me an' Fred, not that we know of. Well, honey, what Mrs. Pike liked was the pygmies. They've got these pygmies down there, too, an' Mrs. Pike was just wild about 'em. You know, the tee-nini-est men in the universe? Well honey, they can rest back on their little bohunkus an' roll around an' you can't hardly tell if they're sittin' or standin'. That'll give you some idea. They're about forty-two years old. Just suppose it was your husband!''

''Well, Mr. Fletcher is five foot nine and one half,'' said Mrs. Fletcher quickly.

''Fred's five foot ten,'' said Leota, ''but I tell him he's still a shrimp, account of I'm so tall.'' She made a deep wave over Mrs. Fletcher's other temple with the comb. ''Well, these pygmies are a kind of a dark brown, Mrs. Fletcher. Not bad-lookin' for what they are, you know.''

''I wouldn't care for them,'' said Mrs. Fletcher. ''What does that Mrs. Pike see in them?''

''Aw, I don't know,'' said Leota. ''She's just cute, that's all. But they got this man, this petrified man, that ever'thing ever since he was nine years old, when it goes through his digestion, see, somehow Mrs. Pike says it goes to his joints and has been turning to stone.''

''How awful!'' said Mrs. Fletcher.

''He's forty-two too. That looks like a bad age.''

''Who said so, that Mrs. Pike? I bet she's forty-two,'' said Mrs. Fletcher.

''Naw,'' said Leota, ''Mrs. Pike's thirty-three, born in January, an Aquarian. He could move his head—like this. A course his head and mind ain't a joint, so to speak, and I guess his stomach ain't either—not yet, anyways. But see—his food, he eats it, and it goes down, see, and then he digests it''—Leota rose on her toes for an instant—''and it goes out to his joints and before you can say 'Jack Robinson,' it's stone—pure stone. He's turning to stone. How'd you like to be married to a guy like that? All he can do, he can move his head just a quarter of an inch. A course he *looks* just *terrible*.''

''I should think he would,'' said Mrs. Fletcher frostily. ''Mr. Fletcher takes bending exercises every night of the world. I make him.''

''All Fred does is lay around the house like a rug. I wouldn't be surprised if he woke up someday and couldn't move. The petrified man just sat there moving his quarter of an inch though,'' said Leota reminiscently.

''Did Mrs. Pike like the petrified man?'' asked Mrs. Fletcher.

''Not as much as she did the others,'' said Leota deprecatingly. ''And then she likes a man to be a good dresser, and all that.''

''Is Mr. Pike a good dresser?'' asked Mrs. Fletcher skeptically.

''Oh, well, yeah,'' said Leota, ''but he's twelve or fourteen years older 'n her. She ast Lady Evangeline about him.''

''Who's Lady Evangeline?'' asked Mrs. Fletcher.

''Well, it's this mind reader they got in the freak show,'' said Leota. ''Was real good. Lady Evangeline is her name, and if I had another dollar I wouldn't do a thing but have my other palm read. She had what Mrs. Pike said was the 'sixth mind' but she had the worst manicure I ever saw on a living person."

"What did she tell Mrs. Pike?" asked Mrs. Fletcher.

"She told her Mr. Pike was as true to her as he could be and, besides, would come into some money."

"Humph!" said Mrs. Fletcher. "What does he do?"

"I can't tell," said Leota, "because he don't work. Lady Evangeline didn't tell me near enough about my nature or anything. And I would like to go back and find out some more about this boy. Used to go with this boy got married to this girl. Oh, shoot, that was about three and a half years ago, when you was still goin' to the Robert E. Lee Beauty Shop in Jackson. He married her for her money. Another fortune-teller tole me that at the time. So I'm not in love with him any more, anyway, besides being married to Fred, but Mrs. Pike thought just for the hell of it, see, to ask Lady Evangeline was he happy."

"Does Mrs. Pike know everything about you already?" asked Mrs. Fletcher unbelievingly. "Mercy!"

"Oh yeah, I tole her ever'thing about ever'thing, from now on back to I don't know when—to when I first started goin' out," said Leota. "So I ast Lady Evangeline for one of my questions, was he happily married, and she says, just like she was glad I ask her, 'Honey,' she says, 'naw, he idn't. You write down this day, March 8, 1941,' she says, 'and mock it down: three years from today him and her won't be occupyin' the same bed.' There it is, up on the wall with them other dates—see, Mrs. Fletcher? And she says, 'Child, you ought to be glad you didn't git him, because he's so mercenary.' So I'm glad I married Fred. He sure ain't mercenary, money don't mean a thing to him. But I sure would like to go back and have my other palm read."

"Did Mrs. Pike believe in what the fortune-teller said?" asked Mrs. Fletcher in a superior tone of voice.

"Lord, yes, she's from New Orleans. Ever'body in New Orleans believes ever'thing spooky. One of 'em in New Orleans before it was raided says to Mrs. Pike one summer she was goin' to go from State to State and meet some gray-headed men, and, sure enough, she says she went on a beautician convention up to Chicago. . . ."

"Oh!" said Mrs. Fletcher. "Oh, is Mrs. Pike a beautician too?"

"Sure she is," protested Leota. "She's a beautician. I'm goin' to git her in here if I can. Before she married. But it don't leave you. She says sure enough, there was three men who was a very large part of making her trip what it was, and they all three had gray in their hair and they went in six States. Got Christmas cards from 'em. Billy Boy, go see if Thelma's got any dry cotton. Look how Mrs. Fletcher's a-drippin'."

"Where did Mrs. Pike meet Mr. Pike?" asked Mrs. Fletcher primly.

"On another train," said Leota.

"I met Mr. Fletcher, or rather he met me, in a rental library," said Mrs. Fletcher with dignity, as she watched the net come down over her head.

"Honey, me an' Fred, we met in a rumble seat eight months ago and we was practically on what you might call the way to the altar inside of half an hour," said Leota in a guttural voice, and bit a bobby pin open. "Course it don't last. Mrs. Pike says nothin' like that ever lasts."

"Mr. Fletcher and myself are as much in love as the day we married," said Mrs. Fletcher belligerently as Leota stuffed cotton into her ears.

"Mrs. Pike says it don't last," repeated Leota in a louder voice. "Now go git under the dryer. You can turn yourself on, can't you? I'll be back to comb you out. Durin' lunch I promised to give Mrs. Pike a facial. You know—free. Her bein' in the business, so to speak."

"I bet she needs one," said Mrs. Fletcher, letting the swing-door fly back against Leota. "Oh, pardon me."

A week later, on time for her appointment, Mrs. Fletcher sank heavily into Leota's chair after first removing a drugstore rental book, called *Life Is Like That,* from the seat. She stared in a discouraged way into the mirror.

"You can tell it when I'm sitting down, all right," she said.

Leota seemed preoccupied and stood shaking out a lavender cloth. She began to pin it around Mrs. Fletcher's neck in silence.

"I said you sure can tell it when I'm sitting straight on and coming at you this way." Mrs. Fletcher said.

"Why, honey, naw you can't," said Leota gloomily. "Why, I'd never know. If somebody was to come up to me on the street, and say, 'Mrs. Fletcher is pregnant!' I'd say, 'Heck, she don't look it to me.' "

"If a certain party hadn't found it out and spread it around, it wouldn't be too late even now," said Mrs. Fletcher frostily, but Leota was almost choking her with the cloth, pinning it so tight, and she couldn't speak clearly. She paddled her hands in the air until Leota wearily loosened her.

"Listen, honey, you're just a virgin compared to Mrs. Montjoy," Leota was going on, still absent-minded. She bent Mrs. Fletcher back in the chair and, sighing, tossed liquid from a teacup onto her head and dug both hands into her scalp. "You know Mrs. Montjoy—her husband's that premature-gray-headed fella?"

"She's in the Trojan Garden Club, is all I know," said Mrs. Fletcher.

"Well, honey," said Leota, but in a weary voice, "she come in here not the week before and not the day before she had her baby—she come in here the very selfsame day, I mean to tell you. Child, we was all plumb scared to death. There she was! Come for her shampoo an' set. Why, Mrs. Fletcher, in a hour an' twenty minutes she was layin' up there in the Babtist

Hospital with a seb'm-pound son. It was that close a shave. I declare, if I hadn't been so tired I would of drank up a bottle of gin that night."

"What gall," said Mrs. Fletcher. "I never knew her at all well."

"See, her husband was waitin' outside in the car, and her bags was all packed an' in the back seat, an' she was all ready, 'cept she wanted her shampoo an' set. An' havin' one pain right after another. Her husband kep' comin' in here, scared-like, but couldn't do nothin' with her a course. She yelled bloody murder, too, but she always yelled her head off when I give her a perm'nent."

"She must of been crazy," said Mrs. Fletcher. "How did she look?"

"Shoot!" said Leota.

"Well, I can guess," said Mrs. Fletcher. "Awful."

"Just wanted to look pretty while she was havin' her baby is all," said Leota airily. "Course, we was glad to give the lady what she was after— that's our motto—but I bet a hour later she wasn't payin' no mind to them little end curls. I bet she wasn't thinkin' about she ought to have on a net. It wouldn't of done her no good if she had."

"No, I don't suppose it would," said Mrs. Fletcher.

"Yeah man! She was a-yellin'. Just like when I give her her perm'nent."

"Her husband ought to make her behave. Don't it seem that way to you?" asked Mrs. Fletcher. "He ought to put his foot down."

"Ha," said Leota. "A lot he could do. Maybe some women is soft."

"Oh, you mistake me, I don't mean for her to get soft—far from it! Women have to stand up for themselves, or there's just no telling. But now you take me—I ask Mr. Fletcher's advice now and then, and he appreciates it, especially on something important, like is it time for a permanent—not that I've told him about the baby. He says, 'Why dear, go ahead!' Just ask their *advice*."

"Huh! If I ever ast Fred's advice we'd be floatin' down the Yazoo River on a houseboat or somethin' by this time," said Leota. "I'm sick of Fred. I told him to go over to Vicksburg."

"Is he going?" demanded Mrs. Fletcher.

"Sure. See, the fortune-teller—I went back and had my other palm read, since we've got to rent the room again—said my lover was goin' to work in Vicksburg, so I don't know who she could mean, unless she meant Fred. And Fred ain't workin' here—that much is so."

"Is he going to work in Vicksburg?" asked Mrs. Fletcher. "And—"

"Sure. Lady Evangeline said so. Said the future is going to be brighter than the present. He don't want to go, but I ain't gonna put up with nothin' like that. Lays around the house an' bulls—did bull—with that good-for-nothin' Mr. Pike. He says if he goes who'll cook, but I says I never get to eat anyway—not meals. Billy Boy, take Mrs. Grover that *Screen Secrets* and leg it."

Mrs. Fletcher heard stamping feet go out the door.

"Is that that Mrs. Pike's little boy here again?" she asked, sitting up gingerly.

"Yeah, that's still him." Leota stuck out her tongue.

Mrs. Fletcher could hardly believe her eyes. "Well! How's Mrs. Pike, your attractive new friend with the sharp eyes who spreads it around town that perfect strangers are pregnant?" she asked in a sweetened tone.

"Oh, Mizziz Pike." Leota combed Mrs. Fletcher's hair with heavy strokes.

"You act like you're tired," said Mrs. Fletcher.

"Tired? Feel like it's four o'clock in the afternoon already," said Leota. "I ain't told you the awful luck we had, me and Fred? It's the worst thing you ever heard of. Maybe *you* think Mrs. Pike's got sharp eyes. Shoot, there's a limit! Well, you know, we rented out our room to this Mr. and Mrs. Pike from New Orleans when Sal and Joe Fentress got mad at us 'cause they drank up some homebrew we had in the closet—Sal an' Joe did. So, a week ago Sat'day Mr. and Mrs. Pike moved in. Well, I kinda fixed up the room, you know—put a sofa pillow on the couch and picked some ragged robins and put in a vase, but they never did say they appreciated it. Anyway, then I put some old magazines on the table."

"I think that was lovely," said Mrs. Fletcher.

"Wait. So, come night 'fore last, Fred and this Mr. Pike, who Fred just took up with, was back from they said they was fishin', bein' as neither one of 'em has got a job to his name and we was all settin' around in their room. So Mrs. Pike was settin' there, readin' a old *Startling G-Man Tales* that was mine, mind you, I'd bought it myself, and all of a sudden she jumps!—into the air—you'd 'a' thought she'd set on a spider—an' says, 'Canfield'—ain't that silly, that's Mr. Pike—'Canfield, my God A'mighty,' she says, 'honey,' she says, 'we're rich, and you won't have to work.' Not that he turned one hand anyway. Well, me and Fred rushes over to her, and Mr. Pike, too, and there she sets, pointin' her finger at a photo in my copy of *Startling G-Man*. 'See that man?' yells Mrs. Pike. 'Remember him, Canfield?' 'Never forget a face,' says Mr. Pike. 'It's Mr. Petrie, that we stayed with him in the apartment next to ours in Toulouse Street in N.O. for six weeks. Mr. Petrie.' 'Well,' says Mrs. Pike, like she can't hold out one secont longer, 'Mr. Petrie is wanted for five hundred dollars cash, for rapin' four women in California, and I know where he is.' "

"Mercy!" said Mrs. Fletcher. "Where was he?"

At some time Leota had washed her hair and now she yanked her up by the back locks and sat her up.

"Know where he was?"

"I certainly don't," Mrs. Fletcher said. Her scalp hurt all over.

Leota flung a towel around the top of her customer's head. "Nowhere else but in that freak show! I saw him just as plain as Mrs. Pike. *He* was the petrified man!"

"Who would ever have thought that!" cried Mrs. Fletcher sympathetically.

"So Mr. Pike says, 'Well, whatta you know about that,' an' he looks real hard at the photo, and whistles. And she starts dancin' and singin about their good luck. She meant our bad luck! I made a point of tellin' that fortune-teller the next time I saw her. I said, 'Listen, that magazine was layin' around the house for a month, and there was five hundred dollars in it for somebody. An' there was the freak show runnin' night an' day, not two steps away from my own beauty parlor, with Mr. Petrie just settin' there waitin'. An' it had to be Mr. and Mrs. Pike, almost perfect strangers.' "

"What gall," said Mrs. Fletcher. She was only sitting there, wrapped in a turban, but she did not mind.

"Fortune-tellers don't care. And Mrs. Pike, she goes around actin' like she thinks she was Mrs. God," said Leota. "So they're goin' to leave tomorrow, Mr. and Mrs. Pike. And in the meantime I got to keep that mean, bad little ole kid here, gettin' under my feet ever' minute of the day an' talkin' back too."

"Have they gotten the five hundred dollars' reward already?" asked Mrs. Fletcher.

"Well," said Leota, "at first Mr. Pike didn't want to do anything about it. Can you feature that? Said he kinda liked that ole bird and said he was real nice to 'em, lent 'em money or somethin'. But Mrs. Pike simply tole him he could just go to hell, and I can see her point. She says, 'You ain't worked a lick in six months, and here I made five hundred dollars in two seconts, and what thanks do I get for it? You go to hell, Canfield,' she says. So," Leota went on in a despondent voice, "they called up the cops and they caught the ole bird, all right, right there in the freak show where I saw him with my own eyes, thinkin' he was petrified. He's the one. Did it under his real name—Mr. Petrie. Four women in California, all in the month of August. So Mrs. Pike gits five hundred dollars. And my magazine, and right next door to my beauty parlor. I cried all night, but Fred said it wasn't a bit of use and to go to sleep, because the whole thing was just a sort of coincidence—you know: can't do nothin' about it. He says it put him clean out of the notion of goin' to Vicksburg for a few days till we rent out the room agin—no tellin' who we'll git this time."

"But can you imagine anybody knowing this old man, that's raped four women?" persisted Mrs. Fletcher, and she shuddered audibly. "Did Mrs. Pike *speak* to him when she met him in the freak show?"

Leota had begun to comb Mrs. Fletcher's hair. "I says to her, I says, 'I didn't notice you fallin' on his neck when he was the petrified man—don't tell me you didn't recognize your fine friend?' And she says, 'I didn't recognize him with that white powder all over his face. He just looked familiar,' Mrs. Pike says, 'and lots of people look familiar.' But she says that ole petrified man did put her in mind of somebody. She wondered who it was! Kep' her awake, which man she'd ever knew it reminded her of. So when she seen the photo, it all come to her. Like a flash. Mr. Petrie. The way he'd turn his head and look at her when she took him in his breakfast."

"Took him in his breakfast!" shrieked Mrs. Fletcher. "Listen—don't tell me. I'd 'a' felt something."

"Four women. I guess those women didn't have the faintest notion at the time they'd be worth a hundred an' twenty-five bucks a piece some day to Mrs. Pike. We ast her how old the fella was then, an' she says he musta had one foot in the grave, at least. Can you beat it?"

"Not really petrified at all, of course," said Mrs. Fletcher meditatively. She drew herself up. "I'd 'a' felt something," she said proudly.

"Shoot! I did feel somethin'," said Leota. "I tole Fred when I got home I felt so funny. I said, 'Fred, that ole petrified man sure did leave me with a funny feelin'.' He says, 'Funny-haha or funny-peculiar?' and I says, 'Funny-peculiar.' " She pointed her comb into the air emphatically.

"I'll bet you did," said Mrs. Fletcher.

They both heard a crackling noise.

Leota screamed, "Billy Boy! What you doin' in my purse?"

"Aw, I'm just eatin' these ole stale peanuts up," said Billy Boy.

"You come here to me!" screamed Leota, recklessly flinging down the comb, which scattered a whole ashtray full of bobby pins and knocked down a row of Coco-Cola bottles. "This is the last straw!"

"I caught him! I caught him!" giggled Mrs. Fletcher. "I'll hold him on my lap. You bad, bad boy, you! I guess I better learn how to spank little old bad boys," she said.

Leota's eleven o'clock customer pushed open the swing-door upon Leota paddling him heartily with the brush, while he gave angry but belittling screams which penetrated beyond the booth and filled the whole curious beauty parlor. From everywhere ladies began to gather round to watch the paddling. Billy Boy kicked both Leota and Mrs. Fletcher as hard as he could, Mrs. Fletcher with her new fixed smile.

"There, my little man!" gasped Leota. "You won't be able to set down for a week if I knew what I was doin'."

Billy Boy stomped through the group of wild-haired ladies and went out the door, but flung back the words, "If you're so smart, why ain't you rich?"

# Research and Popular Culture

## FEMININE DEPENDENCY
### Helen Andelin

A good definition of Feminine Dependency is *a woman's need for masculine care and protection.* Women were designed to be wives, mothers and homemakers and therefore in need of masculine help to make their way through life. The men were assigned to fill this need for women by serving as their guide, protector and provider. Feminine dependency is very attractive to men. Dora was rather helpless and dependent upon men and for this reason made a strong appeal to David's gentlemanly heart. Agnes was too lacking in this ability. She was too self-sufficient and independent, to win David at this stage in his life.

Do not think that protecting a dependent woman is an imposition on a man. *One of the most pleasant sensations a real man can experience is his consciousness of the power to give his manly care and protection. Rob him of this sensation of superior strength and ability and you rob him of his manliness.* It is a delight to him to protect and shelter a dependent woman. The bigger, manlier and more sensible a man is, the more he seems to be attracted by this quality.

### How Men Feel in the Presence of Capable Women

What happens when the average red-blooded man comes in contact with an obviously able, intellectual and competent woman manifestly independent of any help a mere man can give and capable of meeting him or defeating him upon his own ground? He simply doesn't feel like a man any longer. In the presence of such strength and ability in a mere woman, he feels like a futile, ineffectual imitation of a man. It is the most uncomfortable and humiliating sensation a man can experience; so that the woman who arouses it becomes repugnant to him. *A man cannot derive any joy or satisfaction from protecting a woman who can obviously do very well without him. He only delights in protecting or sheltering a woman who needs his manly care, or at least appears to need it.*

84

## How Men Feel in the Presence of
## Dependent Women

When a man is in the presence of a tender, gentle, trustful, dependent woman, he immediately feels a sublime expansion of his power to protect and shelter this frail and delicate creature. In the presence of such weakness, he feels stronger, more competent, bigger, manlier than ever. This feeling of strength and power is one of the most enjoyable he can experience. The apparent need of the woman for protection, instead of arousing contempt for her lack of ability, appeals to the very noblest feelings within him.

## Amelia

An excellent illustration of feminine dependency is found in the character of Amelia in *Vanity Fair.* "Those who formed the small circle of Amelia's acquaintances were quite angry with the enthusiasm with which the other sex regarded her. For almost all men who came near her loved her; though no doubt they would be at a loss to tell you why. She was not brilliant, nor witty, nor wise overmuch, nor extraordinarily handsome. But wherever she went, she touched and charmed everyone of the male sex, as invariably as she awakened the scorn and incredulity of her own sisterhood. I think it was her *weakness* which was her principle charm; a kind of sweet submission and *softness* which seemed to appeal to each man she met for his sympathy and protection."

## Mrs. Woodrow Wilson

Mrs. Wilson was a tender, dependent woman, for her husband wrote to her, "What a source of steadying and of strength it is to me in such seasons of too intimate self-questioning to have one fixed point of confidence and certainty—that even, unbroken, excellent perfection of my little wife, with her poise, her easy capacity in action, her unfailing courage, her quick efficient thought—and the charm that goes with it all, the sweetness, the feminine grace—none of the usual penalties of efficiency—no hardness, no incisive sharpness, no air of command or of unyielding opinion. Most women who are efficient are such terrors."

## The Capable Woman

In describing the capable woman, let me first state that I am referring to a woman's being capable in the *masculine things.* I am not suggesting that a woman be incapable in her own feminine sphere of work. As a homemaker, she must be efficient to succeed. But to be feminine, a woman must eliminate any tendency to masculine capabilities such as efficiency in running an office, skill in fixing a motor or changing a tire, or masculine courage in braving danger. To have such masculine capabilities is to *turn off feminine charm*. This is a widespread problem in our times which needs our consideration.

There are many women, in all walks of life, who possess great personal magnetism, whom all, including the men, admire as great and powerful characters, but who can never change a man's admiration into love. One such woman, a famous Sunday school teacher of young men and women, illustrates this situation. Her magnetic personality and noble character were so much admired that hundreds of young people sought to join her class and thousands of men and women of all ages attended whenever she gave a public lecture. In spite of this almost universal respect and admiration, the average man would never think of seeking her private company, indulging in an intimate conversation or of making her his "little girl" to cherish and protect throughout a lifetime. Everyone knows of such women, healthy, charming, enjoyable, whom men admire greatly but whom they do not seem to be fascinated by. The reason for this is that they lack an air of frail dependency upon men. They are too capable and independent to stir a man's sentiments. The air of being able to "kill your own snakes" is just what destroys the charm of so many business and professional women. And it is the absence of this air that permits many a "brainless doll" to capture an able and intelligent man whom one would expect to choose a more sensible companion.

The kind of woman a man wants is first an angelic being whom he can adore as better than himself, but also a helpless creature whom he would want to gather up in his arms and cherish and protect forever. The admirable women that we just mentioned fulfill the first requirement but fail to fulfill the second. Though it is absolutely necessary to fulfill the first, you cannot afford to do as these women do and neglect the second.

What if you happen to be a big, strong and capable woman, or have a powerful personality or in some other way overpower men? How, then, can you possibly appear to be tender, trustful, delicate and dependent? In the first place, size has nothing to do with the quality of feminine dependency. No matter what your size, your height or your capabilities, you can appear fragile to a man if you follow certain rules and if you will take on an attitude of frailty. It is not important that you actually be little and delicate, but that *you seem so* to the man.

## When the Large Woman Attracts the Little Man

Occasionally we will see a rather small short man, married to a large woman. It is interesting to observe that she does not seem large to him because she has given him the impression of smallness. Such a man is even apt to call her "his little girl." She has managed, in spite of her size, to give him the impression of delicacy. By letting him know that she can't get along without him, that she is utterly dependent upon him, she has been able to disguise her rather large, overpowering figure.

If you are a large, tall or strong woman, you will have to work to disguise these features so that men will have the impression that you are little and delicate. And if you are efficient and capable in masculine things, you will have to "unlearn" these traits.

## The Capable Woman That Men Admire

Occasionally we may notice men who seem to admire women who are capable and efficient in masculine things. They may be exceedingly skilled in managing a department or have ingenious ideas about how to make the business or industrial world "tick." But don't let men's admiration for these women confuse you. Although the man may have a genuine admiration for such a woman, it does not mean he finds her attractive. He undoubtedly admires her as he would another man—with appreciation for her fine ability.

## How to Acquire Feminine Dependency

1. *Attitude*: In acquiring femininity, you must first dispense with any air of strength and ability, of competence and fearlessness and acquire instead an attitude of frail dependency upon men to take care of you. Always let him know that his masculine help is needed and appreciated and that you could not get along in this world very well without him. Women often display a capable attitude in the things they say. For example, a woman may oppose her husband's life insurance by saying, "Oh, if anything happened to you, I could take care of myself well enough." Or in planning a move or a trip they take no thought, in their plans, of needing masculine assistance, care or protection. Their attitude is one of self-sufficiency, of getting along in the world without masculine aid.

2. *Stop Doing the Masculine Work*: Next, you will have to stop doing the man's work—stop lifting heavy boxes, moving furniture, mowing the lawn, painting, fixing motors, cleaning cars, changing tires, carpentry, or anything which is masculine responsibility. Eliminate *heavy* work which is beyond your physical strength, and also eliminate work which is *inappropriate* for women, or unfeminine. Also stop handling the money problems and worries, bossing your husband around, telling him what to do and when to do it. Stop braving the dark, facing the creditors or making long-distance car trips alone. If you are working to provide part of the living, if at

all possible stop working. (If you are an older woman who is working to fill in time or for benevolent service, this may be different.) Stop doing the masculine work, not only to increase your femininity, but *so you will have time for your own feminine work.*

In eliminating the man's work, it is best to first explain your intentions to your husband. Tell him that you feel "unfeminine" doing these things and that you want very much to become a truly feminine woman and live within the bounds of your own role. Then, ask him if he will completely take over all of the masculine responsibility which you have been doing. Discuss each one of these jobs so that he will clearly understand. If your request is feminine, he will probably cooperate. He may, however, resist taking over these jobs, or fail to follow through with a job he has promised to do. The man's failure to do his *home work* is a bone of marital contention, one we will now deal with briefly.

Some women are skeptical about getting the man to do the masculine work around the house. They may say, "Oh, I've tried to get him to do the heavy work, but it doesn't work. Why, I stopped mowing the lawn and it grew a foot high. And, if I didn't paint my kitchen it would never get painted. He won't do these things for me, so I have to resort to doing them myself." This is the common response. The trouble here lies in the fact the woman does not completely stop, but only temporarily. She never *lets go* and turns her back on the man's responsibilities.

"But," the same woman may say, "if I do not do them and he does not, what will happen? Someone must do these things!" But, must they? Must the lawn be mowed and the kitchen painted and the battles won at the expense of feminine charm? "But," she may say, "I cannot stand for the roof to leak and the door to fall from its hinges and the lawn to go un-mowed." If you cannot make these temporary sacrifices, you cannot become the ideal of Angela Human, nor can you awaken the man's chivalry.

When you turn your back on the man's work, don't expect any miracles. If he fails to do his "home work," don't complain, make him feel ashamed or pressure him to get things done. Remember, the jobs are his to do or neglect. If his failures are difficult for you to accept, develop an attitude of humility by asking yourself, "Have I performed my work well today? Was I dressed and well-groomed before breakfast? Did I serve my husband well prepared meals on time today? Is my house clean and orderly? Have I been patient with the children? Am I loving and understanding of my husband?" After you have asked yourself these questions, then ask, "Do I have a right to feel resentful because he neglects *his* duties?" Also, try to understand that what may seem to you like an important job at home, may seem insignificant to him when he compares it to problems he is facing in his work. If you hammer the point on small home repairs, you only display a narrow, self-centered and unsympathetic attitude.

3. *If Stuck with a Masculine Job, Do it in a Feminine Manner*: As you are

trying to unload the masculine work, there may be times you will feel stuck with a masculine job—something that must be done and there is no one to do it but yourself. If this is the case, do the job in a *feminine manner*. It is not up to you to perform masculine tasks with the skill that men do. If you must fix the furnace or the leaking roof or handle the finances, do not try so hard to do it with masculine efficiency. Just be your feminine self, and your husband will soon realize that you need masculine assistance. If you can do a job as well as a man can, *he will never come to your rescue*.

4. *Be Submissive*: Another quality of femininity is submissiveness. This means to be yielding, obedient, to yield to power or authority or leave matters to the opinions, discretion or judgment of another, or others. The opposite of submissiveness is to be defiant, rebellious, unruly, obstinate or stubborn. To be feminine, a woman must be yielding to her husband's rule.

Women should especially guard against having unyielding opinions. Men find it very disagreeable to be in the company of such women. They want them to express their viewpoints and to defend them to a degree, but are offended when a woman takes such a firm stand on an issue that the man cannot convince her of anything, regardless of his sound logic. It is better to be submissive to a man than to try to win an argument with him. It is more feminine. I do not wish to imply that you be yielding in your moral convictions or ideals, but when you find that you clash in principle.

5. *Don't Subdue Fearfulness*: Feminine women tend to have a natural fear of dangers. They are afraid of snakes, and are even known to be afraid of small dangers such as bugs, spiders, mice, the dark, and strange noises, much to the amusement of men. The reason that men seem to enjoy this trait in women is that in the presence of her weakness he naturally feels stronger. If she shrinks from a spider or hops on a chair at the sight of a mouse, how manly he feels that he can laugh at such tremblings and calm her fears. It does a man more good to save a woman from a mouse than a tiger, since he feels so much more superiority over the mouse.

Feminine women are also known to be afraid of the dangers of nature. An illustration of this is the following incident a woman confided to me: Her husband owned a sailboat and was a competent seaman. He loved to take her into dangerous waters and keel the boat over on its side. She was terrified at such times and asked me, "Why does he do this when he knows I am afraid?" I explained that the reason he does is because she *is* so afraid and he is so *unafraid*. Her fearfulness was appealing to him and this is why he kept repeating the dangerous sailing. I suggested that she express her fearfulness in calmer waters and perhaps he would be satisfied and not take her out further. It is a mistake for a women to subdue the tendency of fearfulness in the presence of men, for to do so is to subdue feminine charm.

Feminine women are also uneasy in the presence of heavy traffic. If you take a tiny child to a busy highway and hold it tightly in your arms while the heavy trucks and fast moving traffic rush by, you sense the tremorous fearfulness of the child. Similarly, a feminine woman approaches an intersection with hesitancy. She does not charge forth with all confidence, but hesitates at the curb for a moment, clings to the man's arm a little tighter, waiting for him to lead the way. Here again, the man appreciates her apparent uneasiness and his ability to give protection.

6. *Don't Try to Excel Him:* To be feminine, don't compete with men in anything which requires masculine ability. For example, don't try to outdo them is sports, lifting weights, in running, in repairing equipment, etc. Also, don't compete with men for advancement on a job, for higher pay, or greater honors. Don't compete with them for scholastic honors in men's subjects. It may be all right to win over a man in English or social studies, but you are in trouble if you compete with a man in math, chemistry, public speaking, etc. Don't appear to know more than a man does in world events, the space program, or science or industry. Do not excel men in anything which has to do with the masculine field of endeavor.

7. *Need His Care and Protection:* Let him open doors for you, help you on with your coat, pull up your chair, or offer you his coat in the cold or in a rainstorm. If he does not offer his help, perhaps it is because you did it for yourself too quickly, did not give him time to offer. But if he still does not offer, then work on the other parts of femininity until he does. You can ask him to do some things, like lift in your groceries, open tight jar lids. Take care, however, that you confine your requests to things that women need men for and not for trivial things that women can just as well do for themselves.

8. *Live Your Feminine Role:* Perhaps in no way can a woman develop her femininity more than by living her feminine role as the wife, mother and homemaker. Here, in this area of her life, a woman has a field in which to grow as a woman. Certainly motherhood increases her femininity. And, although she may not realize it, taking feminine work upon her shoulders year after year makes her more of a woman. And if she is a good wife, she will develop understanding, acceptance, forgiveness and sympathy—all gentle traits which make her more feminine.

## What Feminine Dependency Awakens in a Man

Feminine dependency awakens in a man *love and tenderness*. As a man begins to do things for a woman, to shelter her and take care of her, this feeling grows. This is true of any individual that protects and shelters any form of life that is in need of protection. Take our pets, for example. Don't we learn to love them by taking care of them? And the more helplessly dependent they are upon us, the more tenderly we feel for them. Take a little canary, for example. Don't you love him because he is so trustingly dependent upon you for food and water, because his happiness is so obvious when he is rewarded with a bit of food? He will twist his little head with such an air of interest and alertness and yet is so soft, fluttering and helplessly dependent upon you that you cannot think of trusting his care to anyone else. This feeling, magnified a thousand times, is what every mother feels who protects her child and what every man feels who protects his wife and children.

A woman also takes care of and protects her husband, in a different way. She prepares him nourishing meals, washes his shirts, and watches over him to see that he does not neglect his health. She gives him comfort, understanding and sympathy, and the man grows dependent upon her for these things. She also protects him in her own way. She tries to keep others from taking unfair advantage of his generous nature; tries to keep his foolhardy courage from endangering his safety; and tries to make certain that his manly indifference to detail does not lead him into trouble. Thus, she too feels that he is dependent upon her, and she delights in his need of her and her ability to fill the need of such a big, strong, yet helpless man. She, too, feels tenderness toward the one she is caring for.

## The Sweet Promise

Although men are fascinated by frailty in women, there is a balancing quality that they also want to see. They would like the assurance that, with all the women's helplessness, with all of her dependency upon him to take care of her, to protect her and to wait upon her, that she has somewhere hidden within her the ability to meet an emergency. He would like to know that in such circumstances she would have womanly courage, strength and endurance and the ability to solve difficult problems, that she would not, in this case, be helpless. This is known as the "sweet promise." The man needs to be able to detect it somewhere in her character.

There are many women who show forth this promise when put to the test. Take, for example, a young widow who is left with several small children to support. What does she do? She sets out single-handed to battle against all odds. She slaves and struggles, she dares and she suffers in her effort to provide for her children. When defeat stares her in the face, she doesn't even whimper, but taking her lot as a matter of course, she grimly grits her teeth and braves the struggle again. No matter what pain she suffers from overwork, she has always a smile of comfort for the childish fears of her little ones; no matter how weary she is, she is always ready to forget her own weariness at the slightest hint of danger to one of her children. Look to the widows of this earth and you will find that many of them compare to the angels of heaven. This sweet promise is a quality which comes from the development of a noble character, for in it are courage, love, determination, endurance, faith, etc.

## Should Women Be Trained for Careers?

Many parents feel that they should prepare their daughters to make a living in the event of widowhood, divorce or other compelling emergencies. Consider the seriousness of this step from the following viewpoints:

1. If one of the charms of womanhood is feminine dependency, a girl should not center her education around a career, in which she becomes *independent*. By so doing she will lose one of the elements that attracts men to women—her need of manly care, or financial support. She will, in addition, be in danger of acquiring the efficient masculine traits that so many professional women have, thus reducing her feminine charm. There are, of course, some professional women who manage to stay feminine, either through a nature so strongly feminine that it cannot be subdued or by conscious effort. But it seems a mistake for parents to encourage a girl in the direction of a career, when disadvantages could arise which she would always have to work to overcome.

2. Training for careers encourages women to work, both before and after marriage. The effort the girl has put forth in training seems wasted if it is "put on the shelf." She will just naturally be tempted to use her knowledge at some time or another, whether there is a need or not.

3. Requirements for employment change from year to year. The woman who is qualified at one time may be out of date a few years later and must return for further training to qualify for her work.

4. The independence which results from the ability to make money can be a dangerous thing for a woman, serving as an escape. Many difficulties may arise in early marriage. The woman who is independent will have less incentive to make the adjustment. Divorce may seem an easy way out, since she can be self-supporting.

5. It does not seem logical that a woman should train for a career in the event of a rare emergency, if by so doing she bypasses a rich cultural education that would give her a broad picture of life and thus better prepare her for her role ahead as the wife, mother and homemaker. A man may as well train for motherhood and homemaking if this logic is sound.

The best way for a woman to plan for her future is to plan a *broad education*. The background of a liberal education will assist her greatly in being a wonderful mother to her children, in helping to educate them and inspire them with an appreciation for life and in helping them to make the proper adjustments and preparations for their lives ahead. It will help her equally as a wife, since women who are educated in a broad sense are more interesting, more open-minded to new ideas and challenging thoughts. She will also be a better citizen, have a greater appreciation for life and a greater capacity for happiness. This is providing she has a *good* education and puts something into getting the most out of it. As for homemaking classes and family living subjects, these can be of value, too. Somewhere along the line she will have to learn to cook, sew and manage a household. Many girls learn these skills from their mothers, but if not, she will need to have training or at least have a determination to learn on her own. But all of her education should focus around helping her fill her feminine destiny—to create a happy home.

As for meeting a rare emergency, the woman with the broad cultural background has developed creativeness, intelligence and wisdom. When faced with an emergency, she usually has enough ingenuity to solve her problems. If she must work, she can usually find her way into the working world and qualify for a job better than can the woman who was trained for a career ten years earlier and now finds that she is "out of date."

## Summary

As we come to the end of the chapters on femininity, you should have gained a new insight into the subject. Femininity, as you can see, is much more than ruffles and lace. Although a feminine appearance is important, it is of little use without the feminine manner; and neither of them will be of any merit without feminine dependency. Of all the qualities a woman may possess, this one attribute outweighs them all, as far as men are concerned. Without femininity she may have a magnetic personality and she may have a powerful character, but in men's eyes she will not be a woman. A man isn't interested in a great and powerful character. He *wants a woman*, as is evident in the following true experiences:

## It Helped Me to Become Feminine

"Before I found out about Fascinating Womanhood, I was extremely unhappy. I had doubts about whether or not I even wanted to get married, because there are so many marriages that fail. I didn't know if I could make a marriage that would not only survive, but *be happy* in the process. I had been raised to be very aggressive, independent, and competent, and added to that was the fact that I am very tall and non-feminine looking. Fascinating Womanhood helped me to realize my mistaken frame of mind and become a truly fascinating woman. My husband has become more of

a man through my application of the principles, and he says I have made
him so happy he just doesn't know what to do, sometimes. I feel anything
that can change a person like I was into a soft, feminine woman needs to
be taught to every woman, especially women's libbers! They don't know
what they're missing!!''

## I Tried to Do Too Much

"My success story is quite different from most. I had been married two
times before I found Fascinating Womanhood. Now that I have found
Fascinating Womanhood I have married again, and it seems to have been
planned to happen this way. My mistake was different from most women's.
I tried to do too much. My mother was married and divorced many times;
consequently, I wanted to be the 'perfect wife.' Instead, I went to a disap-
pointing extreme.

"The first marriage (to my childhood sweetheart) was when I was 18
and he was 20. He had always been spoiled by his parents and family, and
I was convinced I should do every task for him that I could possible
perform. This included washing cars, earning money on two full-time jobs
so he could attend night classes at college, handling finances, making all
the decisions, serving his breakfast in bed, laying out his clothes each day,
etc. He appeared to enjoy this, and I thought we had a good marriage,
though he was immature.

"Trouble came after two years of marriage, when I become pregnant.
Although we had always planned to have children, this baby was not
planned at this time. He simply could not accept the responsibility. (After
all, he hadn't carried any of our responsibilities yet—I had 'mothered'
him!) He told me I must either get an abortion or immediately sign papers
to give the baby away as soon as it was born. He claimed the baby would
interfere with his completing college and that we would have children later.
He told me if I did not do one of these things immediately, he would leave
me. This threw me into a traumatic state of shock, crying, disappointment,
and I just can't describe the painful hurt feelings. My world had collapsed!

"I decided to leave him. After I moved out, however, I received another
shock. I lost the baby. The doctor said it was due to nervous strain. After
that, everything was fine as far as my husband was concerned, and he
wanted to reconcile. I just couldn't feel the same, so I continued to live
alone. After one year and three months, I filed for divorce, still not realizing
I made the mistake by not letting him 'grow.'

"Later I married a man 15 years older than myself. He was very mature
about all things, fun, easy to get along with, kind and considerate, handled
the money, and was definitely 'boss' in our home. He had three children

from a previous marriage (8, 10, and 12 years old) who visited us each weekend. The children would always bring three friends their own age to visit them for the weekend in our home.

"We all got along very well, and I became very close to his children, and they seemed to love me also. In fact, they still come and visit me, even though I have remarried. Because of my husband's heavy financial responsibility, I still worked and tried to make things as easy for him as possible. My husband and I had an understanding before marriage that I would work only one year to pay off some of the bills, and then I could get pregnant and we would have 'our' baby. Well, we paid more and more money to the ex-wife and child support, and my husband had a guilt complex that seemed to get worse each year. He bought them more and more gifts, trying to compensate for not being with them through the week. We were behind in all our bills, and didn't even own a home, or even pay the rent on time. I kept trying to come to his rescue and never be any problem myself or bother him with my needs. I just kept quiet and let the tensions and frustrations build up inside, all along thinking I was doing the right thing. The children would call continually with problems and the ex-wife would call, too. At one time my husband even made the statement: 'You can take care of yourself, but they can't.' I should have heard what he was trying to tell me . . . *you don't need me . . . they do!*

"Finally, after three and one-half years I asked him if we could either buy a house for OUR marriage, and have OUR baby, and if not, I wanted OUT! I wanted to start my life rather than finish up his first marriage. Soon after that I had the marriage annulled on the grounds that he had deceived me when we were married, promising children and then refusing. He said he didn't feel he was doing enough for the three he already had, and did not want to bring another baby into the world and have to support it for twenty years, thus taking away from his three children he already had.

"After the marriage was annulled I felt pretty empty. I had put everything I had into both marriages, but still failed as a wife; I just didn't understand. I thought I was doing all any woman could. Then I found Fascinating Womanhood. I read it, and after doing so, I took a long time deciding whether to ever risk another marriage. Then I met my 'Mr. Wonderful.' He was only five years older than I, had no children from his previous marriage, but wanted a family. He definitely was the 'boss' between us, and seemed to be all the things I wanted and admired. We were married eight months later. I had completed my first Fascinating Womanhood course, and was ready to let go and live it. I am a completely different woman in this marriage. I still do very many special things for my husband, and he comes first. I love him handling the responsibilities of his role, and I stay in my role as a woman.

"I have had my fondest wish granted by my husband. He has allowed me to quit working. I had worked for ten years with the aerospace industry, and held quite a high position. I enjoyed the people and everyone said I would not enjoy staying home, especially with no children. I am busy all day, every day, and I'm happy to say that all those people were wrong. I love being home! I know that Fascinating Womanhood has taught me how to enjoy my home and my role as wife and homemaker. I just light up when 'Mr. Wonderful' comes home for lunch and dinner. We are planning a family, and it is so comforting to have a husband who wants children and is looking forward to our first child.

"I have now completed three Fascinating Womanhood courses and plan to teach in the very near future. Fascinating Womanhood has taught me the true meaning of the happiness in being a woman, and being married to a wonderful man. My husband thinks Fascinating Womanhood is the greatest! He tells his friends if they get a wife only half as good as his, they will really 'luck out.' "

## I Stopped Killing My Own Snakes

"Before I started practicing Fascinating Womanhood, our home was anything but happy. Now I can truthfully say that the harmony we have is more than I had thought possible and it is increasing every day.

"Considering the fact that my husband and I have been Christians for 21 years, it really came as a shock to me to find that I was the one that needed to do the changing. Only when confronted with my self-righteous attitude while reading Fascinating Womanhood could I accept it and change.

"Oh, the heartache I needn't have gone through with our oldest son. He is just 20 years old, and he has had mama telling him what to do and when to do it for too long. Now I can see what caused his rebellion in the first place. (Me!) He returned home this summer to work on the farm for his father, and with the help of Fascinating Womanhood, things went smoother than they have for years. Our 15-year-old daughter is responding, too, and our married daughter is a faithful follower.

"I'm saving the best for last, my husband. He takes me to dinner at least twice a week. He has cancelled his big hunting trip to Alaska, which he has been planning for six months. Says he would rather spend the money taking me to Mexico. When I have gone out of town to shop, he services the car for me, without being asked. The other day he even carried my golf clubs to the car because he thought they were too heavy for me. All this for the girl who has been 'killing her own snakes' for years! He knows how I love flowers and has brought me two bouquets he picked himself. This from the man I've always considered as being cold and unsentimental."

## Assignment

1. Analyze your life's responsibilities to see if you are doing any masculine work.
2. If you are: a) Ask him to take it over. b) Stop doing it and risk the consequences. c) If you feel stuck with it, do it in a feminine manner.

# THE FANTASY OF DIRT

Lawrence S. Kubie

In the course of this paper it will seem at times as though an attempt were being made to claim that there is no such thing as dirt. Such is not our purpose or meaning; but rather to describe the complex system of fantasies which lurk behind the reality of dirt and which manifest themselves both in the structure of the neurosis and in many significant aspects of adult human life. Nevertheless it is true that we acknowledge no "innate" or inherent distinctions between clean and dirty, whether on the basis of consistency, color, form, smell, utility, waste, or any combinations of these.[1] Instead, the concept of dirt is looked upon throughout rather as the outcome of an emotional judgment which is imposed by the environment upon the ego of the developing infant. Furthermore it is found to be infested with a surprising array of conflicting and fantastic implications. It should hardly be necessary to state explicitly what ought to be obvious, namely, that in the concept of dirt there is a nucleus of pragmatic reality; but that because of the unconscious distortions and elaborations of the concept the imaginary components play a far more significant role in daily life than does this realistic kernel. Therefore it is justifiable to emphasize this aspect of the problem by writing of the *fantasy* rather than of the *reality* of dirt.

It is generally understood that the unconscious fantasies which cluster about any reality may have more significance than does the reality itself, but it seems that psychoanalysis has been guided by this principle more consistently when dealing with the concept of mutilation than when dealing with the concept of dirt. Thus it is an accepted fact that every human being faces the possibility of real physical injury, and that an important part of the development of every child is concerned with his efforts to cope with a growing awareness that he can in actuality be mutilated and that he in turn can mutilate others. Over and beyond this, however, it is known that recurrently much of this struggle focuses on the genitalia; and that as the child develops he must master not only a reasonable dread of possible forms of injury or mutilation, but a psychologically more destructive cloud of impossible, unconscious, and fantastic terrors as well. When stress is laid therefore on the fantastic nature of the neurotic yet universal terrors, it is understood that no one is denying that danger itself can be real.

---

1. The reactions of lower animals, primates, and of the infants of different primitive peoples are relevant to this point: but a discussion of these, insofar as the data are available, will have to be reserved for another communication.

The feeling of disgust, on the other hand, is usually treated quite differently, almost as though this reaction in and of itself was enough to settle the question of whether something was or was not dirty, and as though there were no unconscious fantasies to be disentangled from whatever reality may warrant the feeling. Naturally, in outspoken manifestations of misophobia, or in the classical hysterical reversals of affect about libidinal cravings, the pathological nature of the feeling of disgust is recognized; but short of these extreme cases there is a tendency to be significantly uncritical of the responses of people to what they call dirt.

It will be our first task, therefore, to show that we scarcely know what is meant by the word "dirt," that there exists neither a psychoanalytic nor yet a reasonable pragmatic definition of dirt, and that in general our behavior toward things that are usually thought of as "dirty" is replete with paradoxes, absurdities, confused assumptions, and mutually contradictory implications and premises. Also it will appear that our *mores,* our personal idiosyncrasies, our neuroses, and our very analytic theories reflect this confusion.

## The Body as Dirt Factory. Protection of the Outsides from the Insides

In his paper on Character and Anal Erotism, Freud suggests parenthetically that "dirt is matter in the wrong place"; but in the context it is made clear that he himself set little store by this suggestion; and surely it is not merely a translocation in space which makes the difference between honey and slime, between food and feces, or a thousand other similar and perplexing contrasts. Therefore let us seek our definition clinically by observing human behavior. It will then appear that there are objects toward which men behave in a manner which is easily described. They do not consciously want to take these objects into their bodies. They approach them gingerly, if at all. They prefer not to touch them without some intervening protection. And ultimately they feel that they do not want even to *look* at them. These are the qualities of that which is looked upon as dirt, defined in terms of conventionally accepted norms of adult behavior. And now if we turn from the world outside of us to the body itself, we find that there are certain aspects of the body toward which we manifest the same type of behavior. These are the parts of the bodies of animals which are not used as food except under rare and exceptional circumstances, that are not approached freely, and that it is conventional not even to look at openly: to wit, the apertures, and anything which emerges from the apertures.

At this point we must recall that in unconscious language the outside world is never represented by the body, but that the body must always and constantly be represented by the outside world. In other words, and for reasons which we have outlined in a paper on Body Symbolization and the Development of Language, the direction of displacement must always be from the body to the outside world. If this is true, everything in the outside world which is looked upon as dirty or disgusting must represent those aspects of the body and its products to which we react in the same way; and the ethnologist should be able to demonstrate that the distinction between clean and dirty is found in primitive language only after there is segregation of the excretory functions in the community.

It is possible in this way to derive a psychological definition of dirt as being anything which either symbolically or in reality emerges from the body, or which has been sullied by contact with a body aperture. There is here revealed a fantasy which is not the less amazing merely because it is given almost universal and unthinking acceptance, namely, that the body itself creates dirt, and is in fact a kind of animated, mobile dirt factory, exuding filth at every aperture, and that all that is necessary to turn something into dirt is that it should even momentarily enter the body through one of these apertures. Furthermore, and paradoxically, we find that this curious dirt factory, the body, must, despite its own uncleanliness, shun as dirty anything in the outside world which resembles or represents the body's own "dirt," and that above all else it must never allow its own relatively "clean" outsides to become contaminated by contact with the filthy interior of itself or of anyone else. (In this aspect of the fantasy is a clue to certain characteristics of the obsessional neurosis, which are discussed below.)

Let us take a few homely illustrations of these general statements.

If you move your tongue around in your mouth, you will become aware of the saliva. To you that saliva does not seem dirty. If then you contemplate your finger, it also presumably looks "clean." But now if you put your clean finger into your clean mouth, moisten it with your clean saliva, and stroke your neighhbor's cheek with it, he will have to control an impulse to shrink; just as we are troubled if we see a slum mother moisten the corner of her handkerchief with saliva to rub the soot from her baby's nose. Your clean saliva has become his dirt, and not to him alone: now that it has left your mouth you would hesitate to lick it with your own tongue. Thus a lover may shrink from the wetness which his own kisses have left.

Or again, let us think of the very air that we breathe. We do not think of that as being "filthy." It may be dusty and laden with soot, but to that atmosphere we do not react with tension, anxiety, revulsion, and aversion. Let us, however, breathe it into our nasal passages where some of the dust is caught on the ciliated cells of the mucous membranes. Here this dust will be moistened by a fluid exudate. This fluid consists of nothing more appalling than water, salts, and a few diluted molecules of mucoprotein. Nevertheless, when we finally blow this wet and sticky dust out of our nostrils, by the awful alchemy of the body it emerges as filth.

Of food, similar things can be said. Surely it is looked upon as clean when it is taken into our mouths to eat; and none of the chemical processes to which our body subjects it are in any real sense filth-producing. It is split into its assimilable and unassimilable fractions. To the unassimilable fractions are added certain hearty brown and green bile pigments, colors such as every painter uses. Subsequently it is subjected to fermentative processes in the intestinal tracts, which so divide the molecules that volatile fractions are released, which in turn give rise to certain well-known and homely odors. In this way that which is taken into the body as a delicacy emerges as offal.

The fantasies, however, carry us even further. No esthete can take exception to the color of an egg; but many a loving mother swallows hard when a bit of the yolk rolls out of the corner of her baby's mouth and stains his bib. The untouched fried egg which is brought to the table may excite our appetite; but, when washing up, the dried remnants of that same egg on the spoon or plate excite disgust. This is indeed a powerful and surprising magic.

The facile popular explanation of the idea of dirt is "something that smells bad." It is true, of course, that anything that smells in a strange or unexpected fashion is often viewed with mistrust and aversion; but on closer inspection the smell itself often turns out to be identical with some well-known and familiar odor, one which is accepted with equanimity in its usual setting. Furthermore, the examples already given include entirely odorless situations; and conversely there are many foods whose inherent odors are indistinguishable from those of human excrement and sweat (certain cheeses, high game, etc.). In short, the smell or absence of smell cannot in itself be looked upon as the explanation of the distinction between dirt and cleanliness. On the contrary, smells are taken to mean dirt only when they signal either consciously or unconsciously the threat of contamination from a body's interiors. The situation with regard to taste is similar.

One could cite many other homely illustrations of similar things; the reaction to a few wisps of somebody else's hair in the bath-tub, to a strand of hair in the soup, to touching things which have touched the apertures or even the creases in someone else's body, or for that matter, to touching again after an interval something which one has used oneself without first going through some preliminary rite of rinsing and washing. The fact that there is some bacteriological foundation for some of these precautions does not really lessen their fantastic nature. Because once in a hundred times somebody else's toothbrush or spoon might carry to one a pathogenic organism does not mean that in all the other ninety-nine times there is an objective esthetic or bacteriological difference between one's own spittle and that of the rest of the world. It is evident, however, that it is just at this point that the concept of dirt and the concept of danger and disease establish an intimate relationship, the nature of which will have to be dealt with below. Here it is sufficient to point out that there is a tendency to use the bacterial etiology of infectious disease not only as a rationalization of the fear of "dirt," but actually as a form of projection, in order to escape from a deep and terrifying conviction of sickness through masturbation. "It is not *I,* or something dirty *I* have done that will make me sick, it is something dirty from the outside." At this point, therefore, the fear of dirt is strongly reinforced from another quarter.

Without laboring the point further, it becomes evident that so deeply ingrained is this extraordinary notion, that quite without questioning it we make the assumption that the insides of the body are in fact a cistern, that all of the apertures of the body are dirty avenues of approach, dirty holes leading into dirty spaces, and that everything which comes out of the body, with the possible exception of tears, is for that reason alone dirty.[2]

More nearly than anyone else, Ernest Jones has sensed the significance of these facts. He comments on the unconsciously synonymous nature of the words "waste" and "dirty" and "refuse." And after quoting Sadger, who relates an intense dislike of dirt on the body itself to masturbatory experiences, Jones adds: "I find that the anal erotic reaction often extends to the inside of the body, *there being a conviction that everything inside is inherently filthy."* (Italics mine.) "I have known such people to be unwilling even to insert a finger into their own mouths, and to have the custom of drinking large quantities of water daily with the idea of cleansing the dirty insides of the body." Furthermore, the problem is raised in a far more complicated form by Melanie Klein in connection with problems which will be dealt with below.

It would seem hard to doubt that this is the unconscious assumption that lies behind the adult concept of dirt, and that this is the unconscious meaning of the word as it is taught to children.

---

2. To the child the body is not a group of independent systems—a two- or three-family house. Often it is all one room, one cavity; and all the apertures are doors and windows leading by various pathways to one single, undifferentiated, stinking mess.

 The conflicting attitudes to the baby as a body product, and to human milk and semen require special discussion. Toward both, the inconsistencies are at times amazing. The author knows of two young internes in pediatrics who promptly vomited on discovering that they had unwittingly drunk human milk from the supply in the hospital ice-box.

## The Unconscious Hierarchies of Dirt

Out of this fantasy there emerges a tacit hierarchy of dirt; i.e., human beings, although they have no way of measuring different degrees of dirtiness, have "dirt" reactions the intensities of which are quite as finely graded as those which on the positive side of the same scale are looked upon as laws of esthetic tastes. Furthermore, as one might expect, there is a similar hierarchy of the products of the body; so that one can list them in order, from the "cleanest" (beginning probably with tears) to the "dirtiest"; and with two outstanding exceptions there would be little or no disagreement as to the order in which they should be arranged, even if the list included such details as ear-wax, the desquamated cells between the toes, nose pickings, hair clippings, nail clippings, sweat from different parts of the body, urine and feces. The two body-products which could not be placed so exactly in this negative esthetic scale are milk and semen, about which the most perplexing ambivalence would be manifested. Similarly, the various parts of the body can be arranged in such a hierarchy, and the influence of this graded reaction can sometimes be observed in the details of the rituals of an obsessional neurosis.

There are at least four assumptions which one encounters almost universally, and which have their origins in this same fantasy: (1) Softness, wetness, sliminess, and hairiness, respectively, are always looked upon as dirtier than hardness, dryness, and the absence of hair. (2) Old age represents a piling up of undischarged remnants of a lifetime of eating and drinking, and is dirtier than youth.[3] So that growing old means to grow dirty; and infants, although in the unconscious they may be made from feces, are nevertheless and paradoxically cleaner than age. (3) Furthermore, pigmentation obviously means dirt, and dark hair is dirtier than the blond hair which "gentlemen prefer." And (4) finally in general a prominent or out-jutting part of the body carries a presumption of cleanliness, whereas a cavity, or cleft, or hole, or pit in the body carries the presumption of dirt.

It will be seen how these various assumptions fit into the hierarchies which we have mentioned, why the smooth parts of the body are "cleaner" than the wrinkled parts (the penis, for instance, than the scrotum), why those parts of the body which are remote from apertures are "cleaner" than those which surround the apertures, and why thinness is

---

3. This recalls Metchnikoff's once famous theory that senility and death come as the result of microbic action on the contents of the lower bowel—a theory which received indirect scientific investigation in the experiments of Woodruff on the amoeba (cf. Freud's *Beyond the Pleasure Principle*) and pseudo-medical exploitation in theories of intestinal auto-intoxication with their attendant rituals of colonic irrigations and the like. In the lay mind it is reflected in that type of intestinal preoccupation which Osler used to refer to as cases of "bowels on the brain."

presumptively clean and fatness presumably dirty, and why in the mythical physiology of the laity fat people are supposed to have larger bowel movements than thin folk.

*The most important single consequence of this hierarchy of fantasies is an unconscious but universal conviction that woman is dirtier than man.* This belief is diametrically opposed to the conscious popular attitude, i.e., that men are dirty and women clean. Often enough, however, this customary attitude is quite insincere; and those who defend it most chivalrously are often the very ones who shrink with revulsion from direct physical contact with any but "low" women. In reality the reactions of men and women to the body of woman are dominated by this retreat from "dirt"-laden clefts and apertures. We have found this to be true in women as well as men, including those women who are blocked in their heterosexual adjustments and who explain this block as being due to a conscious feeling that in intercourse they are soiled by the man. In this feeling, the idea of semen as dirt is used to obscure the deep personal pain which it costs the woman to regard her own genital aperture as even dirtier.

## The Taboo on the Apertures

In all of this there is implicit the most all-inclusive taboo which we meet in the attitude of adult human beings to the body, namely, the taboo on the apertures. By every means, and by varying degrees at different times and in different civilizations, the apertures have been camouflaged. They have been either hidden or altered; and through displacements and substitutions every aperture has at one time or another been subjected to rituals of this sort. The simplest of these, of course, are the fashions in which the aperture is directly obscured. A woman's hair at one epoch must cover her ears; or in certain Eastern countries her nose and mouth must be hidden behind a veil which she would no more think of lifting than of raising her skirt. A man must wear a moustache and a beard. A polite little boy may at most wriggle an itching ear, but he must not put his fingers in it, nor into his nose or mouth. Nor may any unnecessary noise or smell emanate from an aperture to draw attention to it. It follows inevitably that even soft toothpicks are taboo; and if something is lodged in a crevice between the teeth it must either be dislodged in private or else with surreptitious and genteel manipulations of the tongue. Among many primitive peoples such as the Trobrianders, people turn their backs to one another when they eat; and among East Indians the woman would no more think of eating in the presence of a stranger than of performing any other intimate rite involving one of her body apertures.[4] Indeed so drastic is this

---

4. Dr. A. Kardiner points out that this ceremonial restriction may have other important and coincident determinants. (Personal communication.)

attitude in the Orient that, according to Brill, the Japanese at one time censored all kissing scenes in American movies, and on at least one occasion refused to allow a replica of Rodin's *The Kiss* to be exhibited in an art gallery. Nor can this be attributed to any peculiar intensity of body smells among the Japanese, since, according to Havelock Ellis, they are among the least aromatic of all human races—far less, for instance, than the white races.

## Compulsive Cosmetic Compensations in Woman

That this taboo on the apertures has an intimate relationship to cosmetic rituals must also be quite obvious. It is evident in the compulsive whitening of the nose by the civilized woman, and in the rouging of her lips, or in the gross distortions of the ear lobes, the nose, or the lips in savages.

Either one must obscure the apertures and make them decorous and self-effacing, or where this cannot be done they must be altered, decorated. And since woman has the one aperture whose presence makes the most urgent protest against the taboo, by simple displacement upward her cosmetic rituals become the most compelling and elaborate. Perhaps on the deepest level these may also be a substitute for the genital and excretory cleanliness rites of infancy, for the soaping, patting, powdering and handling that were then enjoyed; but in contradistinction to man, the woman seems to need them in order to free herself from an obsessive conviction that she has one aperture too many, and that a dirty one. In the same way, it is the woman who must never sweat; and who, no matter how severe her cold, must use only a tiny lace handkerchief to prove that there is no dirt inside of her. And it is the woman who must use perfume.

One patient of mine revealed the inner meaning of all of this when, on dropping her compact into the toilet, she roared with uncontrollable laughter, and said, "That's the part of me I'm ashamed of, and not my face—that's what I want to change." Equally clear was the same point as expressed by another patient in her conviction that an ugly mouth always means an ugly genital; or in still another whose exaggerated reaction to a mole on the side of her cheek was traced to her identification of it with a mole on her labia. This, of course, is only an exceptionally transparent example of a well-known fact, namely, that the hands and the head, as the only parts of the body which can always be freely exposed, come to represent all of the hidden parts; and that more particularly the apertures in the head represent the apertures at the other end of the trunk.

Another clear example of this was seen in the behavior of a little girl of five. This little girl had been separated from her father and from her older brother for a few months, and envied this brother deeply. One day she lay on her back with her legs in the air, her genitals exposed; and as she contemplated them she said, "My father won't marry me because I have

an ugly—(here there was a strange break and pause in her speech)—
face."

That the conviction that she has one "dirty" aperture too many is an
important source of woman's incessant discontent with her own body
would seem to be likely. It has manifested itself in endless efforts to alter
her shape, with the emphasis constantly shifting from one part of the body
to another. The feet are squeezed, the neck is stretched, the waist is
confined, the breasts are now crushed flat and again are raised and built
up, the hips are "slenderized" or built out with a bustle. These polymorph-
ous compulsions have as their constant underlying theme the fact that the
body is not accepted as being right as it is and that ultimately all of the
manipulations focus themselves around one or another aperture—the
mouth, the nose, the ears, the breasts, the genitals and the excretory
system, culminating finally in old age in the pathetic struggle against the
dignity of wrinkles.

In this derogatory attitude of woman toward her own body one finds
every gradation from the devastating delusion of a deep depression that
contamination, poison, and overwhelming odors emanate from her body,
to the mild distress of the young actress who felt completely comfortable
on the stage only when she was seated or else hidden from the waist down
behind some piece of furniture.

To avoid misunderstanding it is well to introduce here one necessary
warning. The conscious and unconscious motivations of human conduct
are always complex. It would be absurd to attempt to find in this one
fantasy of the body as a dirt factory the whole explanation of woman's
derogatory attitude to her own body. That this attitude is related also to her
feelings of castration and mutilation is attested abundantly in everyday
analytical experience, and in such cases as those reported by Harnik.
Therefore a sufficient explanation of the manifold eccentricities of dress in
both sexes through the ages must be derived from many sources. The
fantasy of dirt and the related taboo on the apertures constitute only one
force out of the many which have been operative here.

## The Forbidden Interest in Excretory Functions

The taboo on the apertures works in another obvious and important
direction—to forbid the child the right to watch excretory functions. As a
result, a child may stand and watch a machine at work to his heart's
content, but never the body. He may not crouch down to watch even a
dog urinating or defecating without being made to feel as "dirty" as the
thing he wants to observe. Thus human beings are compelled to suppress
(and may therefore repress) all of that frank interest which two dogs will
manifest in each other's apertures; an interest which may then appear in

fantasies or dreams as disguised manifestations of an impulse actually to be in the toilet bowl watching the emergence of the mysterious excretory products of the parents. This is as much a primal scene as is the observation of coitus, and like it, it is infused with excitement and with intense fear of detection and of punishment, and with the direct dread of injury and destruction either by the parents themselves or through their destructive body products.

This group of fantasies was presented with unusual clarity in the dreams of two patients. In one the dream was of "riding the rods" under a train in such a way that the dreamer was enabled to look up through the opened aperture below the toilet into the car above him. The other was the dream of a most proper young lady that she was in the bathroom in the home of her four maiden aunts, and that in the bathroom was a bath-tub which, by some curious alchemy, was not only a cleansing tub but also a toilet bowl, filled with fluid which she or someone else had put there; and in that fluid she bathed, but whether she was getting clean or dirty she did not know. And floating in that fluid was paper, which was equally perplexing because at one and the same time it was pages from the Bible and sheets of toilet paper. (The delightfully witty and ironic reference to the analysis needs no comment.) There is an obscene little nursery jingle about a happy baby named "Sunny Jim," who is in the toilet bowl and finds he can neither swim nor float and who swallows feces. It brings out clearly the lurking curiosity about the excretory functions of parents, the accompanying sense of danger, the link to fears of drowning, the coprophagic fantasies, and the related feelings of shame, disgust, and retribution.

## The Relation to Unreality Feelings in Women

With surprising frequency one finds that a woman's fantasies of dirt lead her in yet another direction, namely, to make an identification with her own state of "dirtiness" so profound that if she loses even momentarily her feeling of being dirty, she develops sudden feelings of unreality. It has been possible to observe this in several women against a background of quite varied clinical pictures; and in men I have detected this only in one who had strong latent homosexual tendencies. His formulation was "All women and I are dirty." The converse of that is expressed in a quotation from a male patient described by Abraham, who said, "Everything that is not me is dirt." This patient, however, was a man with megalomanic tendencies. Certainly all clinical psychiatrists have been impressed by the greater frequency of unreality feelings in women than in men. The mechanism suggested here may be one partial explanation of this difference.

One of the most surprising things which has turned up during the course of these observations on the fantasy of dirt is the occurrence of unreality feelings as the outcome of an analytic reduction of a conviction of personal dirtiness. Shame may exercise so strong an inhibiting influence that it may be difficult to break through the reserves of a patient in this direction even after she has achieved fluent analytic productivity in other matters; but once she becomes free to talk, such a patient reveals feelings that she can *never* get clean. She contaminates a bath faster than a bath can clean her, like Tolstoi's fable of the woman who was trying to clean a table with a dirty rag. Her predicament sheds new light on the "damned spot" and the "perfumes of Arabia" of Lady Macbeth. If she dons clean underclothes she feels "queer," "as though she were a fake," and "unreal." A most attractive young college student said that no matter how clean were her underdrawers when she put them on in the morning, by lunchtime she felt as though they were filthy; yet she could not change them, because if she bathed and dressed again, she would still feel as though it were "all put on." The outside might appear neat, but the inside never was. She struggled, as she put it, between a constant compulsion to prove her cleanliness and simultaneously an actual fear that if she did she would lose her identity. Another said that for her there was no existence apart from her sense of dirt. She said, "A woman is real, like excrement; a man is real, like a penis." When her fiancé was making love to her, she had no feeling of his reality until she touched a pimple on his neck; only then did she feel certain in fact that he had a penis. Another said of herself, "All social presence, clothes and politeness, kindness to others, that is all unreal—a mere imitation." She identified herself completely with the contents of her own body. "I am my own body, and the only reality of that is its products, my bowels and my urine." At times this was associated with an explosive, expulsive protest, to let nothing remain but the feces, underlying which there was a deep unconscious fantasy of world destruction. But at the same time she was caught in a difficult therapeutic impasse. She could not tolerate her sense of dirtiness because it shamed her, made her afraid of people, made her asocial, and in every way cost her all confidence and joy in living. On the other hand, she could not let herself feel clean because that meant an explosion of terrifying feelings of unreality. It was as though she said, "In the absence of a penis, the dirt within is the only reality that is left to me. If I lose that, nothing real remains."

Such patients may at times make impulsive identifications of themselves with every unfortunate cripple and ill-favored person whom they see, by linking such persons with the most unacceptable aspects of their own bodies and their own body products. This is a peculiarly masochistic and self-debasing form of pity.

# HOME

## James Thurber

# Men

# *Fiction*

## FLIGHT
### John Steinbeck

About fifteen miles below Monterey, on the wild coast, the Torres family had their farm, a few sloping acres above a cliff that dropped to the brown reefs and to the hissing white waters of the ocean. Behind the farm the stone mountains stood up against the sky. The farm buildings huddled like little clinging aphids on the mountain skirts, crouched low to the ground as though the wind might blow them into the sea. The little shack, the rattling, rotting barn were gray-bitten with sea salt, beaten by the damp wind until they had taken on the color of the granite hills. Two horses, a red cow and a red calf, half a dozen pigs and a flock of lean, multicolored chickens stocked the place. A little corn was raised on the sterile slope, and it grew short and thick under the wind, and all the·cobs formed on the landward sides of the stalks.

Mama Torres, a lean, dry woman with ancient eyes, had ruled the farm for ten years, ever since her husband tripped over a stone in the field one day and fell full length on a rattlesnake. When one is bitten on the chest there is not much that can be done.

Mama Torres had three children, two undersized black ones of twelve and fourteen, Emilio and Rosy, whom Mama kept fishing on the rocks below the farm when the sea was kind and when the truant officer was in some distant part of Monterey County. And there was Pepé, the tall smiling son of nineteen, a gentle, affectionate boy, but very lazy. Pepé had a tall head, pointed at the top, and from its peak, coarse black hair grew down like a thatch all around. Over his smiling little eyes Mama cut a straight bang so he could see. Pepé had sharp Indian cheekbones and an eagle nose, but his mouth was as sweet and shapely as a girl's mouth, and his chin was fragile and chiseled. He was loose and gangling, all legs and feet and wrists, and he was very lazy. Mama thought him fine and brave, but

110

she never told him so. She said, "Some lazy cow must have got into thy father's family, else how could I have a son like thee." And she said, "When I carried thee, a sneaking lazy coyote came out of the brush and looked at me one day. That must have made thee so."

Pepé smiled sheepishly and stabbed at the ground with his knife to keep the blade sharp and free from rust. It was his inheritance, that knife, his father's knife. The long heavy blade folded back into the black handle. There was a button on the handle. When Pepé pressed the button, the blade leaped out ready for use. The knife was with Pepé always, for it had been his father's knife.

One sunny morning when the sea below the cliff was glinting and blue and the white surf creamed on the reef, when even the stone mountains looked kindly, Mama Torres called out the door of the shack, "Pepé, I have a labor for thee."

There was no answer. Mama listened. From behind the barn she heard a burst of laughter. She lifted her full long skirt and walked in the direction of the noise.

Pepé was sitting on the ground with his back against a box. His white teeth glistened. On either side of him stood the two black ones, tense and expectant. Fifteen feet away a redwood post was set in the ground. Pepé's right hand lay limply in his lap, and in the palm the big black knife rested. The blade was closed back into the handle. Pepé looked smiling at the sky.

Suddenly Emilio cried, "Ya!"

Pepé's wrist flicked like the head of a snake. The blade seemed to fly open in mid-air, and with a thump the point dug into the redwood post, and the black handle quivered. The three burst into excited laughter. Rosy ran to the post and pulled out the knife and brought it back to Pepé. He closed the blade and settled the knife carefully in his listless palm again. He grinned self-consciously at the sky.

"Ya!"

The heavy knife lanced out and sunk into the post again. Mama moved forward like a ship and scattered the play.

"All day you do foolish things with the knife, like a toy-baby," she stormed. "Get up on thy huge feet that eat up shoes. Get Up!" She took him by one loose shoulder and hoisted at him. Pepé grinned sheepishly and came half-heartedly to his feet. "Look!" Mama cried. "Big lazy, you must catch the horse and put on him thy father's saddle. You must ride to Monterey. The medicine bottle is empty. There is no salt. Go thou now, Peanut! Catch the horse."

A revolution took place in the relaxed figure of Pepé. "To Monterey, me? Alone? Si, Mama."

She scowled at him. "Do not think, big sheep, that you will buy candy. No. I will give you only enough for the medicine and the salt."

Pepé smiled. "Mama, you will put the hatband on the hat?"

She relented then. "Yes, Pepé. You may wear the hatband."

His voice grew insinuating. "And the green handkerchief, Mama?"

"Yes, if you go quickly and return with no trouble, the silk green hand-kerchief will go. If you make sure to take off the handkerchief when you eat so no spot may fall on it. . . ."

"*Si*, Mama. I will be careful. I am a man."

"Thou? A man? Thou art a peanut."

He went into the rickety barn and brought out a rope, and he walked agilely enough up the hill to catch the horse.

When he was ready and mounted before the door, mounted on his father's saddle that was so old that the oaken frame showed through torn leather in many places, then Mama brought out the round black hat with the tooled leather band, and she reached up and knotted the green silk handkerchief about his neck. Pepé's blue denim coat was much darker than his jeans, for it had been washed much less often.

Mama handed up the big medicine bottle and the silver coins. "That for the medicine," she said, "and that for the salt. That for a candle to burn for the papa. That for *dulces* for the little ones. Our friend Mrs. Rodriguez will give you dinner and maybe a bed for the night. When you go to the church say only ten Paternosters and only twenty-five Ave Marias. Oh! I know, big coyote. You would sit there flapping your mouth over Aves all day while you looked at the candles and the holy pictures. That is not good devotion to stare at the pretty things."

The black hat, covering the high pointed head and black thatched hair of Pepé, gave him dignity and age. He sat the rangy horse well. Mama thought how handsome he was, dark and lean and tall. "I would not send thee now alone, thou little one, except for the medicine," she said softly. "It is not good to have no medicine, for who knows when the toothache will come or the sadness of the stomach. These things are."

"*Adios,* Mama," Pepé cried. "I will come back soon. You may send me often alone. I am a man."

"Thou art a foolish chicken."

He straightened his shoulders, flipped the reins against the horse's shoulder and rode away. He turned once and saw that they still watched him, Emilio and Rosy and Mama. Pepé grinned with pride and gladness and lifted the tough buckskin horse to a trot.

When he had dropped out of sight over a little dip in the road, Mama turned to the black ones, but she spoke to herself, "He is nearly a man now," she said. "It will be a nice thing to have a man in the house again." Her eyes sharpened on the children. "Go to the rocks now. The tide is going out. There will be abalones to be found." She put the iron hooks into their hands and saw them down the steep trail to the reefs. She brought the smooth stone *metate* to the doorway and sat grinding her corn to flour and looking occasionally at the road over which Pepé had gone. The noonday came and then the afternoon, when the little ones beat the abalones on a rock to make them tender and Mama patted the tortillas to make them thin. They ate their dinner as the red sun was plunging down toward the ocean. They sat on the doorsteps and watched the big white moon come over the mountain tops.

Mama said, "He is now at the house of our friend Mrs. Rodriguez. She will give him nice things to eat and maybe a present."

Emilio said, "Some day I too will ride to Monterey for medicine. Did Pepé come to be a man today?"

Mama said wisely, "A boy gets to be a man when a man is needed. Remember this thing. I have known boys forty years old because there was no need for a man."

Soon afterwards they retired, Mama in her big oak bed on one side of the room, Emilio and Rosy in their boxes full of straw and sheepskins on the other side of the room.

The moon went over the sky and the surf roared on the rocks. The roosters crowed the first call. The surf subsided to a whispering surge against the reef. The moon dropped toward the sea. The roosters crowed again.

The moon was near down to the water when Pepé rode on a winded horse to his home flat. His dog bounced out and circled the horse yelping with pleasure. Pepé slid off the saddle to the ground. The weathered little shack was silver in the moonlight and the square shadow of it was black to the north and east. Against the east the piling mountains were misty with light; their tops melted into the sky.

Pepé walked wearily up the three steps and into the house. It was dark inside. There was a rustle in the corner.

Mama cried out from her bed. "Who comes? Pepé, is it thou?"

"Si, Mama."

"Did you get the medicine?"

"Si, Mama."

"Well, go to sleep, then. I thought you would be sleeping at the house of Mrs. Rodriguez." Pepé stood silently in the dark room. "Why do you stand there, Pepé? Did you drink wine?"

"Si, Mama."

"Well, go to bed then and sleep out the wine."

His voice was tired and patient, but very firm. "Light the candle, Mama. I must go away into the mountains."

"What is this, Pepé? You are crazy." Mama struck a sulphur match and held the little blue burr until the flame spread up the stick. She set light to the candle on the floor beside her bed. "Now, Pepé, what is this you say?" She looked anxiously into his face.

He was changed. The fragile quality seemed to have gone from his chin. His mouth was less full than it had been, the lines of the lips were straighter, but in his eyes the greatest change had taken place. There was no laughter in them any more, nor any bashfulness. They were sharp and bright and purposeful.

He told her in a tired monotone, told her everything just as it had happened. A few people came into the kitchen of Mrs. Rodriguez. There was wine to drink. Pepé drank wine. The little quarrel—the man started toward Pepé and then the knife—it went almost by itself. It flew, it darted before Pepé knew it. As he talked, Mama's face grew stern, and it seemed to grow more lean. Pepé finished. "I am a man now, Mama. The man said names to me I could not allow."

Mama nodded. "Yes, thou art a man, my poor little Pepé. Thou art a man. I have seen it coming on thee. I have watched you throwing the knife into the post, and I have been afraid." For a moment her face had softened, but now it grew stern again. "Come! We must get you ready. Go. Awaken Emilio and Rosy. Go quickly."

Pepé stepped over to the corner where his brother and sister slept among the sheepskins. He leaned down and shook them gently. "Come, Rosy! Come, Emilio! The mama says you must arise."

The little black ones sat up and rubbed their eyes in the candlelight. Mama was out of bed now, her long black skirt over her nightgown. "Emilio," she cried. "Go up and catch the other horse for Pepé. Quickly, now! Quickly!" Emilio put his legs in his overalls and stumbled sleepily out the door.

"You heard no one behind you on the road?" Mama demanded.

"No, Mama. I listened carefully. No one was on the road."

Mama darted like a bird about the room. From a nail on the wall she took a canvas water bag and threw it on the floor. She stripped a blanket from her bed and rolled it into a tight tube and tied the ends with string. From a box beside the stove she lifted a flour sack half full of black stringy jerky. "Your father's black coat, Pepé. Here, put it on."

Pepé stood in the middle of the floor watching her activity. She reached behind the door and brought out the rifle, a long 38-56, worn shiny the whole length of the barrel. Pepé took it from her and held it in the crook of his elbow. Mama brought a little leather bag and counted the cartridges into his hand. "Only ten left," she warned. "You must not waste them."

Emilio put his head in the door. "'Qui 'st 'l caballo, Mama."

"Put on the saddle from the other horse. Tie on the blanket. Here, tie the jerky to the saddle horn."

Still Pepé stood silently watching his mother's frantic activity. His chin looked hard and his sweet mouth was drawn and thin. His little eyes followed Mama about the room almost suspiciously.

Rosy asked softly, "Where goes Pepé?"

Mama's eyes were fierce. "Pepé goes on a journey. Pepé is a man now. He has a man's thing to do."

Pepé straightened his shoulders. His mouth changed until he looked very much like Mama.

At last the preparation was finished. The loaded horse stood outside the door. The water bag dripped a line of moisture down the bay shoulder.

The moonlight was being thinned by the dawn and the big white moon was near down to the sea. The family stood by the shack. Mama confronted Pepé. "Look, my son! Do not stop until it is dark again. Do not sleep even though you are tired. Take care of the horse in order that he may not stop of weariness. Remember to be careful with the bullets—there are only ten. Do not fill thy stomach with jerky or it will make thee sick. Eat a little jerky and fill thy stomach with grass. When thou comest to the high mountains, if thou seest any of the dark watching men, go not near to them nor try to speak to them. And forget not thy prayers." She put her lean hands on Pepé's shoulders, stood on her toes and kissed him formally on both cheeks, and Pepé kissed her on both cheeks. Then he went to Emilio and Rosy and kissed both of their cheeks.

Pepé turned back to Mama. He seemed to look for a little softness, a little weakness in her. His eyes were searching, but Mama's face remained fierce. "Go now," she said. "Do not wait to be caught like a chicken."

Pepé pulled himself into the saddle. "I am a man," he said.

It was the first dawn when he rode up the hill toward the little canyon which let a trail into the mountains. Moonlight and daylight fought with each other, and the two warring qualities made it difficult to see. Before Pepé had gone a hundred yards, the outlines of his figure were misty; and long before he entered the canyon, he had become a gray, indefinite shadow.

Mama stood stiffly in front of her doorstep, and on either side of her stood Emilio and Rosy. They cast furtive glances at Mama now and then.

When the gray shape of Pepé melted into the hillside and disappeared, Mama relaxed. She began the high, whining keen of the death wail. "Our beautiful—our brave," she cried. "Our protector, our son is gone." Emilio and Rosy moaned beside her. "Our beautiful—our brave, he is gone." It was the formal wail. It rose to a high piercing whine and subsided to a moan. Mama raised it three times and then she turned and went into the house and shut the door.

Emilio and Rosy stood wondering in the dawn. They heard Mama whimpering in the house. They went out to sit on the cliff above the ocean. They touched shoulders. "When did Pepé come to be a man?" Emilio asked.

"Last night," said Rosy. "Last night in Monterey." The ocean clouds turned red with the sun that was behind the mountains.

"We will have no breakfast," said Emilio. "Mama will not want to cook." Rosy did not answer him. "Where is Pepé gone?" he asked.

Rosy looked around at him. She drew her knowledge from the quiet air. "He has gone on a journey. He will never come back."

"Is he dead? Do you think he is dead?"

Rosy looked back at the ocean again. A little steamer drawing a line of smoke sat on the edge of the horizon. "He is not dead," Rosy explained. "Not yet."

Pepé rested the big rifle across the saddle in front of him. He let the horse walk up the hill and he didn't look back. The stony slope took on a coat of short brush so that Pepé found the entrance to a trail and entered it.

When he came to the canyon opening, he swung once in his saddle and looked back, but the houses were swallowed in the misty light. Pepé jerked forward again. The high shoulder of the canyon closed in on him. His horse stretched out its neck and sighed and settled to the trail.

It was a well-worn path, dark soft leaf-mould earth strewn with broken pieces of sandstone. The trail rounded the shoulder of the canyon and dropped steeply into the bed of the stream. In the shallows the water ran smoothly, glinting in the first morning sun. Small round stones on the bottom were as brown as rust with sun moss. In the sand along the edges of the stream the tall, rich wild mint grew, while in the water itself the cress, old and tough, had gone to heavy seed.

The path went into the stream and emerged on the other side. The horse sloshed into the water and stopped. Pepé dropped his bridle and let the beast drink of the running water.

Soon the canyon sides became steep and the first giant sentinel redwoods guarded the trail, great round red trunks bearing foliage as green and lacy as ferns. Once Pepé was among the trees, the sun was lost. A perfumed and purple light lay in the pale green of the underbrush. Gooseberry bushes and blackberries and tall ferns lined the stream, and overhead the branches of the redwoods met and cut off the sky.

Pepé drank from the water bag, and he reached into the flour sack and brought out a black string of jerky. His white teeth gnawed at the string until the tough meat parted. He chewed slowly and drank occasionally from the water bag. His little eyes were slumberous and tired, but the muscles of his face were hard set. The earth of the trail was black now. It gave up a hollow sound under the walking hoofbeats.

The stream fell more sharply. Little waterfalls splashed on the stones. Five-fingered ferns hung over the water and dripped spray from their fingertips. Pepé rode half over in his saddle, dangling one leg loosely. He picked a bay leaf from a tree beside the way and put it into his mouth for a moment to flavor the dry jerky. He held the gun loosely across the pommel.

Suddenly he squared in his saddle, swung the horse from the trail and kicked it hurriedly up behind a big redwood tree. He pulled up the reins tight against the bit to keep the horse from whinnying. His face was intent and his nostrils quivered a little.

A hollow pounding came down the trail, and a horseman rode by, a fat man with red cheeks and a white stubble beard. His horse put down its head and blubbered at the trail when it came to the place where Pepé had turned off. "Hold up!" said the man and he pulled up his horse's head.

When the last sound of the hoofs died away, Pepé came back into the trail again. He did not relax in the saddle any more. He lifted the big rifle and swung the lever to throw a shell into the chamber, and then he let down the hammer to half cock.

The trail grew very steep. Now the redwood trees were smaller and their tops were dead, bitten dead where the wind reached them. The horse plodded on; the sun went slowly overhead and started down toward the afternoon.

Where the stream came out of a side canyon, the trail left it. Pepé dismounted and watered his horse and filled up his water bag. As soon as the trail had parted from the stream, the trees were gone and only the thick brittle sage and manzanita and chaparral edged the trail. And the soft black earth was gone, too, leaving only the light tan broken rock for the trail bed. Lizards scampered away into the brush as the horse rattled over the little stones.

Pepé turned in his saddle and looked back. He was in the open now: he could be seen from a distance. As he ascended the trail the country grew more rough and terrible and dry. The way wound about the bases of great square rocks. Little gray rabbits skittered in the brush. A bird made a monotonous high creaking. Eastward the bare rock mountaintops were pale and powder-dry under the dropping sun. The horse plodded up and up the trail toward a little V in the ridge which was the pass.

Pepé looked suspiciously back every minute or so, and his eyes sought the tops of the ridges ahead. Once, on a white barren spur, he saw a black figure for a moment, but he looked quickly away, for it was one of the dark watchers. No one knew who the watchers were, nor where they lived, but it was better to ignore them and never to show interest in them. They did not bother one who stayed on the trail and minded his own business.

The air was parched and full of light dust blown by the breeze from the eroding mountains. Pepé drank sparingly from his bag and corked it tightly and hung it on the horn again. The trail moved up the dry shale hillside, avoiding rocks, dropping under clefts, climbing in and out of old water scars. When he arrived at the little pass he stopped and looked back for a long time. No dark watchers were to be seen now. The trail behind was empty. Only the high tops of the redwoods indicated where the stream flowed.

Pepé rode on through the pass. His little eyes were nearly closed with weariness, but his face was stern, relentless and manly. The high mountain wind coasted sighing through the pass and whistled on the edges of the big blocks of broken granite. In the air, a red-tailed hawk sailed over close to the ridge and screamed angrily. Pepé went slowly through the broken jagged pass and looked down on the other side.

The trail dropped quickly, staggering among broken rock. At the bottom of the slope there was a dark crease, thick with brush, and on the other side of the crease a little flat, in which a grove of oak trees grew. A scar of green grass cut across the flat. And behind the flat another mountain rose, desolate with dead rocks and starving little black bushes. Pepé drank from the bag again for the air was so dry that it encrusted his nostrils and burned his lips. He put the horse down the trail. The hooves slipped and struggled on the steep way, starting little stones that rolled off into the brush. The sun was gone behind the westward mountain now, but still it glowed brilliantly on the oaks and on the grassy flat. The rocks and the hillsides still sent up waves of the heat they had gathered from the day's sun.

Pepé looked up to the top of the next dry withered ridge. He saw a dark form against the sky, a man's figure standing on top of a rock, and he glanced away quickly not to appear curious. When a moment later he looked up again, the figure was gone.

Downward the trail was quickly covered. Sometimes the horse floundered for footing, sometimes set his feet and slid a little way. They came at last to the bottom where the dark chaparral was higher than Pepé's head. He held up his rifle on one side and his arm on the other to shield his face from the sharp brittle fingers of the brush.

Up and out of the crease he rode, and up a little cliff. The grassy flat was before him, and the round comfortable oaks. For a moment he studied the trail down which he had come, but there was no movement and no sound from it. Finally he rode out over the flat, to the green streak, and at the upper end of the damp he found a little spring welling out of the earth and dropping into a dug basin before it seeped out over the flat.

Pepé filled his bag first, and then let the thirsty horse drink out of the pool. He led the horse to the clump of oaks, and in the middle of the grove, fairly protected from sight on all sides, he took off the saddle and the bridle and laid them on the ground. The horse stretched his jaws sideways and yawned. Pepé knotted the lead rope about the horse's neck and tied him to a sapling among the oaks, where he could graze in a fairly large circle.

When the horse was gnawing hungrily at the dry grass, Pepé went to the saddle and took a black string of jerky from the sack and strolled to an oak tree on the edge of the grove, from under which he could watch the trail. He sat down in the crisp dry oak leaves and automatically felt for his big black knife to cut the jerky, but he had no knife. He leaned back on his elbow and gnawed at the tough strong meat. His face was blank, but it was a man's face.

The bright evening light washed the eastern ridge, but the valley was darkening. Doves flew down from the hills to the spring, and the quail came running out of the brush and joined them calling clearly to one another.

Out of the corner of his eye Pepé saw a shadow grow out of the bushy crease. He turned his head slowly. A big spotted wildcat was creeping toward the spring, belly to the ground, moving like thought.

Pepé cocked his rifle and edged the muzzle slowly around. Then he looked apprehensively up the trail and dropped the hammer again. From the ground beside him he picked an oak twig and threw it toward the spring. The quail flew up with a roar and the doves whistled away. The big cat stood up: for a long moment he looked at Pepé with cold yellow eyes, and then fearlessly walked back into the gulch.

The dusk gathered quickly in the deep valley. Pepé muttered his prayers, put his head down on his arm and went instantly to sleep.

The moon came up and filled the valley with cold blue light, and the wind swept rustling down from the peaks. The owls worked up and down the slopes looking for rabbits. Down in the brush of the gulch a coyote gabbled. The oak trees whispered softly in the night breeze.

Pepé started up, listening. His horse had whinnied. The moon was just slipping behind the western ridge, leaving the valley in darkness behind it. Pepé sat tensely gripping his rifle. From far up the trail he heard an answering whinny and the crash of shod hooves on the broken rock. He jumped to his feet, ran to his horse and led it under the trees. He threw on the saddle and cinched it tight for the steep trail, caught the unwilling head and forced the bit into the mouth. He felt the saddle to make sure the water bag and the sack of jerky were there. Then he mounted and turned up the hill.

It was velvet dark. The horse found the entrance to the trail where it left the flat, and started up, stumbling and slipping on the rocks. Pepé's hand rose up to his head. His hat was gone. He had left if under the oak tree.

The horse had struggled far up the trail when the first change of dawn came into the air, a steel grayness as light mixed thoroughly with dark. Gradually the sharp snaggled edge of the ridge stood out above them, rotten granite tortured and eaten by the winds of time. Pepé had dropped his reins on the horn, leaving direction to the horse. The brush grabbed at his legs in the dark until one knee of his jeans was ripped.

Gradually the light flowed down over the ridge. The starved brush and rocks stood out in the half light, strange and lonely in high perspective. Then there came warmth into the light. Pepé drew up and looked back, but he could see nothing in the darker valley below. The sky turned blue over the coming sun. In the waste of the mountainside, the poor dry brush grew only three feet high. Here and there, big outcroppings of unrotted granite stood up like mouldering houses. Pepé relaxed a little. He drank from his water bag and bit off a piece of jerky. A single eagle flew over, high in the light.

Without warning Pepé's horse screamed and fell on its side. He was almost down before the rifle crash echoed up from the valley. From a hole behind the struggling shoulder, a stream of bright crimson blood pumped and stopped and pumped and stopped. The hooves threshed on the ground. Pepé lay half stunned beside the horse. He looked slowly down the hill. A piece of sage clipped off beside his head and another crash echoed up from side to side of the canyon. Pepé flung himself frantically behind a bush.

He crawled up the hill on his knees and one hand. His right hand held the rifle up off the ground and pushed it ahead of him. He moved with the instinctive care of an animal. Rapidly he wormed his way toward one of the big outcroppings of granite on the hill above him. Where the brush was high he doubled up and ran, but where the cover was slight he wriggled forward on his stomach, pushing the rifle ahead of him. In the last little distance there was no cover at all. Pepé poised and then he darted across the space and flashed around the corner of the rock.

He leaned panting against the stone. When his breath came easier he moved along behind the big rock until he came to a narrow split that offered a thin section of vision down the hill. Pepé lay on his stomach and pushed the rifle barrel through the slit and waited.

The sun reddened the western ridges now. Already the buzzards were settling down toward the place where the horse lay. A small brown bird scratched in the dead sage leaves directly in front of the rifle muzzle. The coasting eagle flew back toward the rising sun.

Pepé saw a little movement in the brush far below. His grip tightened on the gun. A little brown doe stepped daintily out on the trail and crossed it and disappeared into the brush again. For a long time Pepé waited. Far below he could see the little flat and the oak trees and the slash of green. Suddenly his eyes flashed back at the trail again. A quarter of a mile down there had been a quick movement in the chaparral. The rifle swung over. The front sight nestled in the V of the rear sight. Pepé studied for a moment and then raised the rear sight a notch. The little movement in the brush came again. The sight settled on it. Pepé squeezed the trigger. The explosion crashed down the mountain and up the other side, and came rattling back. The whole side of the slope grew still. No more movement. And then a white streak cut into the granite of the silt and a bullet whined away and a crash sounded up from below. Pepé felt a sharp pain in his right hand. A sliver of granite was sticking out from between his first and second knuckles and the point protruded from his palm. Carefully he pulled out the sliver of stone. The wound bled evenly and gently. No vein or artery was cut.

Pepé looked into a little dusty cave in the rock and gathered a handful of spider web, and he pressed the mass into the cut, plastering the soft web into the blood. The flow stopped almost at once.

The rifle was on the ground. Pepé picked it up, levered a new shell into the chamber. And then he slid into the brush on his stomach. Far to the right he crawled, and then up the hill, moving slowly and carefully, crawling to cover and resting and then crawling again.

In the mountains the sun is high in its arc before it penetrates the gorges. The hot face looked over the hill and brought instant heat with it. The white light beat on the rocks and reflected from them and rose up quivering from the earth again, and the rocks and bushes seemed to quiver behind the air.

Pepé crawled in the general direction of the ridge peak, zigzagging for cover. The deep cut between his knuckles began to throb. He crawled close to a rattlesnake before he saw it, and when it raised its dry head and make a soft beginning whirr, he backed up and took another way. The quick gray lizards flashed in front of him, raising a tiny line of dust. He found another mass of spider web and pressed it against his throbbing hand.

Pepé was pushing the rifle with his left hand now. Little drops of sweat ran to the ends of his coarse black hair and rolled down his cheeks. His lips and tongue were growing thick and heavy. His lips writhed to draw saliva into his mouth. His little dark eyes were uneasy and suspicious. Once when a gray lizard paused in front of him on the parched ground and turned its head sideways he crushed it flat with a stone.

When the sun slid past noon he had not gone a mile. He crawled exhaustedly a last hundred yards to a patch of high sharp manzanita, crawled desperately, and when the patch was reached he wriggled in among the tough gnarly trunks and dropped his head on his left arm. There was little shade in the meager brush, but there was cover and safety. Pepé went to sleep as he lay and the sun beat on his back. A few little birds hopped close to him and peered and hopped away. Pepé squirmed in his sleep and he raised and dropped his wounded hand again and again.

The sun went down behind the peaks and the cool evening came, and then the dark. A coyote yelled from the hillside. Pepé started awake and looked about with misty eyes. His hand was swollen and heavy; a little thread of pain ran up the inside of his arm and settled in a pocket in his armpit. He peered about and then stood up, for the mountains were black and the moon had not yet risen. Pepé stood up in the dark. The coat of his father pressed on his arm. His tongue was swollen until it nearly filled his mouth. He wriggled out of the coat and dropped it in the brush, and then he struggled up the hill, falling over rocks and tearing his way through the brush. The rifle knocked against stones as he went. Little dry avalanches of gravel and shattered stone went whispering down the hill behind him.

After a while the old moon came up and showed the jagged ridge top ahead of him. By moonlight Pepé traveled more easily. He bent forward so that his throbbing arm hung away from his body. The journey uphill was made in dashes and rests, a frantic rush up a few yards and then a rest. The wind coasted down the slope rattling the dry stems of the bushes.

The moon was at meridian when Pepé came at last to the sharp backbone of the ridge top. On the last hundred yards of the rise no soil had clung under the wearing winds. The way was on solid rock. He clambered to the top and looked down on the other side. There was a draw like the last below him, misty with moonlight, brushed with dry struggling sage and chaparral. On the other side the hill rose up sharply and at the top the jagged rotten teeth of the mountain showed against the sky. At the bottom of the cut the brush was thick and dark.

Pepé stumbled down the hill. His throat was almost closed with thirst. At first he tried to run, but immediately he fell and rolled. After that he went more carefully. The moon was just disappearing behind the mountains when he came to the bottom. He crawled into the heavy brush feeling with his fingers for water. There was no water in the bed of the stream, only damp earth. Pepé laid his gun down and scooped up a handful of mud and put it in his mouth, and then he spluttered and scraped the earth from his tongue with his finger, for the mud drew at his mouth like a poultice. He dug a hole in the stream bed with his fingers, dug a little basin to catch water, but before it was very deep his head fell forward on the damp ground and he slept.

The dawn came and the heat of the day fell on the earth, and still Pepé slept. Late in the afternoon his head jerked up. He looked slowly around. His eyes were slits of wariness. Twenty feet away in the heavy brush a big tawny mountain lion stood looking at him. Its long thick tail waved gracefully, its ears were erect with interest, not laid back dangerously. The lion squatted down on its stomach and watched him.

Pepé looked at the hole he had dug in the earth. A half inch of muddy water had collected in the bottom. He tore the sleeve from his hurt arm, with his teeth ripped out a little square, soaked it in the water and put it in his mouth. Over and over he filled the cloth and sucked it.

Still the lion sat and watched him. The evening came down but there was no movement on the hills. No birds visited the dry bottom of the cut. Pepé looked occasionally at the lion. The eyes of the yellow beast drooped as though he were about to sleep. He yawned and his long thin red tongue curled out. Suddenly his head jerked around and his nostrils quivered. His big tail lashed. He stood up and slunk like a tawny shadow into the thick brush.

A moment later Pepé heard the sound, the faint far crash of horses' hooves on gravel. And he heard something else, a high whining yelp of a dog.

Pepé took his rifle in his left hand and he glided into the brush almost as quietly as the lion had. In the darkening evening he crouched up the hill toward the next ridge. Only when the dark came did he stand up. His energy was short. Once it was dark he fell over the rocks and slipped to his knees on the steep slope. But he moved on and on up the hill, climbing and scrabbling over the broken hillside.

When he was far up toward the top, he lay down and slept for a little while. The withered moon, shining on his face, awakened him. He stood up and moved up the hill. Fifty yards away he stopped and turned back, for he had forgotten his rifle. He walked heavily down and poked about in the brush, but he could not find his gun. At last he lay down to rest. The pocket of pain in his armpit had grown more sharp. His arm seemed to swell out and fall with every heartbeat. There was no position lying down where the heavy arm did not press against his armpit.

With the effort of a hurt beast, Pepé got up and moved again toward the top of the ridge. He held his swollen arm away from his body with his left hand. Up the steep hill he dragged himself. A few steps and a rest, and a few more steps. At last he was nearing the top. The moon showed the uneven sharp back of it against the sky.

Pepé's brain spun in a big spiral up and away from him. He slumped to the ground and lay still. The rock ridge top was only a hundred feet above him.

The moon moved over the sky. Pepé half turned on his back. His tongue tried to make words, but only a thick hissing came from between his lips.

When the dawn came, Pepé pulled himself up. His eyes were sane again. He drew his great puffed arm in front of him and looked at the angry wound. The black line ran up from his wrist to his armpit. Automatically he reached in his pocket for the big black knife, but it was not there. His eyes searched the ground. He picked up a sharp blade of stone and scraped at the wound, sawed at the proud flesh and then squeezed the green juice out in big drops. Instantly he threw back his head and whined like a dog. His whole right side shuddered at the pain, but the pain cleared his head.

In the gray light he struggled up the last slope to the ridge and crawled over and lay down behind a line of rocks. Below him lay a deep canyon exactly like the last, waterless and desolate. There was no flat, no oak trees, not even heavy brush in the bottom of it. And on the other side a sharp ridge stood up, thinly brushed with starving sage, littered with broken granite. Strewn over the hill there were giant outcroppings, and on the top the granite teeth stood out against the sky.

The new day was light now. The flame of the sun came over the ridge and fell on Pepé where he lay on the ground. His coarse black hair was littered with twigs and bits of spider web. His eyes had retreated back into his head. Between his lips the tip of his black tongue showed.

He sat up and dragged his great arm into his lap and nursed it, rocking his body and moaning in his throat. He threw back his head and looked up into the pale sky. A big black bird circled nearly out of sight, and far to the left another was sailing near.

He lifted his head to listen, for a familiar sound had come to him from the valley he had climbed out of; it was the crying yelp of hounds, excited and feverish, on a trail.

Pepé bowed his head quickly. He tried to speak rapid words but only a thick hiss came from his lips. He drew a shaky cross on his breast with his left hand. It was a long struggle to get to his feet. He crawled slowly and mechanically to the top of a big rock on the ridge peak. Once there, he arose slowly, swaying to his feet, and stood erect. Far below he could see the dark brush where he had slept. He braced his feet and stood there, black against the morning sky.

There came a ripping sound at his feet. A piece of stone flew up and a bullet droned off into the next gorge. The hollow crash echoed up from below. Pepé looked down for a moment and then pulled himself straight again.

His body jarred back. His left hand fluttered helplessly toward his breast. The second crash sounded from below. Pepé swung forward and toppled from the rock. His body struck and rolled over and over, starting a little avalanche. And when at last he stopped against a bush, the avalanche slid slowly down and covered up his head.

# A CHANGE OF AIR

Ivan Gold

## Prologue

Bobbie Bedner at the age of nineteen during the course of three warm August days and nights lost not her virginity which she had long before misplaced in the back of an automobile but the memory of it, and almost, along with this, the capacity to remember. What she knew when she awoke on the first of the August mornings was that on such a fine sunny morning one had to be completely out of one's head to go to work in a button factory what with a hundred better nicer cleaner things to do, and damn her mother and the button factory, she would go for a long walk out of doors or maybe to a movie. What she knew as well (but not as loudly) as her not going to work was exactly where she was going and why. But what she did not know . . . what she could not possibly know when she got on the bus (which passed one park and two movie houses on its journey along an avenue of New York's lower East Side, but which also stopped almost directly outside the clubroom of the silk-jacketed Werewolves, membership thirty-five, and many friends) was that when she returned home seventy-two hours later, she would do so minus her underwear, the greater part of her emotional stability, her future in the button factory, and eleven pounds.

For the two or three young men of her acquaintance whom she expected to find in the clubroom at this early hour (they living there, being otherwise unhoused and temporarily unemployed) she found in the clubroom, running win, place, and show in a fabulous, all-night, seven-man stud poker game, and consequently filled to overflowing with philanthropy (love for one's fellow man). She walked in boldly, then hesitated, seeing seven card players and three hecklers, ten in all, counted on Tony, Frank, and Fat Andy for the protection she thought she wanted, found them extremely interested in her presence, but averse to any plan of action which did not include their intimates at the card table, who were now poorer (and they richer) by three hundred dollars. Decided finally, persuaded by Frank's embraces and the uniqueness (ten of them—why not the hecklers too—on the same day) of the prospect, communicated her decision by her slightly hysterical laugh, running crazily up the scale and halfway down, and thereby set out to make East Side of New York (and possibly national) history.

For . . . although unrecorded in the Werewolves' minutes, or in any other written source (ignoring the possibility that one or more of the half-dozen or so twelve- to fifteen-year-old young men she devirginized during the three-day period was sentimental enough to keep a diary), it is proved beyond any doubt by an unchallengeable number of oral affirmations that Bobbie Bedner (although expressing some desire to leave about four o'clock of the same afternoon when the situation seemed to be getting out of hand) nevertheless was taken, or rather had, one hundred and sixty times during seventy hours by a total of fifty-three persons (the entire membership of the Werewolves, their younger brothers and friends) of all nationalities and sizes, slept a grand total of seven hours during the three days and nights, consumed a bottle of milk, two of beer, a number of pretzels and a ham sandwich, called her mother on the evening of the first day to assure her that everything was under control and (it was Friday) she was spending the night at a friend's house and did not know exactly when she would be home, and returned home two and one-half days later when one of the Werewolves, preparing to make the trip for the third time, suddenly and concernedly noticed how peaked she was. They put her on a bus at eight o'clock on Monday morning, thoughtfully providing her with carfare, warning her to keep it quiet which they did not have to do since she truly bore them no animosity, and she returned home, eleven pounds less of her, to her mother and to the police who had preceded her by only twenty minutes, and fainted in the doorway.

When she awoke, tight-lipped, in a hospital, heard the doctor proclaim to the police and nurse the girl has suffered an ordeal, been without food and raped many times, laughed her crazy laugh, and had to say you screwy sawbones you it wasn't rape and how many times and laughed the crazy laugh for many minutes at the doctor's guess of thirty and the nurse's forty the police's fifty, told them how many times (having kept a careful count), told them laughing crazily it was all her own idea and she might have a go at it again, but worth less than nothing to the forces of law and order in the names and places department.

They sent her away. They had to. Her mother wrung her hands, cursed her God and the memory of her husband. They sent her away for two years. When she returned from Rehabilitation School she had regained the eleven pounds and five additional. There were other apparently deeper changes.

*Franklin Cripple DeTorres,* carrying himself well at five foot-seven, absolutely sound of limb and body, derived his middle name, twenty-five cents, and a good part of his reputation as a result of an encounter in (and with) a subway. Always sure of himself, acutely conscious of his heritage—Puerto Rico (for his birth and the year afterward), New York and bravery—never more so than at five A.M. on a liquored Sunday morning. Cripple (Crip to his friends) conjectured aloud on the fate of his foot provided he left it where it was, hanging over the parapet above the tracks, a void soon to be filled by an incoming subway train.

His friends, not realizing the full extent of his courage, liking him and wishing (in good spirits) to create the opportunity to apply to him a large number of defamatory epithets (which they would be in a position to do when he snatched his foot out of danger), offered (one of them did) the sum of twenty-five cents to the soon-to-be-martyred if he left his foot there until and after the train arrived. It was not the money which decided him, but the attitude which prompted its offer. Placing his foot up to the heel (with which he clutched the edge of the parapet for support) over the parapet, Cripple waited. The train came. He did not even flinch, not until the train (with its agonized conductor) hit him, and then he did not flinch but fell down parallel to the tracks, landing on his elbows, the foot which earned him the name the money the reputation seemingly unhurt, and shouted very loudly, unhysterically, but with great conviction, get me to the hospital.

His ten weeks in the hospital he found dull but not unbearable, being able to leaf through the books previously stolen from the bookstore where he stockclerked, being always interested in culture, and favored daily by visits from his friends, the entire membership of the Werewolves, most calling his act of bravery the stupidest thing anyone had ever done, but all admiring, and the six weeks after that when he walked with an ever-lessening limp were just that, six weeks, so he suffered nothing finally except the money he did not make (more than compensated for by the quarter which he had framed and hung in the Werewolves' clubroom threatening death and other penalties to anyone who removed it), and he gained a name which it seemed to outsiders should offend him, until they learned the manner of its origination.

On the day Bobbie Bedner did not go to work, Frank Cripple DeTorres won one hundred and forty dollars. It was the largest longest most expensive poker game ever played in the Werewolf clubroom, it was the most money he had ever won, and although by no means feeling guilty (perhaps even seeing a way to call a halt to the contest before his luck began to change), Cripple, when he saw her walk in, felt that the least he could do for the boys he had taken over was to get them to the slut as long as she happened to be around. He was the first on line, then, as the affair began to mushroom (something he did not foresee but which did not make any difference), thirty-first and again one hundred and sixth. He was sorry to hear (he did not hear, but deduced from her absence) that the girl had been sent to a reformatory.

When the Werewolves disbanded (after a police raid which led to the twelve Werewolves present at the club spending some time at headquarters, and the two of them identified by the badly battered grocery proprietor remaining after the others were allowed to leave) Cripple devoted himself to intellectual pursuits, spending most of his evenings at Gelber's Chess Club on Seventeenth Street. He went usually with Joe Muneco, or met him there. They were the only two young men (except for occasional visits from Joe's friends) in what was otherwise a storm center for the old. Together, these two, they either beat (they played well) or talked down every old man in the place.

A problem to Early Environmentalists (the key to personality lies in the first three or five or nine or eleven years), *Joseph Muneco* (of whom they had never heard) spent the first three years of his life running around the streets of San Juan, Puerto Rico, the next fourteen years escaping policemen (for playing stickball on New York City streets and mugging usually close-to-penniless passersby), then, being expelled from three high schools (for non attendance of classes and smoking marijuana), finally happening across a novel by Thomas Wolfe, impressed enough to read this author's entire works, discovering James Joyce, and in his twentieth year, and his fourth high school, becoming the editor (and first-prize winner in a national short story contest) of his high school literary magazine.

Made many friends in this high school (at home on all intellectual strata), fell in love with and was loved by the editor of the high school newspaper (a Jewish girl of orthodox parents who were destined to object to their daughter's keeping company with a Gentile, and with a Spanish Gentile, and with one who looked so typically and unhealthily Spanish), went to a city college (his girl and he), saw the girl every day and on Saturday nights, and devoted the rest of his social time alternately to Cripple (alone or with mutual acquaintances, members of the long-defunct Werewolves) and to his other high school friends (the last high school), cream of the intellectual crop, the boys who read the books, who thought about writing them (as he did—although he only thought), and who by fairly frequent remarks pertaining to his dual heritage (the literate hoodlum, and variants, with lots of laughter, although he had for a long time now adhered to the straight and narrow path) contributed to the growth of his impassioned unusual campaign of self-justification.

Impassioned unusual campaign of self-justification . . . not with his girl Anne, with whom he was in love; nor with Cripple and with these friends with whom he fitted in so perfectly that there was no need of it; but with the others. . . .

With *Phillip Zand,* literary critic until his junior year at college, thinking now of psychology, seeing it as a back door to the world he didn't live in; a great reader and a great listener to music, and a self-styled neurotic, finding himself replete with wrong things to say (to women), and not enough women to say them to; not pretty, but (not that this mattered) not as unpretty as he thought he was, weakly contemptuous of the others, his close circle of friends, in the only regions where he was qualified to be contemptuous, books and music, finding them in these regions, although reasonably well-informed, nevertheless with sufficient (for the purposes of ridicule) misinformation. . . .

With *Lee Miller,* a college man, sporadically read in Schopenhauer, Nietzsche, and Philip Wylie, with some Havelock Ellis (being interested in sex); contentious but without a conciliatory delivery (far from it; always unpleasant, not going out of his way to be unpleasant, but being that way because it came easiest), with the result that among his group of friends, he had no friend; cherubic in appearance (and thus with a number of con- quests to his credit which Phil Zand—by no means accidentally—was forever hearing about, but still . . .), a lecher at nineteen, being famed (and given no peace) for the most amazing collection of pornographic snapshots and literature perhaps ever assembled, delighting in lending certain parts of his collection to Phil since he knew what he used them for, a good but strange mind; a flair for chess, a match for Joe Muneco, a terrific and serious rivalry building between them, a result of and a further prod to mutual dislike. . . .

With *Benjamin Brock,* the only one of them attending a college which it required money to attend, assuming therefore a certain superiority in the quality of his education, never having to mention the felt superiority for them to know that it was there; doubting especially (again tacitly, or if not tacitly, then blatantly in jest) Muneco's claim to higher understanding (Joe having not written since the days of his high school triumphs—Ben writing all the time—two long years ago, unable to take his typewriter out of pawn, and besides, being busy—with his girl and with Cripple—being happy), Muneco feeling Ben's doubts, and the doubts of the others, knowing the realm of the intellect to be his as well as (if not more than) theirs, but feeling it always necessary to prove it to them, and so. . . .

Joseph Muneco's impassioned unusual campaign of self-justification, the utilization of a phenomenal memory, an almost photographic memory, committing to it the equivalent of three large volumes of verse, from Sap- pho to Cummings, and considerable prose, quoting some part of his reper- toire at the least provocation, creating his own provocation, irrelevant (the quoting) to anything occurring or even said in his immediate environment, but illustrating to Phil and to Lee and to Ben and to anyone else around that he, Joseph Muneco, had a sizable portion of the world's literature at his fingertips, had the best that man's mind has yet created stored (with an understanding of it, if anyone pursued the matter) in his memory, that he, Joseph Muneco was, whatever else he might also be, an intellectual.

With this and these in mind, we can begin the story.

## The Story

Gelber's Chess Club was partly that. More, it was a place to play cards and a place to stay, on cold winter nights and dull summer ones. In the back of the club, away from the two windows overlooking Seventeenth Street, was a small room with a stove in which Mrs. Gelber made and sold coffee and sandwiches. The long, large room which was the club was divided by common consent into the section for chess players and for card players; there were the few benches in the chess player section for those who wished to sleep, to think, or to read the paper. On the door of the club was a sign reading FOR MEMBERS ONLY and inside the club a sign said MEMBERSHIP DUES, ONE DOLLAR A YEAR. Neither of these mattered. Gelber was friendly, did not need the money, and owned the building. The signs were put up at the insistence of his wife and Gelber neither desired to, nor did he, reinforce them. The club had been on Seventeenth Street for twenty-two years, and although the faces changed, at intervals, the mean age of the members did not. The men at the club—and they were all men aside from Gelber's wife—averaged fifty-five years of age. If not for the presence of Joseph Muneco and Franklin DeTorres, who came often enough to necessitate their inclusion in any mathematical calculations, the average age of the members of Gelber's Chess Club would have been fifty-seven.

Frank DeTorres was talking to Joe Muneco.

"Okay Ace," he said. "Push the pawn. Before the place closes, Ace. I guarantee the safety of the pawn move."

Frank had arrived at 11 o'clock and had played chess with the old men. He won more than he lost and enjoyed his conversation and the reactions to it. At one o'clock Joe Muneco walked in, earlier than usual for a Saturday night, but his girl had gotten sick and he took her home early, leaving her a block from where she lived in case one of her parents happened to be looking from the window. Meeting her on Saturday nights was no problem since she had a job ushering at concerts in a school auditorium in his neighborhood, and he could meet her afterward, at nine-thirty. On this Saturday night she became ill and he took her home. When he got to the club, he and Frank DeTorres played chess. Muneco was the better of the two but against each other they played carelessly, and games were not won or lost in accord with their ability.

At DeTorres' remark, Joe became angry for the three old men who made up his audience.

"Take it easy, Ace," he said. "Any time you want to play three seconds a move, you let me know, Ace. The pawn move is for the fushas. I give you this." He moved his bishop along its diagonal. One of the old men grunted approval and smiled a toothless smile. Frank addressed him.

"Doesn't he play like a master?" he said. "He is a true Morphy in the way he plays this game. I admire your manipulation of the pieces, Ace," he said to Joe. He looked swiftly at the board and made his move. "Try this one," he said.

Joe guffawed. "Swish, Ace," he said, swooping down upon DeTorres' unprotected queen, removing it, and upsetting four or five pieces on both sides of the board.

"I didn't see, Ace," Frank said, beginning to smile. Two of the old men laughed. The third yawned noisily and moved toward one of the benches leaning against the wall.

Frank resigned. He began to set up his pieces in preparation for another game. At one-thirty Phil Zand and Lee Miller walked in. They had gone to a movie, had coffee, and come to the chess club looking for Joe Muneco. They knew that he could be found here on Sunday mornings at this time after taking his girl home.

"Watch him!" Joe said agitatedly to Phil, glancing momentarily at Lee, as the two came over and sat down. "You shouldn't have taken him off the leash. He's liable to rape small boys."

"No need," Lee said. "I was refreshed last night. A very sweet young thing I met at a dance. How's Anne?"

The query might have been solicitous, but it was very poorly placed. Suddenly Muneco was no longer amusing or amused.

"She's all right," he said, looking at Lee. "Unless you just killed her by mentioning her name."

Lee laughed. He laughed unpleasantly, the only way he knew how.

"I thought you had signed a nonaggression pact," Phil said.

"Only verbal," Joe said. "It can be busted at any time."

"What's new?" Frank said to Phil.

"I'm glad you asked," Phil said. "My profession. I'm going to be a psychologist."

"That's nice," Frank said. "We are in need of psychologists. But you've got to gain weight if you want to be healthy enough to pursue your studies. You're very thin, in spite of your weight lifting."

Phil laughed.

" 'I am thy father's spirit.' " Joe said. " 'Doomed for a certain term to walk the night, and for the day confined to fast in fires, till the foul crimes done in my days of nature are burnt and purged away. But that I am forbid,' " he said, " 'to tell the secrets of my prison-house, I could a tale unfold whose lightest word would harrow up thy soul,' checkmate Ace," he said.

"You're a genius, Muneco," Lee said, sitting in the chair Frank had just vacated. Frank visited Mrs. Gelber for some coffee.

"You didn't like that?" Joe inquired. "Maybe you'd prefer an excerpt from Krafft-Ebing. 'George K., longshoreman, locked in the embraces of Mollie F., housewife suffering from vaginismus, found it difficult to extricate. . . .' "

"No moves back," Lee said, making his first move.

"Make it touch move," Joe said, unsmiling. "Better than that we measure the Galvanic Skin Response. If I catch you thinking about a piece, you got to move it."

"Agreed," Lee said.

Phil laughed: at their seriousness, and at the incongruity which it seemed to him the technical term had in Muneco's mouth.

"What do you know about the Galvanic Skin Response?" he said.

"Nothing," Joe said. "Now that you're a psychologist I know nothing about the Galvanic Skin Response. Just as when previously you were a literary critic I knew nothing about literature. And as in consequence of your large record collection, I know nothing about music. If I ever again say anything implying I know anything at all about psychology, may I suffer excruciating pain."

"Okay," Phil laughed. "I'm sorry. You're an intellectual."

Frank returned with his coffee. He knew these two, Lee and Phil, and also Ben, because of their friendship with Joe Muneco. They had graduated from high school with Joe three years ago, and he had continued seeing them, about once a week, since then. They were not particularly interesting, Frank thought, although they were supposed to be bright, and he guessed that this was what Joe saw in them. He could talk to them in Joe's presence, but doubted if he could find anything to say to them under other circumstances. These never arose since he ran into them only when he was with Muneco. Now he returned with the coffee and he saw skinny Phil leaning on the table, his hair mussed, smiling at Muneco, and it struck him what a particularly dull life Phil must lead.

"Hey Phil, you still got it?" he said.

"Got what?"

"Your chastity. Last time I heard, you had still got it."

"Still got it," Phil said, smiling ruefully, but resignedly, as if talking about an amputated arm.

"I can't understand it, Ace," Frank said. "What's the good of going to college if they don't teach you about life? That's why I didn't go to college, because they had no courses in screwing."

"That's right, Ace," Joe mumbled, engrossed in the game.

"You should have gone," Lee said. "You're a great loss to the academic world."

Frank had begun to understand that the things Lee said in jest were no different in tone from the things that he said when he was being nasty. It was just the way he talked, everything seeming an insult. He thought for a moment, and decided from the context that Lee was jesting.

"I appreciate this," Frank said.

Frank sat down to kibitz the game, and Phil read the Sunday *Times*. If no one else arrived and even if someone else did, they would spend an hour or two at the chess club, then go downstairs and across the street into the all-night cafeteria (it was too cold in January for the groups to gather in Union Square Park), spend some time there over their coffee, and then go home at four or five o'clock in the morning. They would take Phil, who became tired before anyone else, and who lived the greatest distance (fourteen blocks) from Seventeenth Street, home first, then would walk three blocks uptown to where Lee lived; and finally walk back to the chess club, and three blocks beyond it, to the street on which Frank and Joe lived, in adjoining tenement buildings.

But Ben Brock arrived. Even this wouldn't have made any difference, for Ben Brock often arrived without noticeably disturbing the Saturday night ritual. But Ben Brock arrived with the family car, which meant, if nothing else, that they would all be driven home. It meant however enough more than that on this Saturday night to change the entire texture of the evening.

"Okay," he said, when he saw them around the chess table. "Drop everything. The bus awaits. Let me take you away from all this."

"You park it in the hallway?" Joe said.

"Stop, I can't stand the irony," Ben said. "The car is parked downstairs, three picas from the curb. How many times do I have to tell you, Muneco, I can park a car?"

"Perhaps," Joe said. "As soon as Krafft-Ebing here resigns his lost game."

"Lost game!" Lee said, angrily incredulous. "You talk like a chess player," he said. "But rather than destroy your ego, I agree to a ride in Brock's convertible."

"Anything," Phil said, "for a change of scenery."

Frank sat behind a board, set up the pieces, and beckoned to an old man who sat, half dozing, on a bench. The old man smiled and came toward him.

"Spot me a rook, Kurtz." Frank said.

The old man smiled. "Why not both?" he said. He sat down opposite Frank.

"Hey Crip, you coming?" Joe said to him.

"You college men go for a ride in the car," Frank said. "Driving . . ." (he groped for the cliché) ". . . exerts no appeal on me. I'm gonna teach

Kurtz here how to play this game." The others were already outside and down the one landing to the street.

"Okay Ace," Joe said. "Castle early and open up a rook file. I'll see you." He turned and walked toward the door.

"So long Ace," Frank said.

The car was riding north, along First Avenue, toward Forty-second Street.

"Are we going to Times Square?" Phil said.

"If that's what you want," Ben said. "Although I was going to drive you down to Miami. It's time you phony authors and literary critics and psychologists and perverts learned that the East Side of New York is not the center of the world."

"How do you know that?" Joe said.

"Hearsay." Ben said. "But it sounds logical."

"We'll go to Miami next time," Phil yawned. "I've got to wake up early tomorrow."

On the corner of Twenty-sixth Street Ben stopped for a light. Muneco, sitting up front, glanced from the window. "Hey," he said suddenly. Ben, following Joe's eye, saw a figure turn the corner of Twenty-sixth Street and walk out of his range of vision. "Was that Barbara Bedner?" Joe said.

"I don't know," Ben said. "Shall we find out?"

"Who's Barbara Bedner?" Phil said.

"What difference does it make?" Lee said. "It's a girl's name."

The light changed and Ben turned the corner. "I've told you about her," Joe said, peering from the window. The street was dark and he could not be sure. "That's the girl they sent up for the impairment of everybody's morals. The record holder. I didn't know they'd let her out."

"Is it her?" Ben said, slowing down a few yards behind the girl.

"I can't tell," Joe said.

The girl turned off and walked up to a stoop leading to the entrance of a building.

"Well you'd better find out if you're going to find out," Lee said.

Joe opened his window.

"Barbara," he called. "Is that Bobbie Bedner?"

The girl turned, startled. It was late at night and she had not heard the car turn the corner. She saw the car but could not see who was inside. The car was a 1950 model, a red convertible. Ben and his father had washed and polished it that same day. It looked like a new car. Bobbie Bedner came, looking very curious, down the stairs and up to the open window.

"Hello," Joe said cheerfully. "I thought it was you. Do you remember me?"

"Yeah," Bobbie said, smiling blankly. "Yeah, I remember you. What's your name?"

Joe grinned. "Joe," he said. "I used to belong to the Werewolves. Remember the Werewolves?"

Bobbie grinned innocently back at him. "Yeah, I remember," she said. "How is everybody? How's Fat Andy?"

"He's fine," Joe said. "He got caught with a stolen car. He won't be around for a while."

"Gee, that's a shame," Bobbie said, meaning it. She laughed. "How's Tony?" she asked.

"I haven't seen him around," Joe said. "I think he's in the army. But where have you been all this while?" he asked her, knowing she would lie, anxious to see how badly. "I haven't seen you for a long time."

Bobbie giggled. "Oh, I been away. I just got back to New York last week."

"You live in this house?" Lee said to her.

For the first time she took notice of the other occupants of the car.

"Yeah," she said, wary, but not unfriendly. Then to Joe: "Who are your friends?"

"Shall I introduce you?" Joe said. She nodded, laughing.

"Bobbie Bedner," Joe said. "This is Brock, the driver and part-owner of the car. This is Miller," and he gestured toward the back of the car, "consultant in pornography, and this is Zand, who is interested in people."

Bobbie laughed, taking her cue from his tone. "What are you doing out so late?" she said. "Just driving around?"

"Yeah," Lee said, anxious to make his presence felt. "How about you?"

"I went to a dance," Bobbie said. "At the Twenty-eighth Street Y."

"Did you have a nice time?" Lee said.

"Not so bad," Bobbie said, laughing.

There was a pause. Ben thought he might as well. She was standing there with her hand resting on the edge of the lowered window.

"Would you like to go for a ride?" he said.

Bobbie laughed uncertainly. "I don't know," she said. "My mother expected me home early, and it's late already."

"So," Joe said, "if it's late already it won't hurt if you come in a little later. Come on," he said persuasively, "we'll go for a ride."

"Where are you going?" the girl asked.

"We don't know," Ben said drily. "That's what makes it so exciting. We might go almost anywhere. Maybe you can help find us a destination."

The girl stood there, her hand on the window. Joe opened the door suddenly and beckoned to her. "Come on," he said. "Any place you say. When you're ready to come back, we'll bring you back."

"It's a nice car," she said.

Joe laughed. He reached out his hand and pulled her one step closer to the car. Then he let go and moved closer to Brock, making room for her. Bobbie Bedner laughed and got into the car.

Ben backed the car to the corner and they went back on First Avenue. He rode to Fourteenth Street and stopped for a light.

"You're looking well," Joe said. "You're looking much better than when I saw you last."

"Yeah," Bobbie said. "I gained a lot of weight."

She had changed. She had gotten into the car, but it wasn't as easy as it once would have been. Joe decided to let DeTorres find out how matters stood with the girl. Although he could have done so his friends might interpret his efforts as illustrating a lack of sensibility. Or it might give them something to laugh about.

"Drive back to the club," Joe said. "We'll pick up Cripple."

"What club?" Bobbie asked alarmedly. "Who's Cripple?"

"Just a chess club," Joe said soothingly. "You remember Cripple. That's Frank, Frank DeTorres. You remember Frank, don't you?"

"What do you want to see him for?" Bobbie said.

"We don't want to see him," Joe said. "We just thought after all this time, he would be glad to see you. He won't hurt you."

Bobbie laughed. "I know he won't hurt me," she said. "I just thought we were going for a ride."

"We will," Ben said, knowing what was on Muneco's mind. "Just as soon as we pick up Frank."

He turned left on Seventeenth Street, pulled up in front of Gelber's Chess Club, and parked the car.

Frank was happy to have Muneco back and happier still when he saw who was with him. The presence of Bobbie Bedner, he felt sure, would liven up the evening. He thought immediately of his pigeon coop and its steam-heating. When Ben Brock came upstairs, after parking the car, he found Frank and Joe seated near the window, Frank talking earnestly to Bobbie, and Lee and Phil standing some distance away leaning against a chess table. He walked over to these two.

"Set'em up," he said to Lee. "You can have the white pieces."

"I'll have to beat you in five moves," Lee appologized. "Don Juan is operating, and I don't know how long we'll be here."

"If he's got to operate," Ben said, "you may be here a long time. If this girl is the girl she's cracked up to be she should be on her hands and knees begging for it."

Joe came over.

"How does it look?" Lee said.

"I don't know," Joe said. "Frank is trying to get her to go to his place but she doesn't like pigeon coops."

"Ask her about bar-bell clubs," Phil said. "I've got the key to the club. There won't be anyone up there this time of night."

"I'll keep you posted," Joe said. He walked back to Frank and the girl.

"Your move," Lee said.

Ben looked at him. "I can't understand your hanging around, Miller," he said to him, "in the hope of laying a broad who has already been on intimate terms with everyone in the neighborhood. Haven't you got any standards?"

"Very funny," Lee said. "In this respect I'm like you. When it comes to women, anywhere and anytime."

"Are you looking forward to this prospect?" Ben said to Phil.

"Why not?" Phil said.

"Hell," Ben said, "you've had it so long you might as well save it for your wife. Listen to me," he said earnestly, "and don't throw yourself away on this harlot. Somewhere, there's a sweet, young, innocent girl who has been ordained by heaven to. . . ."

"Balls to you," Phil said.

Muneco returned.

" 'The outlook wasn't brilliant for the Mudville nine that day,' " Joe began, with every intention of completing the poem.

"Can it," Ben said. "What's the latest?"

"She met a psychiatrist in reform school, " Joe said. "He told her the reason she did what she did was her father died when she was six years old and she missed male attention. She agrees with his diagnosis and she's turning over a new leaf."

"You mean all the psychiatrist did was tell her?" Phil asked professionally.

"I don't know," Joe said. "She's been away for two years. Maybe she underwent intensive therapy. Whatever happened, she's metamorphosized."

"So?" Lee said.

"We're going to take her downstairs, try to soften her up," Joe said. "Give me the keys to the car," he said to Ben.

"You going somewhere?" Lee said suspiciously.

"Hey," Muneco laughed, taking the keys from Ben. "You think we'd run out on you, Miller? We can't leave you. This whole party is in Phil's honor. After Phil lays her we're going to nail her over his fireplace for a trophy." He jingled the keys at DeTorres and walked to the door. Frank got up, took the girl by the hand, and followed Muneco. She went without protesting but she did not look happy.

"Does Cripple have a driver's license?" Lee said.

Ben nodded.

"If those guys pull anything," Lee said, "I'm going to make Muneco pay for it."

"You wouldn't tell his mother, would you?" Ben said.

"No," Lee said. "I'll tell his girl. I'll call his girl and let her know how Muneco spends his Saturday nights." He looked toward the window. Phil, following his glance, walked over and looked out.

"The car's still there," Phil said. "Save your money."

"Your move," Ben said.

Lee moved.

"How long we going to wait here?" he said.

"Give them five more minutes," Ben said.

Phil walked over and looked out the window.

"Hey Zand," Ben called to him.

"What?"

"You're basing your life on a lie," Ben said. "You want to become a clinical psychologist. You want to help the malajusted. Now here is this girl who has been abnormal, at least quantitively, but has since been returned to normalcy by a practicing psychiatrist. Instead of trying to keep her there you're party to a scheme whose aim is to tear down her defenses and re-sink her in the morass of abnormality."

He looked sternly at Phil; then disgustedly shook his head.

"Look," Phil said. "Better her than me. She's neurotic from too much of it and I'm neurotic from too little. It's her or me. And I've got my career at stake."

"He thinks it's the panacea," Lee sneered. "Once he gets laid, he's solved all his problems. What an idiot."

"Okay," Ben said. "I resign. Let's go downstairs."

They got up and put on their coats. "Hey, Kurtz," Ben called to the old man who had been sitting on a bench watching them. "A lineup. Anybody else, we're charging two-fifty. For you, a buck and a half. How about it?"

The old man coughed up some phlegm and spit it into a handkerchief. He was unimpressed. "If I couldn't do better," he said, standing and stretching himself, "I'd shoot myself."

The three left the club.

Ben looked in at the back window of the car. Joe and Frank were in the front seat with the girl between them. Frank had his arm around the girl and was bending over her. Ben motioned the others to wait. After a while the girl worked an arm free from behind her and pushed Frank's face away. Ben walked to the side of the car and knocked on the window. Muneco opened the door.

"Come on in," he said. "We'll go for a ride."

Lee and Phil got into the back of the car. Ben squeezed into the driver's seat. There were four people in the front of the car. Joe moved over, making room for Ben, at the same time pushing Bobbie closer to Frank. Frank was talking into her ear.

"What's the matter baby? Don't you want to kiss me? Just a little kiss?"

"No-o," the girl said, indicating that she had said it many times before. Frank leaned over her and kissed her. After a great many seconds had passed she pushed his face away.

"I don't know what's happened to the way you kiss," Frank said to her. "It's not like you used to. Who ever heard of a girl kissing with her mouth closed?"

"I don't want to kiss you." Bobbie said primly.

"Two years ago," Frank said, "I wouldn't kiss you. I would screw you. That's more fun, isn't it? What's happened to you in two years?"

"I told you," Bobbie said laughing. Her laugh was heavy, like her voice, and unsteady, but it was not the way she used to laugh. "I don't do that anymore."

"For nobody?"

Bobbie laughed. "I don't know," she said. "But not for you."

"I'm truly sorry to hear that," Frank said. "I guess I'll go home and go to bed. Drive me home, Brock," he said. He leaned over the girl.

Ben made a right turn on Third Avenue and drove to Twentieth Street. He stopped once for a light. On Twentieth a sanitation truck was double parked and he slowed down to squeeze past it. During all this time, Frank, using all his art, was kissing the girl.

"You're home," Ben said.

"Yeah," Frank said. "We're home. Come on," he said to the girl. "We'll go upstairs to the pigeon coop and have a party."

"No," Bobbie said. "I don't like pigeon coops."

"Do you like parties?" Joe said.

"Not that kind," she said, laughing slyly.

"Look," Frank said. "Look what I got for you." He took her hand and pulled it to him, but she wrenched it free.

"I don't want it," she said, annoyed. "Leave me alone."

Ben became slightly annoyed by the proceedings. Not by the proceedings as much as by their lack of success.

"All right Frank, you drew a blank," he said. "We forgive you. If you can't convince this girl, she cannot be convinced. Go to bed." He looked at Bobbie. "I'll drive you home."

"Okay," Frank said. "But I don't know what's happened to this girl. She goes away for a short time and comes back with a whole new system of values. It's something for you college men to figure out."

He got out of the car.

"Don't give up the ship," he said. "A little patience. If this girl is Bobbie Bedner you should lay her before daybreak. I'm going to get some sleep."

The girl laughed as Frank turned his back and walked away. "Don't believe him," she said confidentially. "I don't do any of those things. He's just talking." She directed this primarily at Brock in whom she had mistaken the annoyance with DeTorres' methods for sympathy. Joe smiled. Ben started the car.

"Who's going home first?" he said.

"Home?" The girl was indignant. "I thought we were going for a ride."

"You still want to go for a ride?" Ben said.

"Sure. Let's go to Coney Island."

"No," Joe said to her. "Let's go lift some weights. Phil has the key to his bar-bell club."

The girl laughed. "Ah, die young," she said pleasantly. She recognized that the only serious threat had been Frank, and he was gone. She relaxed now, and looked forward to a good time being chauffeured around.

"You can drive me home," Phil said, seeing the futility of remaining. "I've got to wake up early tomorrow."

"How about you, Miller?" Ben said.

"No hurry," Lee said. "As a matter of fact you can take me home after you drop her off."

The girl laughed. "You ain't gonna miss nothin'," she said.

Joe laughed. "You're a dead pigeon, Miller," he said. "Even this dumb broad reads you like a book. You're shallower than a wading pool."

"That's extremely funny, Muneco," Lee said.

"I'm not a dumb broad," Bobbie said good-naturedly.

"Then what are you a dumb?" Joe said.

"Oh, die young," the girl said.

"Where would you like to go besides Coney Island?" Ben said.

"What's the matter with Coney Island?"

"There is nothing open and nobody in Coney Island in January," Ben explained patiently. "So I suggest you suggest something else."

"Let's go where there's excitement," Bobbie said. "Maybe we can see a fight somewhere."

"We have just the thing for you," Joe said. "Take her to Brooklyn," he said to Ben.

"That's right," Ben said. "Brooklyn's a wild town."

"What's so wild about Brooklyn?" the girl said.

"Everything goes positively smash in Brooklyn," Ben said. "There's a fight on every street corner. Trunk murders take place in front of your eyes. Also, there's a little cafeteria right across the bridge where we sometimes sober up after a devil-may-carish Saturday night."

"What's *his* name?" Bobbie said to Joe.

"That's Brock," Joe said. "Author and professional chauffeur. Why, do you like him?"

Bobbie laughed. "He's all right," she said.

"Brock has made a conquest," Lee called from the back of the car.

"I guess you're not interested," Joe said. "Maybe we should drive you home."

"Maybe you should," Lee said. "As a matter of fact, I'm sure you should. I've got a date tomorrow night with this girl I just met. I can use some sleep."

"You poor kid, I'll bet she knocks all hell out of you," Ben said.

Ben turned left, a block before the bridge which led to Brooklyn, and brought the car back to First Avenue. He left Paul on the corner of Third Street, and drove Lee to his home on Sixth Street between First and Second Avenues. He was tired, and got to thinking of the difficulty he would have in finding a parking space.

"Who's next?" he said.

He looked at Bobbie, who was about to protest.

"My old man gets up early in the morning," he lied. "He needs the car to get to work. I've got to bring it back before six o'clock."

"Gee," the girl said. "Your father works on Sundays?"

"Yeah," Ben said. "He's a preacher."

"Gee, that's tough," the girl said.

"Take me home first," Joe said, winking at Ben. "She said she likes you. Don't you like him, Bobbie?"

"Yeah, I like him," Bobbie said. "But I just wanted to drive around."

"You first," Ben said to her. He drove her home. She got out of the car and turned toward them.

"Well, so long," she said. She laughed suddenly, "I had a very nice time."

"Glad to hear it," Joe said. "We must get together sometime and do the whole thing over again."

Ben leaned over and waved to her. "So long Bobbie," he said.

"Bye-bye Brock," she said. "It was nice meeting you." She walked up the stoop and was gone, into the building.

They sat there for a while, not talking.

"A hundred per cent American girl," Ben said finally. "I'm convinced you had her pegged wrong."

"A hundred and sixty times," Joe said absently, "in three days. That must have been one hell of a psychiatrist."

"He wasn't an East Side boy," Ben said, shaking his head. "He performed a great disservice to an entire neighborhood. He dissolved the last trace of communal endeavor to which we could proudly point."

"Yeah," Joe said, leaning back on the seat, his hands locked behind his head. "Drive around to Seventeenth Street. What we've got to do now is get some coffee."

# SORROW-ACRE

Isak Dinesen

The low, undulating Danish landscape was silent and serene, mysteriously wide-awake in the hour before sunrise. There was not a cloud in the pale sky, not a shadow along the dim, pearly fields, hills and woods. The mist was lifting from the valleys and hollows, the air was cool, the grass and the foliage dripping wet with morning-dew. Unwatched by the eyes of man, and undisturbed by his activity, the country breathed a timeless life, to which language was inadequate.

All the same, a human race had lived on this land for a thousand years, had been formed by its soil and weather, and had marked it with its thoughts, so that now no one could tell where the existence of the one ceased and the other began. The thin grey line of a road, winding across the plain and up and down hills, was the fixed materialisation of human longing, and of the human notion that it is better to be in one place than another.

A child of the country would read this open landscape like a book. The irregular mosaic of meadows and cornlands was a picture, in timid green and yellow, of the people's struggle for its daily bread; the centuries had taught it to plough and sow in this way. On a distant hill the immovable wings of a windmill, in a small blue cross against the sky, delineated a later stage in the career of bread. The blurred outline of thatched roofs—a low, brown growth of the earth—where the huts of the village thronged together, told the history, from his cradle to his grave, of the peasant, the creature nearest to the soil and dependent on it, prospering in a fertile year and dying in years of drought and pests.

A little higher up, with the faint horizontal line of the white cemetery-wall round it, and the vertical contour of tall poplars by its side, the red-tiled church bore witness, as far as the eye reached, that this was a Christian country. The child of the land knew it as a strange house, inhabited only for a few hours every seventh day, but with a strong, clear voice in it to give out the joys and sorrows of the land: a plain, square embodiment of the nation's trust in the justice and mercy of heaven. But where, amongst cupular woods and groves, the lordly, pyramidal silhouette of the cut lime avenues rose in the air, there a big country house lay.

The child of the land would read much within these elegant, geometrical ciphers on the hazy blue. They spoke of power, the lime trees paraded round a stronghold. Up here was decided the destiny of the surrounding land and of the men and beasts upon it, and the peasant lifted his eyes to the green pyramids with awe. They spoke of dignity, decorum and taste. Danish soil grew no finer flower than the mansion to which the long avenue led. In its lofty rooms life and death bore themselves with stately grace. The country house did not gaze upward, like the church, nor down to the ground like the huts; it had a wider earthly horizon than they, and was related to much noble architecture all over Europe. Foreign artisans had been called in to panel and stucco it, and its own inhabitants travelled and brought back ideas, fashions and things of beauty. Paintings, tapestries, silver and glass from distant countries had been made to feel at home here and now formed part of Danish country life.

The big house stood as firmly rooted in the soil of Denmark as the peasants' huts, and was as faithfully allied to her four winds and her changing seasons, to her animal life, trees and flowers. Only its interests lay in a higher plane. Within the domain of the lime trees it was no longer cows, goats and pigs on which the minds and the talk ran, but horses and dogs. The wild fauna, the game of the land, that the peasant shook his fist at, when he saw it on his young green rye or in his ripening wheat field, to the residents of the country houses were the main pursuit and the joy of existence.

The writing in the sky solemnly proclaimed continuance, a worldly immortality. The great country houses had held their ground through many generations. The families who lived in them revered the past as they honoured themselves, for the history of Denmark was their own history.

A Rosenkrantz had sat at Rosenholm, a Juel at Hverringe, a Skeel at Gammel-Estrup as long as people remembered. They had seen kings and schools of style succeed one another and, proudly and humbly, had made over their personal existence to that of their land, so that amongst their equals and with the peasants they passed by its name: Rosenholm, Hverringe, Gammel-Estrup. To the King and the country, to his family and to the individual lord of the manor himself it was a matter of minor consequence which particular Rosenkrantz, Juel or Skeel, out of a long row of fathers and sons, at the moment in his person incarnated the fields and woods, the peasants, cattle and game of the estate. Many duties rested on the shoulders of the big landowners—towards God in heaven, towards the King, his neighbour and himself—and they were all harmoniously consolidated into the idea of his duties towards his land. Highest amongst these ranked his obligation to uphold the sacred continuance, and to produce a new Rosenkrantz, Juel or Skeel for the service of Rosenholm, Hverringe and Gammel-Estrup.

Female grace was prized in the manors. Together with good hunting and fine wine it was the flower and emblem of the higher existence led there, and in many ways the families prided themselves more on their daughters than on their sons.

The ladies who promenaded in the lime avenues, or drove through them in heavy coaches with four horses, carried the future of the name in their laps and were, like dignified and debonair caryatides, holding up the houses. They were themselves conscious of their value, kept up their price, and moved in a sphere of pretty worship and self-worship. They might even be thought to add to it, on their own, a graceful, arch, paradoxical haughtiness. For how free were they, how powerful! Their lords might rule the country, and allow themselves many liberties, but when it came to that supreme matter of legitimacy which was the vital principle of their world, the centre of gravity lay with them.

The lime trees were in bloom. But in the early morning only a faint fragrance drifted through the garden, an airy message, an aromatic echo of the dreams during the short summer night.

In a long avenue that led from the house all the way to the end of the garden, where, from a small white pavilion in the classic style, there was a great view over the fields, a young man walked. He was plainly dressed in brown, with pretty linen and lace, bare-headed, with his hair tied by a ribbon. He was dark, a strong and sturdy figure with fine eyes and hands; he limped a little on one leg.

The big house at the top of the avenue, the garden and the fields had been his childhood's paradise. But he had travelled and lived out of Denmark, in Rome and Paris, and he was at present appointed to the Danish Legation to the Court of King George, the brother of the late, unfortunate young Danish Queen. He had not seen his ancestral home for nine years. It made him laugh to find, now, everything so much smaller than he remembered it, and at the same time he was strangely moved by meeting it again. Dead people came towards him and smiled at him; a small boy in a ruff ran past him with his hoop and kite, in passing gave him a clear glance and laughingly asked: "Do you mean to tell me that you are I?" He tried to catch him in the flight, and to answer him: "Yes, I assure you that I am you," but the light figure did not wait for reply.

The young man, whose name was Adam, stood in a particular relation to the house and the land. For six months he had been heir to it all; nominally he was so even at this moment. It was this circumstance which had brought him from England, and on which his mind was dwelling, as he walked along slowly.

The old lord up at the manor, his father's brother, had had much misfortune in his domestic life. His wife had died young, and two of his children in infancy. The one son then left to him, his cousin's playmate, was a sickly and morose boy. For ten years the father travelled with him from one watering place to another, in Germany and Italy, hardly ever in other company than that of his silent, dying child, sheltering the faint flame of life with both hands, until such time as it could be passed over to a new bearer of the name. At the same time another misfortune had struck him: he fell into disfavour at Court, where till now he had held a fine position. He was about to rehabilitate his family's prestige through the marriage which he had arranged for his son, when before it could take place the bridegroom died, not yet twenty years old.

Adam learned of his cousin's death, and his own changed fortune, in England, through his ambitious and triumphant mother. He sat with her letter in his hand and did not know what to think about it.

If this, he reflected, had happened to him while he was still a boy, in Denmark, it would have meant all the world to him. It would be so now with his friends and schoolfellows, if they were in his place, and they would, at this moment, be congratulating or envying him. But he was neither covetous nor vain by nature; he had faith in his own talents and had been content to know that his success in life depended on his personal ability. His slight infirmity had always set him a little apart from other boys; it had, perhaps, given him a keener sensibility of many things in life, and he did not, now, deem it quite right that the head of the family should limp on one leg. He did not even see his prospects in the same light as his people at home. In England he had met with greater wealth and magnificence than they dreamed of; he had been in love with, and made happy by, an English lady of such rank and fortune that to her, he felt, the finest estate of Denmark would look but like a child's toy farm.

And in England, too, he had come in touch with the great new ideas of the age: of nature, of the right and freedom of man, of justice and beauty. The universe, through them, had become infinitely wider to him; he wanted to find out still more about it and was planning to travel to America, to the new world. For a moment he felt trapped and imprisoned, as if the dead people of his name, from the family vault at home, were stretching out their parched arms for him.

But at the same time he began to dream at night of the old house and garden. He had walked in these avenues in dream, and had smelled the scent of the flowering limes. When at Ranelagh an old gypsy woman looked at his hand and told him that a son of his was to sit in the seat of his fathers, he felt a sudden, deep satisfaction, queer in a young man who till now had never given his sons a thought.

Then, six months later, his mother again wrote to tell him that his uncle had himself married the girl intended for his dead son. The head of the family was still in his best age, not over sixty, and although Adam remembered him as a small, slight man, he was a vigorous person; it was likely that his young wife would bear him sons.

Adam's mother in her disappointment lay the blame on him. If he had returned to Denmark, she told him, his uncle might have come to look upon him as a son, and would not have married; nay, he might have handed the bride over to him. Adam knew better. The family estate, differing from the neighboring properties, had gone down from father to son ever since a man of their name first sat there. The tradition of direct succession was the pride of the clan and a sacred dogma to his uncle; he would surely call for a son of his own flesh and bone.

But at the news the young man was seized by a strange, deep, aching remorse towards his old home in Denmark. It was as if he had been making light of a friendly and generous gesture, and disloyal to someone unfailingly loyal to him. It would be but just, he thought, if from now the place should disown and forget him. Nostalgia, which before he had never known, caught hold of him; for the first time he walked in the streets and parks of London as a stranger.

He wrote to his uncle and asked if he might come and stay with him, begged leave from the Legation and took ship for Denmark. He had come to the house to make his peace with it; he had slept little in the night, and was up so early and walking in the garden, to explain himself, and to be forgiven.

While he walked, the still garden slowly took up its day's work. A big snail, of the kind that his grandfather had brought back from France, and which he remembered eating in the house as a child, was already, with dignity, dragging a silver train down the avenue. The birds began to sing; in an old tree under which he stopped a number of them were worrying an owl; the rule of the night was over.

He stood at the end of the avenue and saw the sky lightening. An ecstatic clarity filled the world; in half an hour the sun would rise. A rye field here ran along the garden, two roe-deer were moving in it and looked roseate in the dawn. He gazed out over the fields, where as a small boy he had ridden his pony, and towards the wood where he had killed his first stag. He remembered the old servants who had taught him; some of them were now in their graves.

The ties which bound him to this place, he reflected, were of a mystic nature. He might never again come back to it, and it would make no difference. As long as a man of his own blood and name should sit in the house, hunt in the fields and be obeyed by the people in the huts, wherever he travelled on earth, in England or amongst the red Indians of America, he himself would still be safe, would still have a home, and would carry weight in the world.

His eyes rested on the church. In old days, before the time of Martin Luther, younger sons of great families, he knew, had entered the Church of Rome, and had given up individual wealth and happiness to serve the greater ideals. They, too, had bestowed honour upon their homes and were remembered in its registers. In the solitude of the morning, half in jest he let his mind run as it listed; it seemed to him that he might speak to the land as to a person, as to the mother of his race. "Is it only my body that you want," he asked her, "while you reject my imagination, energy and emotions? If the world might be brought to acknowledge that the virtue of our name does not belong to the past only, will it give you no satisfaction?" The landscape was so still that he could not tell whether it answered him yes or no.

After a while he walked on, and came to the new French rose garden laid out for the young mistress of the house. In England he had acquired a freer taste in gardening, and he wondered if he could liberate these blushing captives, and make them thrive outside their cut hedges. Perhaps, he meditated, the elegantly conventional garden would be a floral portrait of his young aunt from Court, whom he had not yet seen.

As once more he came to the pavilion at the end of the avenue his eyes were caught by a bouquet of delicate colours which could not possibly belong to the Danish summer morning. It was in fact his uncle himself, powdered and silk-stockinged, but still in a brocade dressing-gown, and obviously sunk in deep thought. "And what business, or what meditations," Adam asked himself, "drags a connoisseur of the beautiful, but three months married to a wife of seventeen, from his bed into his garden before sunrise?" He walked up to the small, slim, straight figure.

His uncle on his side showed no surprise at seeing him, but then he rarely seemed surprised at anything. He greeted him, with a compliment on his matutinality, as kindly as he had done on his arrival last evening. After a moment he looked to the sky, and solemnly proclaimed: "It will be a hot day." Adam, as a child, had often been impressed by the grand, ceremonial manner in which the old lord would state the common happenings of existence; it looked as if nothing had changed here, but all was what it used to be.

The uncle offered the nephew a pinch of snuff. "No, thank you, Uncle," said Adam, "it would ruin my nose to the scent of your garden, which is as fresh as the Garden of Eden, newly created." "From every tree of which," said his uncle, smiling, "thou, my Adam, mayest freely eat." They slowly walked up the avenue together.

The hidden sun was now already gilding the top of the tallest trees. Adam talked of the beauties of nature, and of the greatness of Nordic scenery, less marked by the hand of man than that of Italy. His uncle took the praise of the landscape as a personal compliment, and congratulated him because he had not, in likeness to many young travellers in foreign countries, learned to despise his native land. No, said Adam, he had lately in England longed for the fields and woods of his Danish home. And he had there become acquainted with a new piece of Danish poetry which had enchanted him more than any English or French work. He named the author, Johannes Ewald, and quoted a few of the mighty, turbulent verses.

"And I have wondered, while I read," he went on after a pause, still moved by the lines he himself had declaimed, "that we have not till now understood how much our Nordic mythology in moral greatness surpasses that of Greece and Rome. If it had not been for the physical beauty of the ancient gods, which has come down to us in marble, no modern mind could hold them worthy of worship. They were mean, capricious and treacherous. The gods of our Danish forefathers are as much more divine than they as the Druid is nobler than the Augur. For the fair gods of Asgaard did possess the sublime human virtues; they were righteous, trustworthy, benevolent and even, within a barbaric age, chivalrous." His uncle here for the first time appeared to take any real interest in the conversation. He stopped, his majestic nose a little in the air. "Ah, it was easier to them," he said.

"What do you mean, Uncle?" Adam asked. "It was a great deal easier," said his uncle, "to the northern gods than to those of Greece to be, as you will have it, righteous and benevolent. To my mind it even reveals a weakness in the souls of our ancient Danes that they should consent to adore such divinities." "My dear uncle," said Adam, smiling, "I have always felt that you would be familiar with the modes of Olympus. Now please let me share your insight, and tell me why virtue should come easier to our Danish gods than to those of milder climates." "They were not as powerful," said his uncle.

"And does power," Adam again asked, "stand in the way of virtue?" "Nay," said his uncle gravely. "Nay, power is in itself the supreme virtue. But the gods of which you speak were never all-powerful. They had, at all times, by their side those darker powers which they named the Jotuns, and who worked the suffering, the disasters, the ruin of our world. They might safely give themselves up to temperance and kindness. The omnipotent gods," he went on, "have no such facilitation. With their omnipotence they take over the woe of the universe."

They had walked up the avenue till they were in view of the house. The old lord stopped and ran his eyes over it. The stately building was the same as ever; behind the two tall front windows, Adam knew, was now his young aunt's room. His uncle turned and walked back.

"Chivalry," he said, "chivalry, of which you were speaking, is not a virtue of the omnipotent. It must needs imply mighty rival powers for the knight to defy. With a dragon inferior to him in strength, what figure will St. George cut? The knight who finds no superior forces ready to hand must invent them, and combat wind-mills; his knighthood itself stipulates dangers, vileness, darkness on all sides of him. Nay, believe me, my nephew, in spite of his moral worth, your chivalrous Odin of Asgaard as a Regent must take rank below that of Jove who avowed his sovereignty, and accepted the world which he ruled. But you are young," he added, "and the experience of the aged to you will sound pedantic."

He stood immovable for a moment and then with deep gravity proclaimed: "The sun is up."

The sun did indeed rise above the horizon. The wide landscape was suddenly animated by its splendour, and the dewy grass shone in a thousand gleams.

"I have listened to you, Uncle," said Adam, "with great interest. But while we have talked you yourself have seemed to me preoccupied; your eyes have rested on the field outside the garden, as if something of great moment, a matter of life and death, was going on there. Now that the sun is up, I see the mowers in the rye and hear them whetting their sickles. It is, I remember you telling me, the first day of the harvest. That is a great day to a landowner and enough to take his mind away from the gods. It is very fine weather, and I wish you a full barn."

The elder man stood still, his hands on his walking-stick. "There is indeed," he said at last, "something going on in that field, a matter of life and death. Come, let us sit down here, and I will tell you the whole story." They sat down on the seat that ran all along the pavilion, and while he spoke the old lord of the land did not take his eyes off the rye field.

"A week ago, on Thursday night," he said, "someone set fire to my barn at Rǿdmosegaard—you know the place, close to the moor—and burned it all down. For two or three days we could not lay hands on the offender. Then on Monday morning the keeper at Rǿdmose, with the wheelwright over there, came up to the house; they dragged with them a boy, Goske Piil, a widow's son, and they made their Bible oath that he had done it; they had themselves seen him sneaking round the barn by night-fall on Thursday. Goske had no good name on the farm; the keeper bore him a grudge upon an old matter of poaching, and the wheelwright did not like him either, for he did, I believe, suspect him with his young wife. The boy, when I talked to him, swore to his innocence, but could not hold his own against two old men. So I had him locked up, and meant to send him in to our judge of the district, with a letter.

"The judge is a fool, and would naturally do nothing but what he thought I wished him to do. He might have the boy sent to the convict prison for arson, or put amongst the soldiers as a bad character and a poacher. Or again, if he thought that that was what I wanted, he could let him off.

"I was out riding in the fields, looking at the corn that was soon ripe to be mowed, when a woman, the widow, Goske's mother, was brought up before me, and begged to speak to me. Anne-Marie is her name. You will remember her; she lives in the small house east of the village. She has not got a good name in the place either. They tell as a girl she had a child and did away with it.

"From five days' weeping her voice was so cracked that it was difficult for me to understand what she said. Her son, she told me at last, had indeed been over at Rødmose on Thursday, but for no ill purpose; he had gone to see someone. He was her only son, she called the Lord God to witness on his innocence, and she wrung her hands to me that I should save the boy for her.

"We were in the rye field that you and I are looking at now. That gave me an idea. I said to the widow: 'If in one day, between sunrise and sunset, with your own hands you can mow this field, and it be well done, I will let the case drop and you shall keep your son. But if you cannot do it, he must go, and it is not likely that you will then ever see him again.'

"She stood up then and gazed over the field. She kissed my riding boot in gratitude for the favour shown to her."

The old lord here made a pause, and Adam said: "Her son meant much to her?" "He is her only child," said the uncle. "He means to her her daily bread and support in old age. It may be said that she holds him as dear as her own life. As," he added, "within a higher order of life, a son to his father means the name and the race, and he holds him as dear as life everlasting. Yes, her son means much to her. For the mowing of that field is a day's work to three men, or three day's work to one man. Today, as the sun rose, she set to her task. And down there, by the end of the field, you will see her now, in a blue head-cloth, with the man I have set to follow her and to ascertain that she does the work unassisted, and with two or three friends by her, who are comforting her."

Adam looked down, and did indeed see a woman in a blue head-cloth, and a few other figures in the corn.

They sat for a while in silence. "Do you yourself," Adam then said, "believe the boy to be innocent?" "I cannot tell," said his uncle. "There is no proof. The word of the keeper and the wheelwright stand against the boy's word. If indeed I did believe the one thing or the other, it would be merely a matter of chance, or maybe of sympathy. The boy," he said after a moment, "was my son's playmate, the only other child that I ever knew him to like or to get on with." "Do you," Adam again asked, "hold it possible to her to fulfill your condition?" "Nay, I cannot tell," said the old lord. "To an ordinary person it would not be possible. No ordinary person would ever have taken it on at all. I chose it so. We are not quibbling with the law, Anne-Marie and I."

Adam for a few minutes followed the movement of the small group in the rye. "Will you walk back?" he asked. "No," said his uncle, "I think that I shall stay here till I have seen the end of the thing." "Until sunset?" Adam asked with surprise. "Yes," said the old lord. Adam said: "It will be a long day." "Yes," said his uncle, "a long day. But," he added, as Adam rose to walk away, "if, as you said, you have got that tragedy of which you spoke in your pocket, be so kind as to leave it here, to keep me company." Adam handed him the book.

In the avenue he met two footmen who carried the old lord's morning chocolate down to the pavilion on large silver trays.

As now the sun rose in the sky, and the day grew hot, the lime trees gave forth their exuberance of scent, and the garden was filled with unsurpassed, unbelievable sweetness. Towards the still hour of midday the long avenue reverberated like a soundboard with a low, incessant murmur: the humming of a million bees that clung to the pendulous, thronging clusters of blossoms and were drunk with bliss.

In all the short lifetime of Danish summer there is no richer or more luscious moment than that week wherein the lime trees flower. The heavenly scent goes to the head and to the heart; it seems to unite the fields of Denmark with those of Elysium; it contains both hay, honey and holy incense, and is half fairy-land and half apothecary's locker. The avenue was changed into a mystic edifice, a dryad's cathedral, outward from summit to base lavishly adorned, set with multitudinous ornaments, and golden in the sun. But behind the walls the vaults were benignly cool and sombre, like ambrosial sanctuaries in a dazzling and burning world, and in here the ground was still moist.

Up in the house, behind the silk curtains of the two front windows, the young mistress of the estate from the wide bed stuck her feet into two little high-heeled slippers. Her lace-trimmed nightgown had slid up above her knees and down from the shoulder; her hair, done up in curling-pins for the night, was still frosty with the powder of yesterday, her round face flushed with sleep. She stepped out to the middle of the floor and stood there, looking extremely grave and thoughtful, yet she did not think at all. But through her head a long procession of pictures marched, and she was unconsciously endeavouring to put them in order, as the pictures of her existence had used to be.

She had grown up at Court; it was her world, and there was probably not in the whole country a small creature more exquisitely and innocently drilled to the stately measure of a palace. By favor of the old Dowager Queen she bore her name and that of the King's sister, the Queen of Sweden: Sophie Magdalena. It was with a view to these things that her husband, when he wished to restore his status in high places, had chosen her as a bride, first for his son and then for himself. But her own father, who held an office in the Royal Household and belonged to the new Court aristocracy, in his day had done the same thing the other way round, and had married a country lady, to get a foothold within the old nobility of Denmark. The little girl had her mother's blood in her veins. The country to her had been an immense surprise and delight.

To get into her castle-court she must drive through the farm yard, through the heavy stone gateway in the barn itself, wherein the rolling of her coach for a few seconds re-echoed like thunder. She must drive past the stables and the timber-mare, from which sometimes a miscreant would follow her with sad eyes, and might here startle a long string of squalling geese, or pass the heavy, scowling bull, led on by a ring in his nose and kneading the earth in dumb fury. At first this had been to her, every time, a slight shock and a jest. But after a while all these creatures and things, which belonged to her, seemed to become part of herself. Her mothers, the old Danish country ladies, were robust persons, undismayed by any kind of weather; now she herself had walked in the rain and had laughed and glowed in it like a green tree.

She had taken her great new home in possession at a time when all the world was unfolding, mating and propagating. Flowers, which she had known only in bouquets and festoons, sprung from the earth round her; birds sang in all the trees. The new-born lambs seemed to her daintier than her dolls had been. From her husband's Hanoverian stud, foals were brought to her to give names; she stood and watched as they poked their soft noses into their mothers' bellies to drink. Of this strange process she had till now only vaguely heard. She happened to witness, from a path in the park, the rearing and screeching stallion on the mare. All this luxuriance, lust and fecundity was displayed before her eyes, as for her pleasure.

And for her own part, in the midst of it, she was given an old husband who treated her with punctilious respect because she was to bear him a son. Such was the compact; she had known of it from the beginning. Her husband, she found, was doing his best to fulfill his part of it, and she herself was loyal by nature and strictly brought up. She would not shirk her obligation. Only she was vaguely aware of a discord or an incompatibility within her majestic existence, which prevented her from being as happy as she had expected to be.

After a time her chagrin took a strange form: as the consciousness of an absence. Someone ought to have been with her who was not. She had no experience in analysing her feelings; there had not been time for that at Court. Now, as she was more often left to herself, she vaguely probed her own mind, She tried to set her father in that void place, her sisters, her music master, an Italian singer whom she had admired; but none of them would fill it for her. At times she felt lighter at heart, and believed the misfortune to have left her. And then again it would happen, if she were alone, or in her husband's company, and even within his embrace, that everything round her would cry out: Where? Where? so that she let her wild eyes run about the room in search for the being who should have been there, and who had not come.

When, six months ago, she was informed that her first young bridegroom had died and she was to marry his father in his place, she had not been sorry. Her youthful suitor, the one time she had seen him, had appeared to her infantile and insipid; the father would make a statelier consort. Now she sometimes thought of the dead boy and wondered whether with him life would have been more joyful. But she soon again dismissed the picture, and that was the sad youth's last recall to the stage of this world.

Upon one wall of her room there hung a long mirror. As she gazed into it new images came along. The day before, driving with her husband, she had seen, at a distance, a party of village girls bathe in the river, and the sun shining on them. All her life she moved amongst naked marble deities, but it had till now never occurred to her that the people she knew should themselves be naked under bodices and trains, waistcoats and satin breeches, that indeed she herself felt naked within her clothes. Now, in front of the looking glass, she tardily untied the ribbons of her nightgown, and let it drop to the floor.

The room was dim behind the drawn curtains. In the mirror her body was silvery like a white rose; only her cheeks and mouth, and the tips of her fingers and breasts had a faint carmine. Her slender torso was formed by the whalebones that had clasped it tightly from her childhood; above the slim, dimpled knee a gentle narrowness marked the place of the garter. Her limbs were rounded as if, at whatever place they might be cut through with a sharp knife, a perfectly circular transverse incision would be obtained. The side and belly were so smooth that her own gaze slipped and glided, and grasped for a hold. She was not altogether like a statue, she found, and lifted her arms above her head. She turned to get a view of her back, the curves below the waistline were still blushing from the pressure of the bed. She called to mind a few tales about nymphs and goddesses, but they all seemed a long way off, so her mind returned to the peasant girls in the river. They were, for a few minutes, idealized into playmates, or sisters even, since they belonged to her as did the meadow and the blue river itself. And within the next moment the sense of forlornness once more came upon her, a *horror vaccui* like a physical pain. Surely, surely someone should have been with her now, her other self, like the image in the glass, but nearer, stronger, alive. There was no one, the universe was empty round her.

A sudden, keen itching under her knee took her out of her reveries, and awoke in her the hunting instincts of her breed. She wetted a finger on her tongue, slowly brought it down and quickly slapped it to the spot. She felt the diminutive, sharp body of the insect against the silky skin, pressed the thumb to it, and triumphantly lifted up the small prisoner between her fingertips. She stood quite still, as if meditating upon the fact that a flea was the only creature risking its life for her smoothness and sweet blood.

Her maid opened the door and came in, loaded with the attire of the day—shift, stays, hoop and petticoats. She remembered that she had a guest in the house, the new nephew arrived from England. Her husband had instructed her to be kind to their young kinsman, disinherited, so to say, by her presence in the house. They would ride out on the land together.

In the afternoon the sky was no longer blue as in the morning. Large clouds slowly towered up on it, and the great vault itself was colourless, as if diffused into vapours round the white-hot sun in zenith. A low thunder ran along the western horizon; once or twice the dust of the roads rose in tall spirals. But the fields, the hills and the woods were as still as a painted landscape.

Adam walked down the avenue to the pavilion, and found his uncle there, fully dressed, his hands upon his walking-stick and his eyes on the rye field. The book that Adam had given him lay by his side. The field now seemed alive with people. Small groups stood here and there in it, and a long row of men and women were slowly advancing towards the garden in the line of the swath.

The old lord nodded to his nephew, but did not speak or change his position. Adam stood by him as still as himself.

The day to him had been strangely disquieting. At the meeting again with old places the sweet melodies of the past had filled his senses and his mind, and had mingled with new, bewitching tunes of the present. He was back in Denmark, no longer a child but a youth, with a keener sense of the beautiful, with tales of other countries to tell, and still a true son of his own land and enchanted by its loveliness as he had never been before.

But through all these harmonies the tragic and cruel tale which the old lord had told him in the morning, and the sad contest which he knew to be going on so near by, in the corn field, had re-echoed, like the recurrent, hollow throbbing of a muffled drum, a redoubtable sound. It came back time after time, so that he had felt himself to change colour and to answer absently. It brought with it a deeper sense of pity with all that lived than he had ever known. When he had been riding with his young aunt, and their road ran along the scene of the drama, he had taken care to ride between her and the field, so that she should not see what was going on there, or question him about it. He had chosen the way home through the deep, green wood for the same reason.

More dominantly even than the figure of the woman struggling with her sickle for her son's life, the old man's figure, as he had seen it at sunrise, kept him company through the day. He came to ponder on the part which that lonely, determinate form had played in his own life. From the time when his father died, it had impersonated to the boy law and order, wisdom of life and kind guardianship. What was he to do, he thought, if after eighteen years these filial feelings must change, and his second father's figure take on to him a horrible aspect, as a symbol of the tyranny and oppression of the world? What was he to do if ever the two should come to stand in opposition to each other as adversaries?

At the same time an unaccountable, a sinister alarm and dread on behalf of the old man himself took hold of him. For surely here the Goddess Nemesis could not be far away. This man had ruled the world round him for a longer period than Adam's own lifetime and had never been gainsaid by anyone. During the years when he had wandered through Europe with a sick boy of his own blood as his sole companion he had learned to set himself apart from his surroundings, and to close himself up to all outer life, and he had become insusceptible to the ideas and feelings of other human beings. Strange fancies might there have run in his mind, so that in the end he had seen himself as the only person really existing, and the world as a poor and vain shadow-play, which had no substance to it.

Now, in senile wilfullness, he would take in his hand the life of those simpler and weaker than himself, of a woman, using it to his own ends, and he feared of no retributive justice. Did he not know, the young man thought, that there were powers in the world, different from and more formidable than the short-lived might of a despot?

With the sultry heat of the day this foreboding of impending disaster grew upon him, until he felt ruin threatening not the old lord only, but the house, the name and himself with him. It seemed to him that he must cry out a warning to the man he had loved, before it was too late.

But as now he was once more in his uncle's company, the green calm of the garden was so deep that he did not find his voice to cry out. Instead a little French air which his aunt had sung to him up in the house kept running in his mind—*"C'est un trop doux effort . . ."* He had good knowledge of music; he had heard the air before, in Paris, but not so sweetly sung.

After a time he asked: "Will the woman fulfill her bargain?" His uncle unfolded his hands. "It is an extraordinary thing," he said animatedly, "that it looks as if she might fulfill it. If you count the hours from sunrise till now, and from now till sunset, you will find the time left her to be half of that already gone. And see! She has now mowed two-thirds of the field. But then we will naturally have to reckon with her strength declining as she works on. All in all, it is an idle pursuit in you or me to bet on the issue of the matter; we must wait and see. Sit down, and keep me company in my watch." In two minds Adam sat down.

"And here," said his uncle, and took up the book from the seat, "is your book, which has passed the time finely. It is great poetry, ambrosia to the ear and the heart. And it has, with our discourse on divinity this morning, given me stuff for thought. I have been reflecting upon the law of retributive justice." He took a pinch of snuff, and went on. "A new age," he said, "has made to itself a god in its own image, an emotional god. And now you are already writing a tragedy on your god."

Adam had no wish to begin a debate on poetry with his uncle, but he also somehow dreaded a silence, and said: "It may be, then, that we hold tragedy to be, in the scheme of life, a noble, a divine phenomenon."

"Aye," said his uncle solemnly, "a noble phenomenon, the noblest on earth. But of the earth only, and never divine. Tragedy is the privilege of man, his highest privilege. The God of the Christian Church Himself, when He wished to experience tragedy, had to assume human form. And even at that," he added thoughtfully, "the tragedy was not wholly valid, as it would have become had the hero of it been, in very truth, a man. The divinity of Christ conveyed to it a divine note, the moment of comedy. The real tragic part, by the nature of things, fell to the executors, not to the victim. Nay, my nephew, we should not adulterate the pure elements of the cosmos. Tragedy should remain the right of human beings, subject, in their conditions or in their own nature, to the dire law of necessity. To them it is salvation and beautification. But the gods, whom we must believe to be unacquainted with and incomprehensive of necessity, can have no knowledge of the tragic. When they are brought face to face with it they will, according to my experience, have the good taste and decorum to keep still, and not interfere.

"No," he said after a pause, "the true art of the gods is the comic. The comic is a condescension of the divine to the world of man; it is the sublime vision, which cannot be studied, but must ever be celestially granted. In the comic the gods see their own being reflected as in a mirror, and while the tragic poet is bound by strict laws, they will allow the comic artist a freedom as unlimited as their own. They do not even withhold their own existence from his sports. Jove may favour Lucianos of Samosata. As long as your mockery is in true godly taste you may mock at the gods and still remain a sound devotee. But in pitying, or condoling with your god, you deny and annihilate him, and such is the most horrible of atheisms.

"And here on earth, too," he went on, "we, who stand in lieu of the gods and have emancipated ourselves from the tyranny of necessity, should leave to our vassals their monopoly of tragedy, and for ourselves accept the comic with grace. Only a boorish and cruel master—a parvenu, in fact—will make a jest of his servants' necessity, or force the comic upon them. Only a timid and pedantic ruler, a *petit-maitre,* will fear the ludicrous on his own behalf. Indeed," he finished his long speech, "the very same fatality, which, in striking the burgher or peasant, will become tragedy, with the aristocrat is exalted to the comic. By the grace and wit of our acceptance hereof our aristocracy is known."

Adam could not help smiling a little as he heard the apotheosis of the comic on the lips of the erect, ceremonious prophet. In this ironic smile he was, for the first time, estranging himself from the head of his house.

A shadow fell across the landscape. A cloud had crept over the sun; the country changed colour beneath it, faded and bleached, and even all sounds for a minute seemed to die out of it.

"Ah, now," said the old lord, "if it is going to rain, and the rye gets wet, Anne-Marie will not be able to finish on time. And who comes there?" he added, and turned his head a little.

Preceded by a lackey a man in riding boots and a striped waistcoat with silver buttons, and with his hat in his hand, came down the avenue. He bowed deeply, first to the old lord and then to Adam.

"My bailiff," said the old lord. "Good afternoon, Bailiff. What news have you to bring?" The bailiff made a sad gesture. "Poor news only, my lord," he said. "And how poor news?" asked his master. "There is," said the bailiff with weight, "not a soul at work on the land, and not a sickle going except that of Anne-Marie in this rye field. The mowing has stopped; they are all at her heels. It is a poor day for a first day of the harvest." "Yes, I see," said the old lord. The bailiff went on. "I have spoken kindly to them," he said, "and I have sworn at them; it is all one. They might as well all be deaf."

"Good bailiff," said the old lord, "leave them in peace; let them do as they like. This day may, all the same, do them more good than many others. Where is Goske, the boy, Anne-Marie's son?" "We have set him in the small room by the barn," said the bailiff. "Nay, let him be brought down," said the old lord; "let him see his mother at work. But what do you say—will she get the field mowed in time?" "If you ask me, my lord," said the bailiff, "I believe that she will. Who would have thought it so? She is only a small woman. It is as hot a day today as, well, as I do ever remember. I myself, you yourself, my lord, could not have done what Anne-Marie has done today." "Nay, nay, we could not, Bailiff," said the old lord.

The bailiff pulled out a red handkerchief and wiped his brow, somewhat calmed by venting his wrath. "If," he remarked with bitterness, "they would all work as the widow works now, we would make a profit on the land." "Yes," said the old lord, and fell into thought, as if calculating the profit it might make. "Still," he said, "as to the question of profit and loss, that is more intricate than it looks. I will tell you something that you may not know: The most famous tissue ever woven was ravelled out again every night. But come," he added, "she is close by now. We will go and have a look at her work ourselves." With these words he rose and set his hat on.

The cloud had drawn away again; the rays of the sun once more burned the wide landscape, and as the small party walked out from under the shade of the trees the dead-still heat was heavy as lead; the sweat sprang out on their faces and their eyelids smarted. On the narrow path they had to go one by one, the old lord stepping along first, all black, and the footman, in his bright livery, bringing up the rear.

The field was indeed filled with people like a market-place; there were probably a hundred or more men and women in it. To Adam the scene recalled pictures from his Bible; the meeting between Esau and Jacob in Edom, or Boas' reapers in his barley field near Bethlehem. Some were standing by the side of the field, others pressed in small groups close to the mowing woman, and a few followed in her wake, binding up sheaves where she had cut the corn, as if thereby they thought to help her, or as if by all means they meant to have part in her work. A younger woman with a pail on her head kept close to her side, and with her a number of half-grown children. One of these first caught sight of the lord of the estate and his suite, and pointed to him. The binders let their sheaves drop, and as the old man stood still many of the onlookers drew close round him.

The woman on whom till now the eyes of the whole field had rested—a small figure on the large stage— was advancing slowly and unevenly, bent double as if she were walking on her knees, and stumbling as she walked. Her blue head-cloth had slipped back from her head; the grey hair was plastered to the skull with sweat, dusty and stuck with straw. She was obviously totally unaware of the multitude round her; neither did she now once turn her head or her gaze towards the new arrivals.

Absorbed in her work she again and again stretched out her left hand to grasp a handful of corn, and her right hand with the sickle in it to cut it off close to the soil, in wavering, groping pulls, like a tired swimmer's strokes. Her course took her so close to the feet of the old lord that his shadow fell on her. Just then she staggered and swayed sideways, and the woman who followed her lifted the pail from her head and held it to her lips. Anne-Marie drank without leaving her hold on her sickle, and the water ran from the corners of her mouth. A boy, close to her, quickly bent one knee, seized her hands in his own, and steadying and guiding them, cut off a gripe of rye. "No, no," said the old lord, "you must not do that, boy. Leave Anne-Marie in peace to her work." At the sound of his voice the woman, falteringly, lifted her face in his direction.

The bony and tanned face was streaked with sweat and dust; the eyes were dimmed. But there was not in its expression the slightest trace of fear or pain. Indeed amongst all the grave and concerned faces of the field hers was the only one perfectly calm, peaceful and mild. The mouth was drawn together in a thin line, a prim, keen, patient little smile, such as will be seen in the face of an old woman at her spinning-wheel or her knitting, eager on her work, and happy in it. And as the younger women lifted back the pail, she immediately again fell to her mowing, with an ardent, tender craving, like that of a mother who lays a baby to the nipple. Like an insect that bustles along in high grass, or like a small vessel in heavy sea, she butted her way on, her quiet face once more bent upon her task.

The whole throng of onlookers, and with them the small group from the pavilion, advanced as she advanced, slowly and as if drawn by a string. The bailiff, who felt the intense silence of the field heavy on him, said to the old lord: "The rye will yield better this year than last," and got no reply. He repeated his remark to Adam, and at last to the footman, who felt himself above a discussion on agriculture, and only cleared his throat in answer. In a while the bailiff again broke the silence. "There is the boy," he said and pointed with his thumb. "They have brought him down." At that moment the woman fell forward on her face and was lifted up by those nearest to her.

Adam suddenly stopped on the path, and covered his eyes with his hand. The old lord without turning asked him if he felt incommoded by the heat. "No," said Adam, "but stay. Let me speak to you." His uncle stopped, with his hand on the stick and looking ahead, as if regretful of being held back.

"In the name of God," cried the young man in French, "force not this woman to continue." There was a short pause. "But I force her not, my friend," said his uncle in the same language. "She is free to finish at any moment." "At the cost of her child only," again cried Adam. "Do you not see that she is dying? You know not what you are doing, or what it may bring upon you."

The old lord, perplexed by this unexpected animadversion, after a second turned all round, and his pale, clear eyes sought his nephew's face with stately surprise. His long, waxen face, with two symmetrical curls at the sides, had something of the mien of an idealized and ennobled old sheep or ram. He made sign to the bailiff to go on. The foreman also withdrew a little, and the uncle and nephew were, so to say, alone on the path. For a minute neither or them spoke.

"In this very place where we now stand," said the old lord, then, with hauteur, "I gave Anne-Marie my word."

"My uncle!" said Adam. "A life is a greater thing even than a word. Recall that word, I beseech you, which was given in caprice, as a whim. I am praying you more for your sake than for my own, yet I shall be grateful to you all my life if you will grant me my prayer."

"You will have learned in school," said his uncle, "that in the beginning was the word. It may have been pronounced in caprice, as a whim, the Scripture tells us nothing about it. It is still the principle of our world, its law of gravitation. My own humble word has been the principle of the land on which we stand, for an age of man. My father's word was the same, before my day."

"You are mistaken," cried Adam. "The word is creative—it is imagination, daring and passion. By it the world was made. How much greater are these powers which bring into being than any restricting or controlling law! You wish the land on which we look to produce and propagate; you should not banish from it the forces which cause, and which keep up life, nor turn it into a desert by dominance of law. And when you look at the people, simpler than we and nearer to the heart of nature, who do not analyse their feelings, whose life is one with the life of the earth, do they not inspire in you tenderness, respect, reverence even? This woman is ready to die for her son; will it ever happen to you or me that a woman willingly gives up her life for us? And if it did indeed come to pass, should we make so light of it as not to give up a dogma in return?"

"You are young," said the old lord. "A new age will undoubtedly applaud you. I am old-fashioned, I have been quoting you texts a thousand years old. We do not, perhaps, quite understand one another. But with my own people I am, I believe, in good understanding. Anne-Marie might well feel that I am making light of her exploit, if now, at the eleventh hour, I did nullify it by a second word. I myself should feel so in her place. Yes, my nephew, it is possible, did I grant you your prayer and pronounce such an amnesty, that I should find it void against her faithfulness, and that we would still see her at her work, unable to give it up, as a shuttle in the rye field, until she had it all mowed. But she would then be a shocking, horrible sight, a figure of unseemly fun, like a small planet running wild in the sky, when the law of gravitation had been done away with."

"And if she dies at her task," Adam exclaimed, "her death, and its consequences will come upon your head."

The old lord took off his hat and gently ran his hand over his powdered head. "Upon my head?" he said. "I have kept up my head in many weathers. Even," he added proudly, "against the cold wind from high places. In what shape will it come upon my head, my nephew?" "I cannot tell," cried Adam in despair. "I have spoken to warn you. God only knows." "Amen," said the old lord with a little delicate smile. "Come, we will walk on." Adam drew in his breath deeply.

"No," he said in Danish. "I cannot come with you. This field is yours; things will happen here as you decide. But I myself must go away. I beg you to let me have, this evening, a coach as far as town. For I could not sleep another night under your roof, which I have honoured beyond any on earth." So many conflicting feelings at his own speech thronged in his breast that is would have been impossible for him to give them words.

The old lord, who had already begun to walk on, stood still, and with him the lackey. He did not speak for a minute, as if to give Adam time to collect his mind. But the young man's mind was in uproar and would not be collected.

"Must we," the old man asked, in Danish, "take leave here, in the rye field? I have held you dear, next to my own son. I have followed your career in life from year to year, and have been proud of you. I was happy when you wrote to say that you were coming back. If now you will go away, I wish you well." He shifted his walking-stick from the right hand to the left and gravely looked his nephew in the face.

Adam did not meet his eyes. He was gazing out over the landscape. In the late mellow afternoon it was resuming its colours, like a painting brought into proper light; in the meadows the little black stacks of peat stood gravely distinct upon the green sward. On this same morning he had greeted it all, like a child running laughingly to its mother's bosom; now already he must tear himself from it, in discordance, and forever. And at the moment of parting it seemed infinitely dearer than any time before, so much beautified and solemnized by the coming separation that it looked like the place in a dream, a landscape out of paradise, and he wondered if it was really the same. But, yes—there before him was, once more, the hunting-ground of long ago. And there was the road on which he had ridden today.

"But tell me where you mean to go from here," said the old lord slowly. "I myself have travelled a good deal in my days. I know the word of leaving, the wish to go away. But I have learned by experience that, in reality, the word has a meaning only to the place and the people which one leaves. When you have left my house—although it will see you go with sadness—as far as it is concerned the matter is finished and done with. But to the person who goes away it is a different thing, and not so simple. At the moment that he leaves one place he will be already, by the laws of life, on his way to another, upon this earth. Let me know, then, for the sake of our old acquaintance, to which place you are going when you leave here. To England?"

"No," said Adam. He felt in his heart that he could never again go back to England or to his easy and carefree life there. It was not far enough away; deeper waters than the North Sea must now be laid between him and Denmark. "No, not to England," he said. "I shall go to America, to the new world." For a moment he shut his eyes, trying to form to himself a picture of existence in America, with the grey Atlantic Ocean between him and these fields and woods.

"To America?" said his uncle and drew up his eyebrows. "Yes, I have heard of America. They have got freedom there, a big waterfall, savage red men. They shoot turkeys, I have read, as we shoot partridges. Well, if it be your wish, go to America, Adam, and be happy in the new world."

He stood for some time, sunk in thought, as if he had already sent off the young man to America, and had done with him. When at last he spoke, his words had the character of a monologue, enunciated by the person who watches things come and go, and himself stays on.

"Take service, there," he said, "with the power which will give you an easier bargain than this: That with your own life you may buy the life of your son."

Adam had not listened to his uncle's remarks about America, but the conclusive, solemn words caught his ear. He looked up. As if for the first time in his life, he saw the old man's figure as a whole, and conceived how small it was, so much smaller than himself, pale, a thin black anchorite upon his own land. A thought ran through his head: "How terrible to be old!" The abhorrence of the tyrant, and the sinister dread on his behalf, which had followed him all day, seemed to die out of him, and his pity with all creation to extend even to the sombre form before him.

His whole being cried out for harmony. Now, with the possibility of forgiving, of a reconciliation, a sense of relief went through him; confusedly he bethought himself of Anne-Marie drinking the water held to her lips. He took off his hat, as his uncle had done a moment ago, so that to a beholder at a distance it would seem that the two dark-clad gentlemen on the path were repeatedly and respectfully saluting one another, and brushed the hair from his forehead. Once more the tune of the garden-room rang in his mind:

> "Mourir pour ce qu'on aime
> C'est un trop doux effort. . ."

He stood for a long time immobile and dumb. He broke off a few ears of rye, kept them in his hand and looked at them.

He saw the ways of life, he thought, as a twined and tangled design, complicated and mazy; it was not given him or any mortal to command or control it. Life and death, happiness and woe, the past and the present, were interlaced within the pattern. Yet to the initiated it might be read as easily as our ciphers—which to the savage must seem confused and incomprehensible—will be read by the schoolboy. And out of the contrasting elements concord arose. All that lived must suffer; the old man, whom he had judged hardly, had suffered, as he had watched his son die, and had dreaded the obliteration of his being. He himself would come to know ache, tears and remorse, and even through these, the fullness of life. So might now, to the woman in the rye field, her ordeal be a triumphant procession. For to die for the one you loved was an effort too sweet for words.

As now he thought of it, he knew that all his life he had sought the unity of things, the secret which connects the phenomena of existence. It was this strife, this dim presage, which had sometimes made him stand still and inert in the midst of the games of his playfellows, or which had, at other moments—on moonlight nights, or in his little boat on the sea—lifted the boy to ecstatic happiness. Where other young people, in their pleasures or their amours, had searched for contrast and variety, he himself had yearned only to comprehend in full the oneness of the world. If things had come differently to him, if his young cousin had not died, and the events that followed his death had not brought him to Denmark, his search for understanding and harmony might have taken him to America, and he might have found them there, in the virgin forests of a new world. Now they had been disclosed to him today, in the place where he had played as a child. As the song is one with the voice that sings it, as the road is one with the goal, as lovers are made one in their embrace, so is man one with his destiny, and he shall love it as himself.

He looked up again, towards the horizon. If he wished to, he felt, he might find out what it was that had brought to him, here, the sudden conception of the unity of the universe. When this same morning he had philosophized, lightly and for his own sake, on his feeling of belonging to this land and soil, it had been the beginning of it. But since then it had grown; it had become a mightier thing, a revelation to his soul. Some time he would look into it, for the law of cause and effect was a wonderful and fascinating study. But not now. This hour was consecrated to greater emotions, to a surrender to fate and to the will of life.

"No," he said at last. "If you wish it I shall not go. I shall stay here."

At that moment a long, loud roll of thunder broke the stillness of the afternoon. It re-echoed for a while amongst the low hills, and it reverberated within the young man's breast as powerfully as if he had been seized and shaken by hands. The landscape had spoken. He remembered that twelve hours ago he had put a question to it, half in jest, and not knowing what he did. Here it gave him its answer.

What it contained he did not know; neither did he inquire. In his promise to his uncle he had given himself over to the mightier powers of the world. Now what must come must come.

"I thank you," said the old lord, and made a little stiff gesture with his hand. "I am happy to hear you say so. We should not let the difference in our ages, or of our views, separate us. In our family we have been wont to keep peace and faith with one another. You have made my heart lighter."

Something within his uncle's speech faintly recalled to Adam the misgivings of the afternoon. He rejected them; he would not let them trouble the new, sweet felicity which his resolution to stay had brought him.

"I shall go on now," said the old lord. "But there is no need for you to follow me. I will tell you tomorrow how the matter has ended." "No," said Adam, "I shall come back by sunset, to see the end of it myself."

All the same he did not come back. He kept the hour in his mind, and all through the evening the consciousness of the drama, and the profound concern and compassion with which, in his thoughts, he followed it, gave to his speech, glance and movements a grave and pathetic substance. But he felt that he was, in the rooms of the manor, and even by the harpsichord on which he accompanied his aunt to her air from *Alceste,* as much in the centre of things as if had stood in the rye field itself, and as near to those human beings whose fate was now decided there. Anne-Marie and he were both in the hands of destiny, and destiny would, by different ways, bring each to the designated end.

Later on he remembered what he had thought that evening.

But the old lord stayed on. Late in the afternoon he even had an idea; he called down his valet to the pavilion and made him shift his clothes on him and dress him up in a brocaded suit that he had worn at Court. He let a lace-trimmed shirt be drawn over his head and stuck out his slim legs to have them put into thin silk stockings and buckled shoes. In this majestic attire he dined alone, of a frugal meal, but took a bottle of Rhenish wine with it, to keep up his strength. He sat on for a while, a little sunk in his seat; then, as the sun neared the earth, he straightened himself, and took the way down to the field.

The shadows were now lengthening, azure blue along all the eastern slopes. The lonely trees in the corn marked their site by narrow blue pools running out from their feet, and as the old man walked a thin, immensely elongated reflection stirred behind him on the path. Once he stood still; he thought he heard a lark singing over his head, a spring-like sound; his tired head held no clear perception of the season; he seemed to be walking, and standing, in a kind of eternity.

The people in the field were no longer silent, as they had been in the afternoon. Many of them talked loudly among themselves, and a little farther away a woman was weeping.

When the bailiff saw his master, he came up to him. He told him, in great agitation, that the widow would, in all likelihood, finish the mowing of the field within a quarter of an hour.

"Are the keeper and the wheelwright here?" the old lord asked him. "They have been here," said the bailiff, "and have gone away, five times. Each time they have said that they would not come back. But they have come back again, all the same, and they are here now." "And where is the boy?" the old lord asked again. "He is with her," said the bailiff. "I have given him leave to follow her. He has walked close to his mother all afternoon, and you will see him now by her side, down there."

Anne-Marie was now working her way towards them more evenly than before, but with extreme slowness, as if at any moment she might come to a standstill. This excessive tardiness, the old lord reflected, if it had been purposely performed, would have been an inimitable, dignified exhibition of skilled art; one might fancy the Emperor of China advancing in like manner on a divine procession or rite. He shaded his eyes with his hand, for the sun was now just beyond the horizon, and its last rays made light, wild, many-coloured specks dance before his sight. With such splendour did the sunset emblazon the earth and the air that the landscape was turned into a melting-pot of glorious metals. The meadows and the grass-lands became pure gold; the barley field near by, with its long ears, was a live lake of shining silver.

There was only a small patch of straw standing in the rye field, when the woman, alarmed by the change in the light, turned her head a little to get a look at the sun. The while she did not stop her work, but grasped one handful of corn and cut it off, then another, and another. A great stir, and a sound like a manifold, deep sigh, ran through the crowd. The field was now mowed from one end to the other. Only the mower herself did not realize the fact; she stretched out her hand anew, and when she found nothing in it, she seemed puzzled or disappointed. Then she let her arms drop, and slowly sank to her knees.

Many of the women burst out weeping, and the swarm drew close round her, leaving only a small open space at the side where the old lord stood. Their sudden nearness frightened Anne-Marie; she made a slight, uneasy movement, as if terrified that they should put their hands on her.

The boy, who had kept by her all day, now fell on his knees beside her. Even he dared not touch her, but held one arm low behind her back and the other before her, level with her collar-bone, to catch hold of her if she should fall, and all the time he cried aloud. At that moment the sun went down.

The old lord stepped forward and solemnly took off his hat. The crowd became silent, waiting for him to speak. But for a minute or two he said nothing. Then he addressed her, very slowly.

"Your son is free, Anne-Marie," he said. He again waited a little, and added: "You have done a good day's work, which will long be remem-bered."

Anne-Marie raised her gaze only as high as his knees, and he under-stood that she had not heard what he said. He turned to the boy. "You tell your mother, Goske," he said, gently, "what I have told her.'

The boy had been sobbing wildly, in raucous, broken moans. It took him some time to collect and control himself. But when at last he spoke, straight into his mother's face, his voice was low, a little impatient, as if he were conveying an everyday message to her. "I am free, Mother," he said. "You have done a good day's work that will long be remembered."

At the sound of his voice she lifted her face to him. A faint, bland shadow of surprise ran over it, but still she gave no sign of having heard what he said, so that the people round them began to wonder if the exhaustion had turned her deaf. But after a moment she slowly and waveringly raised her hand, fumbling in the air as she aimed at his face, and with her fingers touched his cheek. The cheek was wet with tears, so that at the contact her fingertips lightly stuck to it, and she seemed unable to overcome the infinitely slight resistance, or to withdraw her hand. For a minute the two looked each other in the face. Then, softly and lingeringly, like a sheaf of corn that falls to the ground, she sank forward onto the boy's shoulder, and he closed his arms round her.

He held her thus, pressed against him, his own face buried in her hair and head-cloth, for such a long time that those nearest to them, frightened because her body looked so small in his embrace, drew closer, bent down and loosened his grip. The boy let them do so without a word or a movement. But the woman who held Anne-Marie in her arms to lift her up, turned her face to the old lord. "She is dead," she said.

The people who had followed Anne-Marie all through the day kept standing and stirring in the field for many hours, as long as the evening light lasted, and longer. Long after some of them had made a stretcher from branches of the trees and had carried away the dead woman, others wandered on, up and down the stubble, imitating and measuring her course from one end of the rye field to the other, and binding up the last sheaves, where she had finished her mowing.

The old lord stayed with them for a long time, stepping along a little, and again standing still.

In the place where the woman had died the old lord later on had a stone set up, with a sickle engraved on it. The peasants on the land then named the rye field "Sorrow-Acre." By this name it was known a long time after the story of the woman and her son had itself been forgotten.

# Research and Popular Culture

## WHO'S IN CHARGE?

Dan Benson

*Woe to the house where the hen crows and the rooster keeps still.*
SPANISH PROVERB

In spite of its fantasies and weaknesses, television reveals a lot about contemporary thinking.

Take society's view of the family man. "Little House on the Prairie" looks back into the nineteenth century, where Charles Ingalls is an honest, sincere, hard-working farmer. No matter how tough Ingalls' day is, he always takes the time to love, talk, and play with his children. Mrs. Ingalls submits lovingly to Charles' leadership—not because he lords it over her, but out of a geniune respect for her husband. Charles Ingalls seems to relish his wife's input as he contemplates a decision, yet they both know that the decision is his. There is harmony in the Ingallses' household.

"The Waltons" moves us ahead several decades to the mid-30's. In this program the spotlight is primarily on the children, but we begin to see a changing view of the father image. John Walton works hard in his family lumber business to make ends meet during the depression, and there is no doubt about his love and loyalty to his family. There is often some question, however, about who exactly is in charge in his family. Walton's authority is sometimes ursurped by his wife and even by Grandma Walton. In one episode, for example, John-Boy (their eldest son, striving to become a writer) was about to sign a contract to have his first book published. "Don't you think you ought to read it first, son?" Mr. Walton suggested, to which his wife replied, "Oh, John, let him go ahead." John let his son proceed, only to discover later that the contract was for a vanity publishing firm—to which an author must pay a handsome sum in order to see his book published. Walton, although trying his best to be a good husband and father, will sometimes sit it the backgroud while his wife or mother makes the family rules and decisions.

"Happy Days," a nostalgia-inspired comedy set in the late '50s, depicts the contemporary dad as a somewhat rotund, henpecked man who sits in the living room with his paper and pipe after a hard day at the office. "Mr.

C" is usually the straight man for the family jokes, the fall-guy for Richie and Fonzie's escapades, and a generally frustrated man who can never seem to get on top of a situation. Whenever he does display some authority to either his wife, son, or daughter, he is usually talked or conned out of it.

Commercials of the '70s have further emasculated men to the point where more than one commercial has the man whining, "I'm going home to mother." A little pipsqueak with Coke bottle glasses and 1940s bow tie tells us about his problems with diarrhea. In the numerous husband-wife commercials, the husband is often the dummy to whom the wife must explain, over and over, the virtues of Brand X over Brand Y.

If television doesn't *form* the thinking of a nation, it certainly *reveals* it. Our nation is going through an identity crisis in marital leadership, a crisis in which we see several different attitudes taking place:

1. The husband is The Leader, and that means *"Fall in!* There will be no dissension, no disagreement, no 'doing your own thing' while I'm in charge. You're here, wife, to serve me and raise the kids."

2. The husband is trying to assert himself as leader, but his wife won't tolerate it. There is no agreement at the beginning of the marriage regarding the chain of command in the household. The husband has acted weakly, or not at all. Now, we hear the husband saying, "I *will* be the boss of this house, and I will *not* come out from under this bed!"

3. Both spouses have agreed that the husband is responsible for family leadership, but not for family dictatorship. He realizes the value of his wife's mentality and experiences, and feels it only wise to get maximum input from her before making a final decision. They work together as a team of "equals"—but realize that every team, for the sake of avoiding chaos, needs a captain.

4. The husband and wife live together in a sort of no-leader coexistence. This is a fairly recent occurrence, a more militant outgrowth of the feminist movement. Anthropologists, zoologists, and sociologists will tell us that in any given group of human beings or animals, a leader will soon emerge through either election or power struggle. Living creatures *need* a chain of command to exist in a group. For the modern, "liberated" husband and wife to agree to a leaderless coexistence is to agree to a life of frustration in which there is no established procedure for resolving problems.

5. The wife is the leader, usually taking over the responsibility because her husband has failed to lead during the early years of marriage. It happens when the husband prefers being silent to communicating openly; his noncommittal attitude, when the young wife eagerly waits for him to assert himself, prompts her to begin doing the talking, then the thinking, for the family. Our society calls him the "henpecked husband" and her the

"domineering wife." It's happened in more homes than husbands would care to admit.

From this confusion, it is obvious that a basic principle of leadership is needed for the home to be happy. It must be a principle which demeans no one, which provides for open discussion and even dissenting opinions, yet allows for an efficient system of goal-setting and decision-making.

God created marriage knowing that any grouping of two or more people needs such a principle of leadership. He wants marriage to work. And in Ephesians 5:21-25 he has prescribed the principle for us to follow:

> Honor Christ by submitting to each other. You wives must submit to your husband's leadership in the same way you submit to the Lord. For a husband is in charge of his wife in the same way Christ is in charge of his body the church. (He gave his very life to take care of it and be its Savior!)...And you husbands, show the same kind of love to your wives as Christ showed to the church when he died for her.

Here, God has made it quite clear that he has given you, the husband, *responsibility for leadership* in your marriage. *I* didn't say it. Masters and Johnson didn't say it. *God* said it! It is your duty to "take charge"—to maintain a home atmosphere where your wife and children have no question of who is watching out for them. You are responsible for the mood and direction of the household. But God has qualified that ordination with two other important stipulations.

The first is to *submit to each other.* The verse later speaks of a wife submitting to her husband's authority, but take note: *this command is for the husband as well.*

Mutual submission does not mean "let thyself become henpecked." It is simply each spouse saying, "Up to now, as a single person, I have been naturally self-centered. But now we are two becoming one. So I yield to you my right to selfishness. Instead of *me,* from now on it is *we.* Partners. Best friends. Confidantes."

As the husband and wife grow together in unity of body, mind, and spirit, agreement on procedures and decisions become more and more natural because their two sets of values are being molded into one. But *impasses* will happen, and to prevent chaos or stalemate a decision must be made. As designated leader, you are responsible for that final decision.

But remember, too, that mutual submission does not entitle you to lord it over her. It is instead an assurance that God created man and woman as *equal* in personhood, different only in the responsibilities they are to fulfill. This does *not* exclude the wife from the decision-making process. In fact, it is your responsibility to encourage, seek out, and listen to her viewpoint, evaluate it objectively, and then decide in favor of her opinion if she indeed shows the greater wisdom.

Which tends to bother us a little, doesn't it? As a man, I pride myself on being rational, and when I make a decision I want it to be the right one. But frequently when I'm about to decide, Kathy comes up with something entirely different—a woman's point of view. Sometimes it's nothing more than an intuition. But deep down, I know that she may be right. Her opinion might in this case be a wiser one than mine. And it bugs me.

I'm bothered because Kathy's exercies of her mental wisdom challenges my leadership. Shouldn't I be making the decisions around here?

This is where "submit to each other" comes in.

I am *responsible* for the decision made, but that does not allow for despotism on my part. The fact is, I would be stupid not recognize that God gave Kathy a brain. She can think and reason, too—in some areas, more clearly than I can. It would be wasteful not to utilize her thinking as we contemplate a goal, a budgetary decision, or even one of marriage's necessary little disagreements.

So it needn't threaten me at all. I'm learning now to be thankful for Kathy's input. God has given her to me to complete the team of home leadership. If I'm smart, I recognize her opinion not as a threat to my decision-making ability, but as a complement to it.

Submitting to each other can also employ the tool of *delegation*. I may not be present to make a decision, or there could be several areas in which my wife is far more qualified than I. Last month, for example, Kathy needed a new steam iron. Now she was a Home Economics minor in college, and the closest I ever get to an iron is to loft a golf ball onto the green. So instead of my deciding which iron to buy, I delegated the decision to her. Of course, she chose a good one. But it would look awfully funny in my golf bag. Likewise, when I'm out of town, or busy on a project, I'll delegate certain financial and household decisions for Kathy to handle. She enjoys the challenge, and her wisdom hasn't ever disappointed me.

Marriage is actually a partnership among equals in which God seems to have intended a president/vice president relationship between husband and wife. A company vice president is no less a *person* than the company president. The only difference is in their responsibilities. Each is equally vital to the success of the company. A shrewd president will in fact maintain close communication with his vice president, consulting on decisions to be made, taking the initiative to work out problems and differences, forming policy together, even delegating decisions and responsibilities.

The second condition under which God gave us leadership responsibility is *love*. In marriage the two are inseparable. Love without leadership can result in chaos. And leadership without love can result in tyranny.

And as in everything else, the Creator of marriage has provided a perfect example of the kind of love that works:

"And you husbands, show the same kind of love to your wives as Christ showed to the church when he died for her."

"The church" means you and me. Just as Christ loves us, so we are to love our wives.

We may or may not have that euphoric, ooey-gooey feeling that the world has termed "love." We may be good providers, good at giving gifts and taking her out to dinner, or good sex partners. But where we often hit a snag is in giving of *ourselves*. It's hard. It's contrary to our selfish human nature. But it's what our wives need the most.

What is Christlike love?

His life shows us several key attributes:

1. *Love is unconditional.* "No ifs, ands, or buts about it, I love you!" Do we *deserve* Christ's love? Never! But he loves us just the same, and nothing will ever change or weaken that love.

Perhaps you've heard of the three major types of love. The first is *eros* or sensuous love. For this reason alone many couples enter into marriage, only to lose their attraction for one another and discover that "we don't love each other any more." The second is *phileo,* the love of friendship. *Phileo* is a tremendous asset to marriage, for the husband and wife should be best friends to each other. But *phileo* is still an insufficient bond for permanence. There are simply too many times in marriage when you don't feel friendly to your spouse. In argument, disagreement, or during the inevitable moods, something else is needed or the marriage bond can wear thin.

That's where *agape* comes in. *Agape* is a term introduced by Christ himself which means "I love you although I may disagree with you. I love you in spite of any unattractiveness, arguments, or moods. Nothing you do will change the fact that I love you." Without the motivating Spirit of Christ inside you, you're capable of mustering only a cheap imitation of *agape* love. The real thing is nothing short of permanent, weathering storms of argument, tragedy, loss of physical appeal, sexual temptation. *Agape* lasts because it seeks the best for the other person.

Marriage as God designed it is a beautiful combination of all three types of love, but *agape* is what holds it all together. Love in spite of. Unconditional.

2. *Love is sacrificial.* Yes, Christ died for us, and a true man will protect his loved ones with his own life—but Christ also gave of something much more common. His time.

Does my use of time show my wife that I love her more than my job, my hobby, or things-I-just-gotta-do? A man once told me that he could never figure out why his wife always seemed to need that long hug, that extra assurance of his love, just when he was rushing out the door in a big hurry. "When my schedule is free, she'll always keep herself busy," he said. "But whenever I'm in a hurry to go somewhere or accomplish a job, she seems to hang to me. I feel awful leaving her."

"You can count on it," I told him. "Because as long as you act as though you don't have time for her, she'll wonder how important she is to you."

Sacrificial love *makes the time* for the important things when there are often much more "urgent" things to do. It is inherent in *agape* love, for it puts her needs before your own.

3. *Love is acting like a servant.* "What?" I hear some of you saying. "A servant to my wife?"

Not in a Royal Guard sense. Let's look at Christ for a moment. One day, confident in his power and leadership, Jesus Christ humbly stooped down to wash his disciples' feet—a custom of comfort and hygiene after a long, dusty trip. Christ's disciples objected when he did this, for they considered it a job too lowly for him. But his purpose was to back up a claim he had made earlier: "Anyone wanting to be a leader among you must be your servant." In other words, he who really cares about the needs of people, and takes action to meet those needs, is best qualified to be a leader.

Men of the Archie Bunker variety expect to have the beer and paper rushed to them by a doting Edith as they sit in their overstuffed thrones. Christ turned the tables on that concept. A true family leader is the man confident enough in his masculinity to pitch in when he can and help make his wife's job easier.

And the amazing thing is, helping her out like that doesn't spoil her concept of you one bit. It's just another indication that you think she's worth it all.

4. *Love is being a spiritual leader.* Christ's ultimate objective while on earth was to show us a liberating way to know God personally and have eternal life after physical death. So he was above all a spiritual leader teaching and guiding his men in the truth that the abundant life is the Christ-centered life.

Our task of loving is incomplete, men, if we fail our wives in this area. And unfortunately, this is where a lot of us have been the biggest duds.

First Corinthians 11:3 tells us that ". . .a wife is responsible to her husband, her husband is responsible to Christ, and Christ is responsible to God." God has made it clear that we are responsible for the spiritual climate in our home as well as for the climate of love and direction.

This is not to be interpreted as a cop-out on the part of your wife, for she still has the free will to choose whether she will trust Jesus Christ with her life. It is, though, a command for us men to center our family life around the love of God. We are to take the initiative in prayer, in Bible reading and study, in thanking God for his provisions, in teaching our children spiritual truths from his Word. We are responsible for creating a climate in which Christ himself would feel welcome. Such a climate makes marriages and families joyful.

These, then, are God's two qualifying clauses when he commands you to take charge in your household:

First, *submit to one another*—giving her freedom to be herself, to contribute fully in the decision making-process. Being liberated enough to admit when you are wrong, without letting it threaten your sense of masculinity.

Then, *love her*—so wholeheartedly that she'll rarely doubt your love or resent your leadership. Firmness, tempered with gentleness. Christlike love.

Who's in charge at your house?

A big part of your wife's sense of security is your strong, consistent leadership in the home. Be a take-charge man. Lead her, with love.

# THE MALE SEX ROLE:
## OUR CULTURE'S BLUEPRINT
## OF MANHOOD,
## AND WHAT IT'S DONE FOR US LATELY

Deborah S. David and Robert Brannon

By the latest count there are approximately 2,439,028 books currently in print devoted largely or entirely to psychology, sociology, anthropology, and other social sciences.[1] Browsing in the New York Public Library I find whole aisles of books about racial prejudice, juvenile delinquency, personality theory, learning, attitude change, speech defects, sexual deviations. There's an impressive and scholarly book concerned with public attitudes toward the profession of dentistry; an account of cross-cousin speech among the Tikopia; a report on prisons and jails in the state of New Jersey.

But there are no books on the male sex role, no entries of: "Sex Role—Male" in the index of any textbook I pull from the shelves.[2] Between "Maladjustment" and "Management"—nothing. Apparently this topic I'm interested in is so obscure, unimportant, or self-evident that it merits no serious attention from the thousands of scholars and researchers busily engaged in the struggle to understand the deepest of all mysteries, human behavior.

The purpose of this essay, and indeed this book, is to present an argument which almost every reader will find incredible—at first. Yet I believe that it's true, and the more I think about it the surer I become. This idea is that human sex roles of male and female, and specifically the male role itself, have shaped and molded the social structure and social world we live in more deeply and extensively than any other single influence one could name.

## Dimensions of the Male Sex Role

Now let's return to the specifics of the male sex role in our own culture. We already know some of the broad outlines, but there are seeming inconsistencies in the common-sense view of masculinity. One senses that there is not one ideal image of the "real man" in our society but several. Consider for example the following male stereotypes, each of which in one way or another strikes us as distinctively masculine:

- The football player: big, tough, and rugged, though not precisely a towering intellect

1. Office of Information, Library of Congress of The United States, Washington, D.C.

2. Since this writing, I am glad to report, they have begun to appear.

174

- The jet set playboy: usually sighted in expensive restaurants or fast convertibles, accompanied by a beautiful woman (whom he's ignoring)
- The blue-collar brawler: a quick temper with fists to match; nobody better try to push *him* around
- The big-shot businessman: the Babbitt traveling salesman Rotary Club booster type of expansive back-slapper
- The Don Juan: he's smooth, smoldering, and totally irresistible to women; a super-stud on the prowl
- The strong, simple working man: he's honest, solid, direct, and hard-working
- The Truly Great Man: a statesman, prophet, scientist, deep thinker, awesome genius

They don't look, act or sound very much alike, but somehow these images all seem distinctively masculine to at least some of us. Does this mean that the male role is so infinitely flexible that anything a man does can seem "manly"? No; most male images and examples are by no means as masculine as these selected examples. The image of the "average guy," the man-in-the-street, is not especially masculine; many successful, familiar, and popular male personalities seem anything but manly.

The answer is that the male role is demanding but, except on a few points, not very specific. There seem to be several basic routes, and many specific variations, to fulfilling the minimum demands of the role. A man can in some sense choose what to "specialize" in—how to project a viable masculine image, choosing from among the options the role provides. In choosing, he is likely to be influenced by his age, class, ethnic subgroup, and physique, as well as individual talents and capacities. There are many acceptable combinations and certain styles become "fads" after they're popularized by movie stars or public personalities. As with other cultural fashions, there are changes over time. Beneath all the permutations, however, are a small number of basic themes which pervade and ultimately define the male sex role. I believe that there are four such general themes, or dimensions, which underlie the male sex role we see in our culture. Each has subparts and complexities and at some points they overlap, but the following four themes seem to comprise the core requirements of the role:

1. No Sissy Stuff: The stigma of all stereotyped feminine characteristics and qualities, including openness and vulnerability
2. The Big Wheel: Success, status, and the need to be looked up to
3. The Sturdy Oak: A manly air of toughness, confidence, and self-reliance
4. Give 'Em Hell!: The aura of aggression, violence, and daring

There may seem to be a mechanistic quality to such an inflexible listing, and a model which proposes to examine sex roles in terms of four (or any other number of) components. Obviously such a model overstates what is definitely known about sex roles. Remember also that there are many human traits and characteristics (e.g., generosity, loyalty), which are not strongly associated with either male or female sex roles. Some widely admired male images—*Zorba The Greek*, or Sam-the-Lion in *The Last Picture Show* are good examples—combine masculine qualities with unmasculine ones in a very appealing way. But our focus here is on the pure case, the purely masculine part of a man's image. This discussion is focused primarily on the male role in the present-day United States. Much of it is relevant to other areas of Western culture, but there are also national variations which we won't be able to consider here.

Finally, a note about the kinds of evidence we shall consider. As a behavioral scientist I look for and prefer experimental data where it's available. Only a controlled experiment can definitively prove causal relationships between variables (Cronbach 1957, Campbell and Stanley 1963). However, such evidence is necessarily limited to factors which can be manipulated by the experimenter. Observational and correlational studies are less conclusive, but have greater scope, for nature has been experimenting since the dawn of time on a far grander scale than man can contemplate. By carefully studying covariations among events social scientists can extend the scope of science far beyond the controlled certainty of the laboratory.

Writers and novelists have no "controls" at all, but sometimes they show enormous powers of analysis. It has often been observed that novelists are among the greatest psychologists. Freud acknowledged the genius of those writers who can draw "from the whirlpool of their emotions the deepest truths, to which we others have to force our way"; "they draw on sources not yet accessible to science" (quoted in Stone and Stone 1966). Men and masculinity have provided the subject matter for countless great writers in all ages. So to explore this familiar but strangely uncharted domain of masculinity, we'll consider material and insights from all these sources.

## 1.  No Sissy Stuff: the Stigma of Anything Vaguely Feminine

*The earliest lesson: Don't be like girls, kid, be like...like...well, not like girls.* Children of both sexes initially identify most strongly with their mothers, the usual caretakers of infants and children (Hartley 1959, Lynn 1969). As a child gradually becomes aware that there are two adult sexes, one of which he or she will grow up to be, the first major difference in the psychological development of males and females takes place. While the young female may continue to identify with her mother, the boy must gradually switch to a new source of identification, a process often made difficult by the absence of the father during daytime hours:

> The girl has her same-sex parental model for indentification with her more hours per day than the boy has his same-sex model with him. Even when home, the father does not usually participate in as many intimate activities with the child as does the mother, e.g., preparation for bed and toileting. . . . Despite the shortage of male models for direct imitation, a somewhat stereotyped and conventional masculine role is spelled out for the boy, often by his mother, women teachers, and peers in the absence of his father and male models. . . . Consequently, males tend to identify with a culturally defined masculine role, whereas females tend to identify with their mothers. (Lynn 1969, pp. 24-26)

Since boys must learn to perform a masculine role for which there are few models in their immediate environment, one might expect that adults would be relatively tolerant of early mistakes. The reality is that parents are substantially more concerned that boys conform to the male role than girls to the female; both parents, but especially fathers, express substantial displeasure when boys display "feminine" qualities (Lansky 1967, Goodenough 1957). Summarizing a number of studies of preschool children, Hartley concludes:

> Demands that boys conform to social notions of what is manly come much earlier and are enforced with much more vigor than similar attitudes with respect to girls...and at an early age, when they are least able to understand either the reasons for or the nature of the demands. Moreover, these demands are frequently enforced harshly, impressing the small boy with the danger of deviating from them, while he does not quite understand what they are. (Hartley 1959, p. 458)

Surrounded by adult females, offered few positive images of what he is expected to be, but chastised and sometimes shamed for being a "sissy" if he emulates girls and women, the young male child is likely to feel:

> ...an anxiety which frequently expresses itself in over-straining to be masculine, in virtual panic at being caught doing anything traditionally defined as feminine, and in hostility toward anything even hinting at "femininity," including females themselves. (Ibid., p. 458)

The terror of being a sissy, at an age when the child can hardly understand the meaning of that accusation, let alone ignore it, apparently leaves a deep wound in the psyche of many males. It has a clear embodiment in the adult male sex role:

A *"real man" must never, never resemble women, or display strongly stereotyped feminine characteristics.* This simple rule is applied to almost every aspect of life and explains a great deal about what is and isn't considered masculine. Women are smaller, have less hair and higher-pitched voices, so boys lucky enough to be big, hairy, and deep-voiced start off with an advantage. People automatically describe such males as more masculine (Gilkinson 1937). "Develop a deep, manly voice," advises the Charles Atlas home improvement course, "and watch your confidence improve."

Women are thought to be neat and tidy, so a man who seems too fastidious will draw wisecracks. Will Rogers' mother tried scolding and begging her defiant youngster to keep his shirt tail in, all to no avail. Finally she found a sure-fire method: she simply sewed a patch of frilly white lace to the tail of every shirt he owned.

Women wear cosmetics and sweet-smelling toilet waters too, so no two-fisted man would be caught dead in that junk. "Men are actually hungry to buy scents and cosmetics," one product-researcher confided. "But the product has to have a name like Command, Tackle, Brut, Bullwhip, or Hai Karate, and have FOR MEN stamped all over the goddam bottle." (One favorite men's scent was originally a women's cologne—until it was renamed *English Leather*.) When teen-agers first began to wear their hair longer in the late 1960's, most older men were incredulous, sometimes outraged. This was no harmless fad . . . those kids look like . . . like . . . well . . . women!

The stigma of femaleness applies to almost everything: vocabulary, food, hobbies, and even choice of profession. Pastimes such as knitting, flower arranging, and needlepoint are so strongly regarded as feminine that it made the news when a professional football player (a linesman, at that) revealed his hobby of *needlepoint*. "Aren't you afraid people will think you're a sissy?" an incredulous reporter asked the 230-pound giant. Art, poetry, music, and virtually all "fine arts" are seen as somewhat feminine pursuits; men who enjoy, create, or even write about these things are widely assumed to be less manly than men who ignore them. Male ballet dancers train harder and are actually in better physical shape than the average professional football player (Chass 1974), yet their masculinity is highly suspect to most American males. Sports writers, coaches, truck drivers, engineers, and military men, in contrast, are automatically seen as masculine regardless of their physical condition. Their professions place them safely in a man's world—far away from anything that might interest a woman. The threat to this masculine isolation probably explains more of the opposition to women's attempts to enter professional sports than the economic competition reasons usually cited.

If everything associated with females is so potentially stigmatizing, it's not hard to guess how much real intimacy with women themselves a manly man is expected to want. Writing about the social life of men in the typical Western adventure movie, Manville concludes:

> Girls are nice to take your hat off to on Sunday morning when you meet one of them on her way to church, and there's another kind of lady with whom you enjoy a drink in the saloon on a Saturday night when you're ready for fun . . . But a woman as a friend, or deeply moving lover, or equal-partner wife? Never! (Manville 1969)

Men who are most intensely concerned with their own masculinity seldom desire close contact with women. "A highly intelligent man should take a primitive woman," wrote another hard-driving bully-boy, Adolf Hitler; "Imagine if on top of everything else I had a woman who interfered with my work." (cf. Spiegelman and Schneider 1974)

*Openness and Vulnerability.* Women are permitted and even expected to be "emotional": they're allowed to show when they're feeling anxious, depressed, frightened, happy, loving, and so forth. This kind of openness about feelings, especially ones which cast the feeler in a weak or "unfavorable" light, is strongly prohibited for men. It's not that men can never show *any* emotions. Open displays of anger, contempt, impatience, hostility or cynicism, are not difficult for most men. But emotions suggesting vulnerability, and even extremely positive feelings such as love, tenderness, and trust are almost never acceptable.

Try to imagine two rugged he-men standing eye to eye and saying: "I've been so upset since we had that argument I could hardly sleep last night. Are you sure you're really not mad at me?" "Heck, Jim, you mean so much to me, I get so much from our friendship . . . I was just afraid that you'd hold a grudge against me." Men do have these emotions and feelings, but we try like hell never to show them. When a male friend does start to say something like that, there are husky cries of "Get a grip on yourself," "Pull yourself together, man" or "Stiff upper lip, old boy."

Some men become so skilled at hiding feelings that their wives and closest friends don't know when they're scared, anxious, depressed, or in pain. They didn't get to be that way accidentally though. Marc Fasteau remembers consciosly practicing the style while in college:

> I tried to maintain a flat, even tone in conversation. I discussed only issues, the larger the better. I worried about every instance of doubt,

of self-consciousness, of emotion, of not being in control of groups I
was in. The men I admired seemed to feel none of these things. Since
I did, how could I play the game? (Fasteau 1974, p.125)

Probably no action is more stereotypically feminine or humiliating for a
man than crying. One businessman who had an outstanding performance
record with his company learned at an executive meeting that a project he
had spent a year developing was being taken over by someone else, for
fairly arbitrary reasons; he broke down and cried. He was told later that he
was totally discredited with his colleagues, had no future with the company, and should look for another job (Fasteau 1974, p. 123).

Jourard (1971) has developed an index of how much personal information people reveal to others with whom they interact. He finds that men
reveal far less than women, no matter who the audience, and that both
sexes reveal less to men than to women. Revealing yourself to a man can
be dangerous.

Once as a freshman in college I found myself sitting with a stranger in the
college cafeteria. I had been undergoing a lot of changes in my thinking
about religion that year, and I guess I was in a talkative mood, because I
told him all about it: what I'd believed until recently, and the changes I was
going through. "Very interesting," he said, puffing on his cigarette with a
bored, distant look: not one word about his own religious doubts, or
convictions. I felt like such a damn fool it was all I could do to get through
the meal and leave the table.

Years later, in a men's consciosness-raising group, I met a man who was
incredibly open about his feelings. He could and did say that he loved our
group, and what it had meant in his life, and even—get this!—how much
he *cared* about another man, right to his face! We had a lot of other things
in common and I was enormously drawn to him—but hell! Didn't he know
how "uncool" that was? When he would reveal himself in that way, I
would involuntarily look at the floor and squirm in embarrassment. I'd like
to say I don't react that way to men any more—but I can't.

*Male Friendship and the (Gulp!) Unspoken Fear.* When men want to
express affection to one another, their means are rather limited. In the
place of directness, we've developed ritualized gestures which are safer,
and a lot more ambiguous; often in fact they parody hostility and aggression. Two old friends will celebrate their reunion by slugging each other on
the arm. Instead of "I hope you make a good impression today," we say
"Give 'em hell."

The unspoken fear which bedevils friendships between men is, of
course, the fear of being seen as a homosexual. Surveys have shown that a

majority of all men have been worried about being latent homosexuals at some point in their lives. Almost 40% told Kinsey they had actually had what they thought was a homosexual experience since adolescence, yet their descriptions of these events sounded more friendly than erotic (Kinsey, Pomeroy, and Martin 1948). Fears of being a latent homosexual are many times more common among men than among women (Hoffman 1969). Why?

The answer is that the male role so totally prohibits tenderness and affection toward members of the same sex that few men can live a normal lifetime without experiencing supposedly forbidden feelings. Many men inevitably find that they care deeply for—and even love—another man, but believe these warm feelings abnormal and unnatrual. Thus the secret, gnawing fear that "I must be one of *those* . . .''

Like a majority of men (as I was greatly relieved to find out later!), I secretly feared at one time in my life that I was a "latent homosexual." In college the affection and caring I felt for my three roommates worried me, because I could sense that it wasn't really *all that* different from the affection I felt for the girlfriends I knew best and liked most. If the truth be known, I cared more genuinely for my male friends at this time than for any female I knew. What's worse, when we were sprawled out somewhere watching TV or reading, and our legs or arms would touch comfortably, it was . . . well, pleasant! Once one of my roommates and I were lying on our old sofa, talking and drinking beer. For some reason—as I recall there wasn't much room— he put his head in my lap with some wisecrack about getting comfortable. We continued talking. But I felt a closeness, a sort of emotional bond that hadn't been there before. And . . . after a while, I felt a very real desire to lightly stroke his hair, the way I would have done had he been a woman. Finally, I said something brilliant, like "Get off me you lazy sonofabitch, you're gettin' heavy."

That seems pretty stupid now, but I don't think my fears were unusual, or my caution unjustified. Men do not take "mistakes" of this sort lightly.

## 2. The Big Wheel: Success, Status, and the Need to Be Looked Up To.

*A man can't go out the way he came in, Ben; a man has got to add up to something!* (Willie Loman in *Death of a Salesman*)

One of the most basic routes to manhood in our society is to be a success: to command respect and be looked up to for what one can do or has achieved. There are several basic ways to accomplish this, but by definition this kind of status is a limited commodity which not every man can achieve.

*Wealth and Fame.* The most visible and sought-after source of status in our society is what we loosely refer to as "being a success." Success is usually defined in terms of occupational prestige and achievement, wealth, fame, power, and visible positions of leadership. These things usually tend to be correlated: however, *extremely* high standing on any one of them seems to have a very special status quality. The tycoon, the congressman, the movie star, and the sports hero enjoy an automatic kind of status, and will often be viewed as masculine role-models on this basis alone. There's something ineffably masculine about the word "millionaire," or even "the richest man in town." It's also quite helpful to be President of the United States, author of a best-selling novel, or even conductor of a symphony orchestra. Really massive doses of success at almost *anything*, in fact, seem so inherently manly that the "World's Greatest" artist, pianist, chef, hairdresser, or tiddlywink player is to some extent protected from the taint of unmasculine activity which surrounds less successful members of his profession. Intellectual prominence is also valuable in the right circles, but for most people nothing succeeds quite so well as money. "If Karl, instead of writing a lot about capital, had made a lot of it," said Anna Marx about her famous son, "it would have been much better" (Spiegelman and Schneider 1974, p. 49).

*The Symbols of Success.* Simply being a doctor, lawyer, or moderately successful businessman is enough to qualify as success in most social circles. A man who has launched a successful career and is earning an impressive salary can usually enjoy the respect of his family, friends, relatives, co-workers, employees—everyone who is *aware* of his accomplishments. Unfortunately though, neighbors, casual visitors, passing motorists, and the waiter at The Ritz may not happen to know who's Vice President For Local Sales at Crump Amalgamated—to them he's just a middle-aged schlepper with thinning hair and a pot belly. The answer is simple: a $300 hand-made suit, glove-leather Gucci shoes, and a hand-made attache case of unborn calf.

These symbols are wasteful of course, but in another more psychological way, they make sense. Quadraphonic stereos playing dusty old Lawrence Welk albums; hosts serving Chivas Regal to business friends who couldn't tell it from Old Overshoe; we may chuckle at what seem to be foolish excesses, but the rewards are not what they seem. What's a little wasted money compared with the precious feeling of Being A Man?

What about men to whom real financial success is out of reach, temporarily or permanently, for reasons of age, social class, or race? Many hunger for it anyway, and seize on its smallest symbols in a parody of material success, for even the fleeting feeling of "being a man" can be precious. Kenneth Clark (1965) has described young black men with menial jobs, who carry empty briefcases to and from work. One such young-ster wore a white shirt and tie downtown each day to what he said was his "management trainee" job in a large department store; in reality he was a stock-boy.

*Other Routes to Status.* Men who haven't "made it" by the standards of the mainstream often find other battlegrounds to fight on, other routes to status before smaller but highly appreciative audiences. A neighborhood bar may have a champion dart thrower, with a standing bet to lick any man in the house. A mailroom may have its fastest sorter, a men's club its stalwart whose record for beer drinking has never been equaled. In truth almost anything pursued seriously can become a source of status. Specialized subgroups often develop their own status ranking systems, sometimes very different from or even opposite to the mainstream male role. Aggressive violence plays a minor part in the general cultural male role, as we'll see later, but in certain juvenile street gangs it serves as the major "currency" on which reputations are based. Miller (1967) reports that lower-status gang members committed four to six times as many violent, illegal crimes as the high-status members, who had already "made it." Once the low-status men have acquired reputations for bloodthirsty recklessness, they too can "retire" to the relative ease (and safety) of senior status.

One of the most interesting examples of subgroup status is found in the encounter-group, clinically oriented "human potential" movement. In the mainstream male role, showing tender or fearful emotions is distasteful and embarrassing, while being "sensitive" to other people's emotions is fairly irrelevant. In the clinical counterculture, sensitivity and being "in touch with one's emotions" have been redefined as extremely good. Naturally, the subgroup leaders who are most awesomely in touch with every emo-tion and can "sense" things in other people that no one else can are . . . men! At such gatherings as Humanistic Psychology and Orthopsychiatry conventions, these super-sensitive Gurus glide around like whacked-out birds of paradise in beads and Indian gowns, followed by their retinues of admirers.

*Being "Competent."* "Ask any man a factual question and you'll get an answer," says a single woman I know. "He may not know a damn thing about it, but he'll make up something rather than say he doesn't know." Men feel a strong need to seem knowledgeable, on top of things, and generally equal to any situation that arises. When a husband and wife are driving in a car and get lost, it's almost always the woman who suggests stopping to ask directions of someone. When a car won't start, men gather around like flies to peer intently at the mysterious innards. "She's probably flooded," somebody grunts knowledgeably.

The act of lovemaking was once considered a natural function, and the male's prerogative at that. With the widespread discussion of female orgasm, not to mention multiple orgasm, and the appearance of hundreds of sex manuals telling men how to bring any woman to the brink of ecstasy in 35 easy steps, a whole new proving ground for male competence (and status) has appeared. "And I didn't have to consult my sex manual even once!" crowed Woody Allen after his night of debauchery in *Play It Again Sam*. "My husband has studied those things so much," said one med student's wife, "I can tell when he's flipping from page forty-one to forty-two."

*The Breadwinner Role.* Most men seek and long for at least part of their lives in which they feel like a "big wheel." Status of course is a relative thing: A man whose wife looks up to him can feel like a "real man" in relation to her, but not necessarily to anyone else. A shopkeeper who is feared and respected by his employees may feel sublimely masculine at work—but he doesn't look or feel manly when he's asking for a loan at the bank or being ignored by the maitre d' in a fancy restaurant. The famous "fragile male ego" that marriage manuals warn women to be so careful of is one symptom of the status vulnerability most average men must endure. ("Better to let him win a few games of checkers than to put up with a sullen, humiliated man for the rest of the evening," one such guide cautions young women.) For many men the need to feel important is most usually met in role-dictated dominance/submission interactions with women, or with traditional labor divisions in the family.

In the traditional nuclear family the male is the only paid worker, the Breadwinner, the Sole Provider. Even if his job is dull and routine, he leaves the home, labors, and returns with "food for the table"—a computerized paycheck with federal, state, and local withholdings, perhaps—but a direct descendant of Neanderthal's haunch of bison. This bastion of status within the family is traditionally available to virtually every male, a haven in which one basic demand of the male role can be satisfied. When unemployment occurs on a wide scale, such as when the chief industry in a small community fails, the psychological consequences to men are often as severe as the economic.

Despite the importance of having a job, an astounding proportion of men do not especially like what they do for a living, the way they spend approximately two-thirds of their waking hours for the better part of their lives. In a series of interviews I conducted to pretest a questionnaire on masculinity, men's answers about their jobs were notably unenthusiastic. "Well, it's a living," said a restaurant manager. "I guess I like it—I been doing it fifteen years," said a window dresser. "Hell, I gotta eat," said a car salesman.

These are all men who are far from the pinnacle of success (as are most of us), so perhaps it's not surprising they don't see their jobs as heaven on earth. But a member of my men's consciousness-raising group had a different problem with his job. He's an executive with one of the largest corporations in America, in his early forties, and was making over $50,000 a year in an assignment he actually enjoyed and was good at. *His* problem was an impending promotion. Having proven his competence at this level of the company hierarchy, he was expected to move on to the next level. It meant more money but a substantially different kind of work, which he was fairly sure he wouldn't like as well, and he'd have to commute a lot further. It made sense to stay where he was . . . but he couldn't. For one thing that would label him as a "quitter" in the company, and his chances of ever being promoted later would evaporate. For another he really couldn't resist the urge to move upward, or live with a reputation as a guy who was headed nowhere. He accepted the promotion, and, as predicted, hated his new assignment.

To the blue-collar worker struggling to make ends meet, such executives are a privileged class of rich mandarins, and obviously, in a way, they are. But based on some close observations I'd say there's another fact that's relevant. They're not very happy.

## 3. The Sturdy Oak: A Manly Air of Toughness, Confidence, and Self-Reliance

*If you can keep your head when all about you*
*Are losing theirs and blaming it on you,*
*If you can trust yourself when all men doubt you,*
*But make allowance for their doubting too; . . .*

*If you can force your heart and nerve and sinew*
*To serve your turn long after they are gone,*
*And so hold on when there is nothing in you*
*Except the Will which says to them: "Hold on!". . .*

*If you can fill the unforgiving minute*
*With sixty seconds' worth of distance run,*
*Yours is the Earth and everything that's in it.*
*And—which is more—you'll be a Man, my son!*

(From "If" by Rudyard Kipling)

You had to have some quality that was hard to pin down, a certain kind of confidence, a little swagger but not in a boastful way, an easiness, a style, an air of casual good nature, of leadership that wasn't sought but seemed to come natural. You couldn't pin it down, but you could see it in a person. (Wakefield 1970, p. 195)

There's another basic theme in our culture's positive prescription for masculinity which has little to do with success or traditional measures of social
status, and has seldom been noticed or mentioned by social science. Some
of the most widely admired figures in American motion pictures are men
who conspicuously *lack* social status: William Holden in *Stalag 17,* Bogart
in *The African Queen,* Paul Newman in *Cool Hand Luke,* Marlon Brando
in *Streetcar Named Desire,* John Wayne in *True Grit,* and many more.
What they have is harder to identify, for it seems more a matter of style
than tangible achievement, and its ingredients are variable. There's a distinct sense of strong manliness however, not usually belligerent or looking
for trouble, but tough and self-possessed, which somehow emerges from
the variable combination of quiet confidence, self-reliance, determination,
indifference to opposition, courage, and seriousness. Most of all, there's a
sense of mental and physical toughness—the big and little signs which
signal that "here is a man," a force to be reckoned with, not a straw that
blows with the changing wind. It doesn't matter so much *what* he's doing,
whether holding "the system" together, like Marshall Dillon of *Gunsmoke,*
or striking at its very foundation, like John Galt of *Atlas Shrugged;* what
matters is *how* he's doing it. There's a self-confidence and seriousness in all
these figures which demands respect even in defeat.

There is something rather unreal about this formidable creature that
every one of us is supposed to be—something illogical, impossible, and for
the most of us, deeply thrilling. Growing up in America as life became
increasingly civilized, urban, and complex, we sat in darkened movie
theatres and watched these unreal men, fashioned as much by a collective
cultural demand as by some Hollywood script writer, larger and far more
compelling than our real lives. We watched Gary Cooper standing all alone
on that long, dusty street, in *High Noon,* watched by the town that would
not stand beside him: ready to die, but not to run. Usually the man we
longed to be was big and fast on the draw like that, but sometimes it was a
seemingly ordinary guy who showed real strength when the chips were
down. Montgomery Clift's unforgettable Corporal Prewitt, in *From Here to
Eternity,* couldn't be broken by anything a whole army could dish out, and
he showed us that "real men" come in all sizes. The moving *Nothing But A
Man* showed us that they come in all colors too: the film's battered hero
finally turns on his Uncle-Tom father-in-law, who is berating him to accept
white supremacy, and delivers the punch line of a powerful film: "You
been bendin' down so long, you don't know how to stand up straight; you
ain't a man at all."

A man can not always win in this world, but he can always stand his
ground win or lose . . . *stand up straight,*[3] something in that metaphor of

---

3. As the Everly Brothers would wail in a popular song called *Cathy's Clown:* "A man can't crawl,
   he's got to stand tall, or he's not a man at all."

standing captures the image of nonbelligerent strength we so admire. A joke about an old German Jew and a young Nazi illustrates it well: A Nazi soldier is watching an old Jew hobble by. As the man passes, he shouts: "Swine!" The old Jew slowly turns and replies: "Cohen. Pleased to meet you." Even in desperate circumstances, a man can stand up and be a *mensch*.

Another of these Sturdy Oak qualities is self-reliance—the idea that a man should always be "his own man," should think for himself. One of the most popular motion pictures in recent years was *A Man For All Seasons* (Best Picture of 1966), the story of Sir Thomas More's fight to the death against Henry VIII. Few of the modern viewers so enthralled by this 16th century story could have had much enthusiasm for More's position—that divorce was immoral. What was so majestic was the spectacle of one man's personal conviction arrayed against the might of imperial England, refusing to accept any compromise which would save his life.

Strong and independent in action, the *style* of such a man is calm and composed, unimpressed by pain or danger. "Of course it hurts," smiled Peter O'Toole as *Lawrence of Arabia,* as a match burned into his fingertips; "The trick, you see, is not to *care* that it hurts." It goes far beyond the mere avoidance of "feminine" emotionality; it's the cultivation of a stoic, imperturbable persona, just this side of catatonia. A "real man" never worries about death or loses his manly "cool."

> "To hell with the handkerchief," said Walter Mitty scornfully. He took one last drag on his cigarette and snapped it away. Then, with that faint, fleeting smile playing about his lips, he faced the firing squad; erect and motionless, proud and disdainful, Walter Mitty the Undefeated, inscrutable to the last. ("The Secret Life of Walter Mitty," Thurber 1964)

*Physical Strength, Athletic Prowess.* For adults, athletic skill by itself is not strongly related to the appearance of masculine toughness. Famous sports figures such as Tom Seaver, Bob Cousy, Sandy Koufax, and Rod Laver are obviously skillful, but they don't have an exceptionally tough, or masculine, public image. Their reputations as celebrities are based as much on status and public exposure as on being sports figures per se. Professional athletes who do have a strong image of manliness aren't always the most successful, but they usually embody one of the traits we'll examine in the next section. They have a reputation for being unnecessarily violent (e.g., Ty Cobb, Derek Sanderson, Marlin McKeever) or they're famous for their off-the-field hell-raising (Paul Hornung, Babe Ruth, Billy Kilmer, Joe Kapp).

Physical size and strength are more directly relevant to the Sturdy Oak image. A physically big man is usually able to stand up to physical intimidation more easily than a small one, so he may be called on less often to prove himself. But when a big man loses to a smaller man, or appears to have no "guts" in the crunch, he becomes an object of scorn, the butt of innumerable jokes and stories. *The Harder They Fall* was a popular Bogart film about a titanic boxer from South America who bowls over his seemingly terrified opponents—in fixed fights. He really can't take a punch, you see, but nobody knows that. When he finally faces an honest fighter he crumbles, and his total disgrace is symbolized by a bout of crying. The hard-bitten sports writer (Bogart), at a fraction of the giant's body weight, is obviously much more of a Man.

*The Sturdy Oak and the Average Guy.* The need to be seen as a tough customer operates on Park Avenue as well as the gridiron. In executive jobs in which effectiveness can't be gauged directly, promotions often go to a man who has built the best reputation for toughness. In one company it's fairly common practice for a new regional manager to fire 15 of his 60 branch managers, without regard to competence, just to show his superiors he's tough enough to handle the new job. At another large corporation it was once arranged for someone to rise from the audience during a presentation by a new manager, walk up to the charts he was using and throw them to the floor, stomp on them, and return to his seat. If the speaker kept his cool while this happened, and then continued his presentation without appearing upset, he had passed the test (Fasteau 1974, p. 123).

The kind of confidence and toughness required by a test like this, and portrayed so often in popular fiction, is an idealized image, not an accurate picture of the way flesh-and-blood males usually behave. Yet this deeply socialized ideal can exert a powerful strain on man's attitudes, values, and judgments; it can kindle a sudden longing in the mildest of men to appear tough and decisive, whether or not the situation calls for it. A businessman may cling to a losing investment rather than concede that he miscalculated. A father may decide on a stern punishment for his son and stick to it, when understanding and support are what's needed. A husband may insist on lifting heavy objects or fighting a fire in the attic by himself. Women sometimes reinforce this need, for reasons related to their own sex role and the desire to feel sheltered and protected. As one young woman candidly put it: "I want a real man, someone I can lean on, depend on." But the man's inner response is often: "Oh God! How can I be that? I don't know the answers; I'm scared as she is." Like Willie Loman in Arthur Miller's *Death of a Salesman,* we often respond with bluster and braggadocio that fools almost no one; how many women must privately say, like Willie's wife: "He's only a little boat looking for a harbor."

## 4. Give 'em Hell: The Aura of Aggression, Violence, and Daring

There is nothing inherently or necessarily bad about being a success, earning respect, or having confidence and determination. It can be oppressive to *have to be* these things, but the qualities themselves are not inherently undesirable by usual standards.

There is another deep and rich vein in the male sex role that also smacks of strength and toughness but is *not* fundamentally wholesome, constructive, or benign. It is the need to hurt, to conquer, to embarrass, to humble, to outwit, to punish, to defeat, or most basically, in Horney's useful phrase, "to move against people." Like the other deep themes in the male role, this behavior takes many forms, some more disguised than others. But whereas what we have called the Sturdy Oak qualities encompass essentially defensive resources, the underlying theme here is one of attack.

This male penchant for moving against people is not always directed at the strong and powerful, however. There is a disturbing experiment by Titley and Viney (1969) in which aggression (in the form of electric shocks) toward a helpless victim was studied. Women tended to deliver less intense shocks to a victim who appeared to be physically disabled than they did to a normal victim. Men did exactly the opposite.

*The Meanings of Aggressiveness.* When a particular man is described as "aggressive" (presumably meaning more so than average for a man) it usually seems to be meant as a compliment. "Aggressive businessman," "aggressive thinker," "aggressive ballplayer" are all relatively favorable images in our culture (as opposed for example to a "passive businessman," "unaggressive ballplayer," etc.) Help-wanted ads refer to great opportunities for "hard-working, aggressive" young men. Businessmen speak admiringly of ruthless executives who fire 50 men at a shot and impose their wills on subordinates at a moment's whim. A *Playboy* cartoon shows a smartly dressed young man ripping the clothes off a startled receptionist, while announcing to her grinning boss: "I think your firm can use a man like me sir! I'm young, aggressive, and won't take 'No' for an answer!" ("He's got the idea all right" chuckle the magazine's readers, "if he can just redirect it a little!")

As these examples suggest there is considerable ambiguity about just what constitutes aggressiveness, and where the line is drawn between approved and frowned-upon male behavior. The dictionary provides two meanings of the word "aggressive": (1) *tending to aggress, making the first attack;* and (2) *energetic, vigorous.* It's no accident that two such basically different meanings are served by the same word, for our society has a deeply ambivalent attitude toward aggression and its less savory first cousin, violence.

*Violence.* Violence, of course, is officially condemned and certified "bad" by our civilized society. It is denounced in sermons, speeches at the UN, and Presidential addresses, and we have a prestigious National Commission on the Causes and Prevention of Violence. Yet violence holds a deep fascination for us, which does not appear to be totally a matter of viewing with alarm. Our favorite entertainments—movies, novels, and television—are literally packed with violence: eight serious violent incidents per hour in prime-time television, according to a recent study (Gerbner 1971). The largest paid audience in the history of mankind was recently assembled, via satellite telecast and rented theatres around the world, to watch a heavyweight boxing championship, and the largest audience prior to that was for another boxing match.

Fathers do not openly condone "violence" to their sons in so many words, but they don't totally condemn and abhor it either. The message is more often "This world is full of dangerous bullies, son, and that's too bad, but you'd better know how to handle them or you're going to have a rough time." "Never *start* fights, boys," one of my friend's father told us out in his garage one afternoon, "but always *finish* them!" My own father gave me this advice about how to handle a bully: "When you see that a guy is planning to give you a hard time, you just wait for an opening, like maybe he shoves you or something. Then you just rare back and knock his head off, that first time, and you won't ever have any more trouble with him." The message behind all this is that a real man never asks for trouble but he can sure handle it when it comes along. Innumerable Hollywood movies (*Straw Dogs, Deliverance, The Quiet Man*) have been built on exactly this theme—a mild-mannered "civilized" man is pushed beyond his limit, and explodes in a blast of awe-inspiring violence.

Yet the line between self-defense and violence for the sheer fun of it is narrow in theory and often ignored in practice, especially among adolescent boys out of sight of adults, where the rule that "might makes right" usually rules supreme. For their fathers, the allure of violence must take other, more disguised forms, such as "contact sports." Take our most popular American sport, football, for example. There is a widespread conviction that football "builds character" in young men, and there are rules against "unnecessary roughness" in the game. No real football player or fan is fooled by this window dressing. College coaches tell their players they want men who "like to hit" (Shaw 1972), and in the pros a great lineman must "enjoy hurting" and "love to hit" (Meggyesy 1971). Sensitive microphones or telescoping booms are placed along the sidelines tracked by the latest in electronic devices and circuitry, so that we can hear the crash of huge bodies colliding. The admiring exclamations of the sportscasters leave little doubt that these gladiators are the real he-men of our pallid age, the ultimate masculinity symbols.

Violence is to some extent a Southern and Western ideal more than Northeastern, and more typically working class than middle class, but it has deep roots in the general American experience. Support for the social use of violence (e.g. police using clubs and guns to stop student demonstrations) are highest in the South and Border States, lowest in the Middle Atlantic and New England States; highest among the least educated, and lowest for those with graduate degrees; highest among Fundamentalist Protestants, and lowest among Jews (Blumenthal et al. 1972, pp. 45-51). Yet 58 percent of *all* American males currently agree that a man has a perfect right to kill a person "to defend his house," and fully 46 percent think that "hurting people" is no worse an offense than stealing or damaging property (Blumenthal 1972, pp. 29, 108).

*Adventure and Daring.* In another variation of the impulse to "Give 'Em Hell," men sometimes direct their defiance more toward life in general than at a specific target. The result is a glamorous idealizing of reckless adventure, daring exploits, and bold excesses of all kinds. William Faulkner recounts the tale of young Sartoris who with Jeb Stuart galloped 40 harrowing miles behind Union lines to get a pot of coffee. After routing a Union General to the woods in his night shirt and capturing half the Yankee staff, Sartoris tossed his life away on a whim by returning to get—a tin of anchovies. In generations to come,

> The tale itself grew richer and richer, taking on a mellow splendor like wine: until what had been a hare-brained prank of two heedless and reckless boys wild with their own youth had become a gallant and finely tragical focal point to which the history of the race had been raised from out the old miasmic swamps of spiritual sloth by two angels valiantly fallen and strayed, altering the course of human events and purging the souls of men. (Faulkner 1953, p. 33)

Decades later, another generation thrilled to Kerouac's *On The Road,* the unforgettable saga of Dean Moriarity and his friends careening stark naked through the desert in a '47 Hudson at 110 flat across a sleeping and sodden continent and plunging through experimental sex, drugs, jazz, scenes, America! in a wildman's search for life and *kicks* and *meaning.* Largely ignored by social scientists, the impetuous, wild-blooded male figure gallops through American literature like the headless horseman, as magnificent in disaster as in victory.

*Aggressiveness, Violence, and Sex.* One of the vivid images of a certain kind of powerful masculinity is Marlon Brando's role of Stanley Kowalski in Williams' famous play and movie, *A Streetcar Named Desire.* As a

coarse, robust, and totally sexual blue-collar man, Kowalski stirs strong
emotions in every audience, and has come to virtually symbolize the working class brute. Stella's relationship with Stanley is deeply and powerfully
sexual, with the explosions of violence serving as foreplay to "making
those colored lights flash." For the genteel sister Blanche, Stanley's appeal
to her sister is at first unfathomable, but the lady doth protest too much; we
finally learn that she too is a rider on that streetcar named Desire and
understands all too well her sister's view that: "There are things that happen between a man and a woman in the dark... that sort of make everything else seem unimportant."

Both men and women grow up in our culture thinking of male aggressiveness as natural and normal, and of men as the sexual aggressors; by
adulthood our private experiences of eroticism and aggression/
submission are often so deeply intertwined that we cannot easily untangle
them. Even among men and women in consciousness-raising groups, ac-
tively working to overcome sex roles, erotic fantasies are often embarras-
singly traditional, with man as the ruthless aggressor, woman the helpless
submittor. We've grown up whispering such euphemisms for making love
as "having," "taking," "getting it"; they pose man as the aggressor and
often still convey a deep thrill, however irrational it may be to mutually
consenting adults. We watched Rhett Butler lift Scarlet O'Hara, kicking
and screaming, and sweep her up that spiral staircase into the velvety
darkness of the boudoir. Our parents may have watched Rudolph Valen-
tino as *The Sheik*, bear the swooning heroine off to his desert tent with
equal fascination.

Some would call this mock conquest "the dance of love," while others
consider it a demeaning and ridiculous charade that subverts real intimacy
and communication. If it stopped here, at the level of mutual role-play, it
would be relatively harmless—but it does not. The marriage of sex and
aggression has spawned in many men something far more sinister and
serious; a sadistic eroticism which thrives on inflicting pain as an end in
itself, widely seen in our culture as erotic rather than sado-masochistic. A
forcible rape is committed every 14 minutes in the United States, or rather
reported; experts believe that from three to ten times more rapes are
committed than reported. Here, a man who raped thirty-three women
fondly recalls his first:

> It was a good clean fuck with no bullshit about it.... Broads really
> want to cut the bullshit too, but society won't let them tell a guy they
> meet for the first time, "Hey, let's make it," so they get repressed and
> it comes out in rape fantasies... a good eight or ten of the broads I
> connected with had orgasms—that's a better percentage than among
> married women. (Youree 1970, p. 57)

Others are more candid, or insightful, about their own motivations:

> The main reason why I do the things I do is that I find rape enormously stimulating and very exciting. *It's fun.* (Csida and Csida 1974, pp. 32-33)

Despite the prevailing notion that rapists are sick, deranged perverts, the most extensive study of rapists (Amir 1971) could find few differences between them and "average" males. Seemingly average men, with regular sexual partners, apparently rape women when opportunities arise. One 22-year-old woman was raped in a public park, and left bleeding and weeping. She screamed to the first man passing by: "Mister, I've been raped, please help me." That man raped her too (*ibid.,* p. 16). A woman gave a man a ride and he asked her to stop at a pool hall. When she stepped inside, the proprietor locked the door and six customers raped her. Meanwhile the proprietor made some phone calls, and ten more arrived and all raped her; she was hospitalized for three months (*ibid.,* p. 16). The most compelling fact of all is that many, perhaps most, men do not regard rape as an especially serious abuse. On a TV documentary on KNXT in Los Angeles in 1973, one construction worker paused on his job and explained, "Hell, I think it's one way of getting sex without having to go out and socialize for it." Another told the reporter: "Rape's not really a serious crime...uh...other than, no more than beatin' up a girl or something like that."

*Average Men and the Aura of Violence.* Most men are not really dangerous brutes, tough customers, or knife-wielding bullies. We fulfill the male role in other, less dangerous ways, and know better than to get into fights with strangers.

> Real violence scares the hell out of most of us. But men are brought up with the idea that there *ought* to be some part of them, under control until released by necessity, that thrives on it. (Fasteau 1974)

We sense that if a man is *too* civilized and predictable and well-mannered, too completely the practical husband and dutiful provider, his image loses much of its "sex appeal." There's no spike in the punch, no hint of danger, of excitement; just good old predictable George, not *exactly* a sissy, but thoroughly domesticated and a little...well, dull.

To be seen as a "real man" then, there should be at least a hint of untamed, primitive force beneath a civilized exterior. We often strive for this effect in superficial ways, and merchandisers play on this strategy. These props can collapse in an instant when reality intrudes: a drunk blocks one's path and demands "spare change," a construction worker shouts an obscene remark at your date. It is a rare male who doesn't feel humiliated and diminished as a man when he wisely (did I say, *"cowardly"*?) lets it pass (did I say, *"runs away"*?).

> Somewhere in me a voice was still saying, even though I haven't been in a fight since high school, "If you were a real man, if you had any guts, you'd get out and knock him on his ass, instead of trading insults from the safety of the car." (Fasteau 1974)

As I sit writing these words in a Northern university, I am thinking back to the region where I was raised, and how deeply the image of masculinity I learned there has affected me, and affects me still. I grew up in the Bible Belt of the Deep South, where Men were Men, or so it always seemed to me. My grandfather was a rough-and-ready frontiersman who killed several "lawbreakers" in his youth and to this day carries a loaded gun in his car, occasionally using it to break up traffic jams on pleasant Sunday afternoons. My father was a powerfully built man, a football star and later a lumberman, who believed a good fistfight was the best way to solve life's little problems. And the inheritor of this proud tradition of rugged manhood was me, an absent-minded 90-pound weakling, with a fondness for far-fetched science projects. I devoted an enormous portion of my teenage years to becoming a man in ways for which I had little talent, and finally achieved a painfully won mediocrity. I played on a city-league football team at a level which matched my physique (we were the Class YYYY Ruby-Throated Hummingbirds, I think) and there on the gridiron, armored in shoulder pads, pants, and helmet, I received the humiliating nickname "birdlegs." But I tackled with such abandon that I broke my leg in the final game, and was named to the league All Star team. I lifted weights... (light ones, as my workout buddies constantly pointed out). I spent hours practicing my wildly erratic jump-shot in a backyard basketball court. By my senior year in high school I was the star of an interclub basketball game played before the whole student body—the zenith of my athletic greatness. My friends and I would take rifles and drive out to the gravel quarry and blaze away at bottles and beer cans or any bird that was foolish enough to fly into that din (we never hit any).

But still at 120 pounds I wasn't exactly what you'd call the violent type, and I backed down from more challenges to fight than I can remember. Once I hid from a boy named Bobby who had promised to bash my head in if I showed up at the bus stop after school. I walked all the way home rather than find out if he could do it, and I felt like crying but couldn't. I doubt if Bobby could remember that incident now for a million dollars (or my name, perhaps), but two decades later I can shut my eyes and see the sidewalk on that miserable walk home, remember the shirt I was wearing.

My experience was wounding because I had been a coward, I had run away from a little violence (I wouldn't really have been killed, after all). I had really just failed to be a man. It always seemed worse in these cases because my own father was such a stupendously powerful and violent man. *My Father, God!* When he got angry he could be terrifying. He had a way of stomping in rage on the floor of our jerry-built ranch house that would make the rafters shake and the china rattle. But even this awesome superman (or so I saw him) was not immune to occasional failures to live up to the male role.

When I was around 15 we had as neighbors a pair of newlyweds we all called Dick and Birdie. One evening after a loud quarrel Dick left in a huff, and when he returned home hours later, he found both the front and back doors locked. He pounded and pounded, to no avail. By now in a blind rage he raced over to our house, seized my boy scout axe, and proceeded to chop his own front door to splinters. The newlyweds apparently settled their differences that night (like Stanley Kowalski and Stella), for the next morning he was cheerfully repairing the mayhem, while the domestic aroma of eggs and bacon drifted across our fence.

Several years later my father attended a poker game with "the boys," not quite like the scene from *Streetcar Named Desire*, but I guess there were drinks, and good times. He had promised to be home by one, but finally stumbled back in the wee hours of the morning—to discover that my mother had locked him out! After knocking and banging around for a while my father left in disgust, probably feeling a little guilty about breaking his promise, and spent the night somewhere else. The misunderstanding was settled the next day, and presumably forgotten. But in the midst of an argument some years later, I heard my mother say to my father: "Well, I'll say this: if you were a *real man*, you'd have chopped down my front door that night I locked you out, the way Dick next door did to Birdie!"

No one less than Attila the Hun could have lived up to that role all the time; we were all losers. But we believed in the values and norms that made us losers, we reinforced them, and we imposed them on others. My father actually felt ashamed, after that conversation, that he hadn't chopped or knocked the door down like a "real man," just as I feel ashamed that I ran away from Bobby. It's hard to believe, and I could claim otherwise, but I still feel ashamed.

# References

AMIR, M. *Patterns in forcible rape*. Chicago: University of Chicago Press, 1971.

BLUMENTHAL, M. D.; R. L. KAHN; F. M. ANDREWS; and K. B. HEAD. *Justifying violence: attitudes of American men*. Ann Arbor, Mich.: Institute for Social Research, 1972.

CAMPBELL, D. T., and J. C. STANLEY. *Experimental and quasi-experimental designs for research*. Chicago: Rand McNally, 1963.

CHASS, M. A gut issue: who shapes up best, athletes or dancers? *New York Times*, August 18, 1974, Section 2, pp. 1, 25.

CLARK, K. *Dark ghetto*. New York: Harper, 1965.

CRONBACH, L. J. The two disciplines of scientific psychology. *American psychologist*, 1957, *12*, 671–684.

CSIDA, J. B., and J. CSIDA. *Rape: how to avoid it and what to do about it if you can't*. Chatsworth, Calif.: Books for Better Living, 1974.

FASTEAU, M. F. *The male machine*. New York: McGraw-Hill, 1974.

FAULKNER, W. *Sartoris*. New York: Signet, 1953. Originally published in 1929.

GERBNER, G. Violence in television drama: trends and symbolic functions. In G. Comstock and E. Rubinstein (eds.), *Television and social behavior*. Volume I: *Content and control*. Washington, D.C. Government Printing Office, 1971.

GILKINSON, H. Masculine temperament and secondary sex characteristics: a study of the relationship between psychological and physical measure of masculinity. *Genetic psychology monographs*, 1937, *19*, 105–154.

GOODENOUGH, E. W. Interest in persons as an aspect of sex difference in the early years. *Genetic psychology monographs*, 1957, *55*, 287–323.

HARTLEY, R. E. Sex-role pressures and the socialization of the male child. *Psychological reports*, 1959, *5*, 457–468.

HOFFMAN, M. *The gay world*. New York: Bantam, 1969. Originally published in 1968.

JOURARD, S. *The transparent self*. New York: Van Nostrand Reinhold, 1971.

KEROUAC, J. *On the road*. New York: Viking, 1955. Signet reprint.

KINSEY, A.; W. POMEROY; and C. MARTIN. *Sexual behavior in the human male*. Philadelphia: Saunders, 1948.

LANSKY, L. M. The family structure also affects the model: sex-role attitudes in parents of preschool children. *Merrill-Palmer quarterly*, 1967, *13*, 139–150.

LYNN, D. B. *Parental and sex-role identification: a theoretical formulation*. Berkeley: McCutchan, 1969.

MANVILLE, W. H. The locker-room boys. *Cosmopolitan*, November 1969, 110–115.

MEGGYESY, D. *Out of their league*. New York: Ramparts, 1971.

MILLER, A. Death of a salesman. In Clurman (ed.), *The portable Arthur Miller*. New York: Viking, 1971.

MILLER, W. B. Violent crimes in city gangs. In T. Dye (ed.), *Politics in the metropolis*. Columbus: Charles Merrill, 1967.

SHAW, G. *Meat on the hoof*. New York: St. Martin's Press, 1972.

SPIEGELMAN, A., and B. SCHNEIDER. *Whole grains: a book of quotations*. New York: Douglas Links, 1974.

STONE, A. A., and S. S. STONE. *The abnormal personality through literature.* Englewood Cliffs, N.J.: Prentice-Hall, 1966.

THURBER, J. The secret life of Walter Mitty. In *The Thurber Carnival.* New York: Delta, 1964.

TITLEY, R. W., and W. VINEY. Expression of aggression toward the physically handicapped. *Perceptual and motor skills,* 1969, *29,* 51–56.

WAKEFIELD, D. *Going all the way.* New York: Delacorte Press, 1970.

YOUREE, G. Jack the raper. *Avant-Garde,* May 1970, 54–61.

# MANISH BOY

Melvin London, McKinley Morganfield, Ellis McDaniels

Now when I was a young boy
At the age of five
My mother said I'll be
The greatest man alive.
But now I'm a man
Way past twenty-one
I don't need a woman,
I have lots of fun.

CHORUS:

I'm a man
I spell M-A-N-child
That represents MAN
No B-
O-child-
Y, that mean manish boy
Man! I'm a full grown man,
Man! I'm a natural born lover's man,
Man! I'm a rollin' stone,
Man! I'm a hootchy-cootchy man.

Settin on the outside
Just me and my mate,
You know I'm made to move, honey
Come up two hours late.

CHORUS:

I'm a man
I spell M-A-N-child
That represents MAN
No B-
O-child-
Y, that mean manish boy
Man! I'm a full grown man,
Man! I'm a natural born lover's man,
Man! I'm a rollin' stone,
Man! I'm a hootchy-cootchy man.

Well! Well! Well! Well!
The lilac suits
Well I never miss
When I make love to a girl
She can't resist
I think I'll go down to old Kansas Town
I'm going to bring back the second cousin
That little Johnnie Cockaroo.
Oh you little girl
Setting out that line,
I could make love to you girl
In five minutes' time.

CHORUS:

I'm a man
I spell M-A-N-child
That represents MAN
No B-
O-child-
Y, that mean manish boy
Man! I'm a full grown man,
Man! I'm a natural born lover's man,
Man! I'm a rollin' stone,
Man! I'm a hootchy-cootchy man.

Well, well, well, well.

# STUDY QUESTIONS

1. Consider why a mother may have more invested in the child's life than has the father. Do your views about this issue conform with Sherwood Anderson's in "Mother"?

2. "Gogol's Wife" obviously represents a man's fantasy of what a "perfect wife" would be like. Describe what you think a woman's fantasy of the "perfect husband" would be.

3. Write an essay in which you discuss who is "petrified" in Eudora Welty's "Petrified Man."

4. In two separate essays, first defend and then dispute Helen Andelin's views in "Feminine Dependency."

5. After reading Kubie's article "The Fantasy of Dirt," consider how you feel about your own genitals and the other sex's genitals. Do your views mirror Kubie's?

6. What are the advantages and the disadvantages for men of being excluded from the home as suggested by the Thurber cartoon "Home"?

7. Does the story "Flight" by John Steinbeck present a *macho* image for men to emulate? Why or why not?

8. Ivan Gold's "A Change of Air" depicts male camaraderie. Some people feel that only men can experience this kind of close friendship. Do you agree?

9. Given the circumstances presented in Isak Dinesen's "Sorrow-Acre," was justice done in the field?

10. Carefully analyze Dan Benson's article "Who's in Charge?" Take a stand of your own in the process.

11. In "The Male Sex Role," David and Brannon present mostly the negative effects of the traditional male role. What are some positive effects of the role?

12. Thinking of contemporary song lyrics with which you may be familiar, discuss the images of masculinity and femininity they present.

# Breaking
# Free of
# Stereotypes

Where are we now? Until recent years psychological studies of sex roles did not go beyond stereotypes. Because people innocently assumed that developing a "masculine identity" was good for boys and that girls should strive toward a "feminine identity," researchers simply questioned where these "healthy" self-concepts came from. What (who) makes boys "masculine"? Where (from whom) does a girl learn her "femininity"? Literary criticism also had gender limitations, one of which is inherent in the nature and purpose of literature. Fiction and poetry reflect life (or, at least, a writer's conception of it). Because, across the centuries, women's roles have generally required subordination to men's, literature naturally mirrors this fact, while often excluding alternatives that have also been possible for both sexes. Another limitation with literature stems from its having been written mostly by men. Males' perceptions of the world, especially before and even into this century, have dominated the literary corpus. A third limitation with sex-role examinations in literary studies runs parallel to the problem encountered by psychologists. Since few people questioned sex-role stereotypes in society, literary critics tended not to discuss them either.

In 1973, however, Carolyn Heilbrun published *Toward a Recognition of Androgyny* in which she resurrected—and for literary critics gave new form to—the androgyny myth. The word "androgyny" is taken from the Greek (*andro*-man, *gyn*-woman). Heilbrun wrote that androgyny "defines a condition under which the characteristics of the sexes, and the human impulses expressed by men and women, are not rigidly assigned. Androgyny seeks to liberate the individual from the confines of the appropriate."[1]

1. Carolyn Heilbrun, *Toward a Recognition of Androgyny* (New York: Harper & Row, 1973), p. x.

Although the myth had been familiar for centuries (Plato in the *Sym-posium* refers to "circular beings who existed *before* the split of humans into male and female halves"[2]), Heilbrun was the first to suggest that it be used as a critical tool for analyzing literature. Great literature, Heilbrun claimed, is androgynous, and in making this claim she meant that fully formed androgynous characters in good fiction are not two-dimensional. They make choices according to their own personal needs and not because of social pressures to conform. In the Greek play *Antigone*, for example, the title heroine is androgynous because she assertively (tra-ditionally considered a "masculine" adverb) disobeys King Creon's order that she not bury her dead brother Polynices. Leopold Bloom in James Joyce's *Ulysses* androgynously states in a dream sequence that he wishes to become a mother because he wants to experience the entire range of human emotions. Both characters act in ways considered unacceptable in their cultures. Women—and men, for that matter—in Antigone's time were not expected to defy the orders of a king. Men in Leopold Bloom's early-twentieth-century Ireland were supposed to enjoy drinking stout and telling off-color jokes with "the lads" at a neighborhood pub.

But Antigone and Leopold Bloom are only two of many characters in literature whom Heilbrun labels androgynous. She also mentions Tiresias who, according to Ovid, was blinded because he claimed that women enjoy lovemaking as much as men.

Heilbrun's theory has generated much controversy in certain critical circles and is considered a benchmark event in literary criticism. Both the book's supporters and detractors would agree that it motivated literary critics to examine sex-role depictions from a new perspective. It caused them to bring new questions to texts, to consider literature in a new way.

Meanwhile, in psychology, much the same shift in orientation was taking place. Beginning in the early 1970s, Sandra Bem developed a research tool, the Bem Sex-Role Inventory, which she hoped would measure and eventually lead to changes in sex-role attitudes. At first, many people were confused about the term used by Bem to describe the healthiest of human psyches. They connected the term androgyny with transsexualism and hermaphroditism. However, Bem was interested in the word's more abstract connotations. She thought of androgyny as a state in which human qualities traditionally regarded as feminine or masculine had be-come incorporated into the mind of a single individual. Carl Jung had earlier used the term in this way, and, in fact, most religions and philosophies—both Eastern and Western—had long ago formulated simi-lar concepts describing the union of opposite/opposing forces.

Bem started with the stereotypes and built outward. Soon she theorized

2. Ibid., p. xiii.

that androgynous individuals may be capable of greater flexibility of behavior than are non-androgynes in that they are more easily capable of functioning effectively in a wider variety of situations. One stereotype that Bem examined is the notion that women conform more to group opinion than do men. What she found was that androgynous students—both male and female—and traditionally masculine males conformed less than traditionally feminine females and males. Tests by others to determine how intellectual performance relates to certain personality characteristics have indirectly shown the value of androgyny. Girls with some "masculine" traits and boys with some "feminine" ones performed better on tests of intelligence and creativity than did the more sex-typed boys and girls.[3]

Important as the androgyny concept is, it may have limitations. Because it draws on the belief that certain fixed differences exist between the sexes, androgyny rests on shaky ground. With few exceptions, research simply has not established that there are these differences. Nevertheless, androgyny has served as a useful guide in identifying stereotypes and in showing us the range of behaviors from which people may choose. Choice is, after all, what people who question clearly defined sex roles seek. It is not necessarily wrong for men to be aggressive and women nurturing, these people would argue. The problem comes when men cannot nurture and women cannot be aggressive, even when they would like to.

Because of these difficulties with the concept of androgyny, psychologists and literary critics are seeking new ways to understand gender. Because people's behavior often changes more quickly than their attitudes, psychologists are studying these basic feelings about gender and how they influence our thoughts and actions. For instance, an individual could take the Bem Sex-Role Inventory, could score "androgynous," yet could hold deep-rooted convictions about gender differences, Even though a person might describe him or herself in androgynous terms, he or she could still believe, for example, that men are essentially more aggressive and women more nurturing. In literature, sex-role attitudes also seem to be important. Critics with a special interest in how readers respond to literature now recognize that the reader's attitudes about sex roles play a part in the reading process. If a reader expects people in real life to behave in rather fixed gender-typed ways, these expectations will surely color the reader's interpretation of what she or he reads. For example, an account of a male character who expresses "feminine" traits such as emotional warmth, tenderness, and nurturing might appear to such a reader as deviant, even disturbed. A reader who does not assume that gender affects behavior in such a fixed way might well view this nurturing character in a different light.

3. Eleanor Maccoby, *The Development of Sex Differences* (Stanford, Calif.: Stanford University Press, 1966).

This point has significance for our discussions of the literature in this book, and perhaps special significance for the selections in Part III. What may seem to some readers to be a "breaking free" of traditional sex roles may seem to others to exemplify a violation of what is appropriate and inherently right. As the fiction selections in Part III illustrate, good literature is open to diverse interpretations.

"Breaking free" is the topic of each fiction selection in Part III, but the manner of "breaking free," if you choose to consider it such, varies considerably. Eudora Welty's "A Worn Path" depicts the trials of a strong old black woman who journeys into town to buy medicine for her grandson. Some might consider her "androgynous" because she is courageous and independent, as well as tender-hearted and devoted to nurturing her grandchild. In order to purchase the medicine, Phoenix Jackson must endure many hardships on her long trip into town. She must walk through an inhospitable wasteland that taxes both her strength and her ingenuity. Once she secures the medication that will prolong her grandson's life, she manages to buy something for him that will also give him joy.

"Biff" is an excerpt from Carson McCullers' *The Heart Is a Lonely Hunter.* It focuses on Biff Brannon, the proprietor of the New York Café, a character sometimes overshadowed by the novel's other protagonists. Biff provides a place for the town's lonely people to come for physical and emotional sustenance. In addition to the food he serves, Biff offers sympathy and help when people need it. Although he wears a wedding ring, Biff's marriage is not a happy one and ends rather early in the novel with his wife's death. Lacking a family of his own, he takes care of those in the community who come to him with their problems. Biff Brannon's strength is not only that he cares for others, but that he can express his caring.

The guerrilla women in Monique Wittig's "A Women's Community" liberate themselves through female friendships, through redefinition of the myths that have formerly imprisoned women, and through revolution against oppression. The selection is taken from Wittig's novel *Les Guérillères.* In contrast to the superficial, even catty relationships of the women in Eudora Welty's "Petrified Man," the friendships of the guerrilla women in Wittig's piece are based on mutually supportive attitudes and positive feelings. Whereas women's bodies are typically viewed with revulsion and embarrassment according to Lawrence Kubie in "The Fantasy of Dirt," women's bodies in "A Women's Community" are viewed with pride and pleasure. The guerrilla women exult in their own genitals, rejoicing in their femininity. Because many of the myths surrounding women have been negative, the guerrilla women revise these stories so that they depict women more favorably. The new myths portray women as assertive, self-assured, and proud. The women's revolution is less a revolt against men than it is a revolt against a world that limits the options of both men and women.

John Irving's "Garp" is excerpted from *The World According to Garp*. T. S. Garp, the title hero, is a wrestling coach and writer who embodies the strength and aggressiveness of an athlete with the sensitivity and expressiveness of an artist. Garp and his wife, Helen, a college professor, have an egalitarian marriage. Being a writer allows Garp to stay at home where he takes charge of many of the household responsibilities. Garp is especially well suited for this role because he enjoys nurturing his two sons and can freely express his affection for them. He also enjoys cooking, and is a rather compulsive housekeeper. Garp also has a stereotypically masculine side. His athletic ability allows Garp to be a champion of children's safety in the neighborhood, but most of his aggressive feelings he channels into writing.

The Research and Popular Culture section of Part III contains three selections dealing with nontraditional behavior for children and adults. Stan and Jan Berenstain's *He Bear She Bear* offers children a variety of things to do and ways to be. This book is one of many published in the last decade that present to preschool-aged children a genderless view of occupations and activities. Boy and girl bears alike can repair and paint things, build and tend things, drive a truck, knit a sock, put out fires, play a tuba, be a firefighter, a teacher, a jet pilot, or an architect. Contrast this example to the careful segregation of boys' and girls' activities in "Hats, Hats, and Hats" and "Boys Like to Play."

The two versions of the Atalanta myth raise a fascinating issue about the nature and use of mythology. One common misconception about myths is that they are artifacts expressing a timeless wisdom. In fact, myths usually present a version of the truth acceptable to a particular age or culture. As cultures change, their myths may be modified to reflect changes in morality or attitudes. Such is the case with the Atalanta myth. The first "Atalanta" selection portrays the classical heroine as described by Edith Hamilton in *Mythology*. Despite this heroine's skill as a runner, she is duped by the wily and more rational male. Like the protagonist in Katherine Mansfield's "Her First Ball," this Atalanta learns that, once the courtship ritual is over, so also is her life of excitement and freedom. Betty Miles' "Atalanta" was written in response to changing views of men's and women's roles. Originally appearing in *Free to Be You and Me*, it describes a new kind of mythic heroine, one who does not give up her strength, independence, and self-sufficiency.

The excerpt from *Modesty Blaise,* the first novel in a series by Peter O'Donnell about the spy heroine, depicts one instance among many in which Modesty Blaise and Willie Garvin work together as equal partners. Each does what she or he is good at; each one is half of an androgynous team. In this episode, Willie has been captured during a perilous mission. Imprisoned far away from his native London, Willie can be saved only by Modesty. Using considerable physical strength and agility, Modesty orchestrates Willie's rescue. Karate, a gas mask, a weapon called a kongo, and a special emergency technique known as "The Nailer" are Modesty's methods of freeing her partner. Of course, Willie also contributes to his own rescue. What is important, however, is the way in which Modesty and Willie rely on one another's strengths and compensate for one another's weaknesses.

# Fiction

## A WORN PATH

Eudora Welty

It was December—a bright frozen day in the early morning. Far out in the country there was an old Negro woman with her head tied in a red rag, coming along a path through the pinewoods. Her name was Phoenix Jackson. She was very old and small and she walked slowly in the dark pine shadows, moving a little from side to side in her steps, with the balanced heaviness and lightness of a pendulum in a grandfather clock. She carried a thin, small cane made from an umbrella, and with this she kept tapping the frozen earth in front of her. This made a grave and persistent noise in the still air, that seemed meditative like the chirping of a solitary little bird.

She wore a dark striped dress reaching down to her shoe tops, and an equally long apron of bleached sugar sacks, with a full pocket; all neat and tidy, but every time she took a step she might have fallen over her shoelaces, which dragged from her unlaced shoes. She looked straight ahead. Her eyes were blue with age. Her skin had a pattern all its own of numberless branching wrinkles and as though a whole little tree stood in the middle of her forehead, but a golden color ran underneath, and the two knobs of her cheeks were illumined by a yellow burning under the dark. Under the red rag her hair came down on her neck in the frailest of ringlets, still black, and with an odor like copper.

Now and then there was a quivering in the thicket. Old Phoenix said, "Out of my way, all you foxes, owls, beetles, jack rabbits, coons and wild animals! . . . Keep out from under these feet, little bob-whites. . . . Keep the big wild hogs out of my path. Don't let none of those come running my direction. I got a long way." Under her small black-freckled hand her cane, limber as a buggy whip, would switch at the brush as if to rouse up any hiding things.

On she went. The woods were deep and still. The sun made the pine needles almost too bright to look at, up where the wind rocked. The cones dropped as light as feathers. Down in the hollow was the mourning dove—it was not too late for him.

The path ran up a hill. "Seem like there is chains about my feet, time I get this far," she said, in the voice of argument old people keep to use with

**207**

themselves. "Something always take a hold of me on this hill—pleads I should stay."

After she got to the top she turned and gave a full, severe look behind her where she had come. "Up through pines," she said at length. "Now down through oaks."

Her eyes opened their widest, and she started down gently. But before she got to the bottom of the hill a bush caught her dress.

Her fingers were busy and intent, but her skirts were full and long, so that before she could pull them free in one place they were caught in another. It was not possible to allow the dress to tear. "I in the thorny bush," she said. "Thorns, you doing your appointed work. Never want to let folks pass, no sir. Old eyes thought you was a pretty little *green* bush."

Finally, trembling all over, she stood free, and after a moment dared to stoop for her cane.

"Sun so high!" she cried, leaning back and looking, while the thick tears went over her eyes. "The time getting all gone here."

At the foot of this hill was a place where a log was laid across the creek. "Now comes the trial," said Phoenix.

Putting her right foot out, she mounted the log and shut her eyes. Lifting her skirt, leveling her cane fiercely before her, like a festival figure in some parade, she began to march across. Then she opened her eyes and she was safe on the other side.

"I wasn't as old as I thought," she said.

But she sat down to rest. She spread her skirts on the bank around her and folded her hands over her knees. Up above her was a tree in a pearly cloud of mistletoe. She did not dare to close her eyes, and when a little boy brought her a plate with a slice of marble-cake on it she spoke to him. "That would be acceptable," she said. But when she went to take it there was just her own hand in the air.

So she left that tree, and had to go through a barbed-wire fence. There she had to creep and crawl, spreading her knees and stretching her fingers like a baby trying to climb the steps. But she talked loudly to herself: she could not let her dress be torn now, so late in the day, and she could not pay for having her arm or her leg sawed off if she got caught fast where she was.

At last she was safe through the fence and risen up out in the clearing. Big dead trees, like black men with one arm, were standing in the purple stalks of the withered cotton field. There sat a buzzard.

"Who you watching?"

In the furrow she made her way along.

"Glad this not the season for bulls," she said, looking sideways, "and the good Lord made his snakes to curl up and sleep in the winter. A pleasure I don't see no two-headed snake coming around that tree, where it come once. It took a while to get by him, back in the summer."

She passed through the old cotton and went into a field of dead corn. It whispered and shook and was taller than her head. "Through the maze now," she said, for there was no path.

Then there was something tall, black, and skinny there, moving before her.

At first she took it for a man. It could have been a man dancing in the field. But she stood still and listened, and it did not make a sound. It was as silent as a ghost.

"Ghost," she said sharply, "who be you the ghost of? For I have heard of nary death close by."

But there was no answer—only the ragged dancing in the wind.

She shut her eyes, reached out her hand, and touched a sleeve. She found a coat and inside that an emptiness, cold as ice.

"You scarecrow," she said. Her face lighted. "I ought to be shut up for good," she said with laughter. "My senses is gone. I too old. I the oldest people I ever know. Dance, old scarecrow," she said, "while I dancing with you."

She kicked her foot over the furrow, and with mouth drawn down, shook her head once or twice in a little strutting way. Some husks blew down and whirled in streamers about her skirts.

Then she went on, parting her way from side to side with the cane, through the whispering field. At last she came to the end, to a wagon track where the silver grass blew between the red ruts. The quail were walking around like pullets, seeming all dainty and unseen.

"Walk pretty," she said. "This the easy place. This the easy going."

She followed the track, swaying through the quiet bare fields, through the little strings of trees silver in their dead leaves, past cabins silver from weather, with the doors and windows boarded shut, all like old women under a spell sitting there. "I walking in their sleep," she said, nodding her head vigorously.

In a ravine she went where a spring was silently flowing through a hollow log. Old Phoenix bent and drank. "Sweet-gum makes the water sweet," she said, and drank more. "Nobody know who made this well, for it was here when I was born."

The track crossed a swampy part where the moss hung as white as lace from every limb. "Sleep on, alligators, and blow your bubbles." Then the track went into the road.

Deep, deep the road went down between the high green-colored banks. Overhead the live-oaks met, and it was as dark as a cave.

A black dog with a lolling tongue came up out of the weeds by the ditch.

She was meditating, and not ready, and when he came at her she only hit him a little with her cane. Over she went in the ditch, like a little puff of milkweed.

Down there, her senses drifted away. A dream visited her, and she reached her hand up, but nothing reached down and gave her a pull. So she lay there and presently went to talking. "Old woman," she said to herself, "that black dog come up out of the weeds to stall you off, and now there he sitting on his fine tail, smiling at you."

A white man finally came along and found her—a hunter, a young man, with his dog on a chain.

"Well, Granny!" he laughed, "what are you doing there?"

"Lying on my back like a June-bug waiting to be turned over, mister," she said, reaching up her hand.

He lifted her up, gave her a swing in the air, and set her down. "Anything broken, Granny?"

"No sir, them old dead weeds is springy enough," said Phoenix, when she had got her breath. "I thank you for your trouble."

"Where do you live, Granny?" he asked, while the two dogs were growling at each other.

"Away back yonder, sir, behind the ridge. You can't even see it from here."

"On your way home?"

"No sir, I going to town."

"Why, that's too far! That's as far as I walk when I come out myself, and I get something for my trouble." He patted the stuffed bag he carried, and there hung down a little closed claw. It was one of the bob-whites, with its beak hooked bitterly to show it was dead. "Now you go on home, Granny!"

"I bound to go to town, mister," said Phoenix. "The time come around."

He gave another laugh, filling the whole landscape. "I know you old colored people! Wouldn't miss going to town to see Santa Claus!"

But something held old Phoenix very still. The deep lines in her face went into a fierce and different radiation. Without warning, she had seen with her own eyes a flashing nickel fall out of the man's pocket onto the ground.

"How old are you, Granny?" he was saying.

"There is no telling, mister," she said, "no telling."

Then she gave a little cry and clapped her hands and said, "Git on away from here, dog! Look! Look at that dog!" She laughed as if in admiration. "He ain't scared of nobody. He a big black dog." She whispered, "Sic him!"

"Watch me get rid of that cur," said the man. "Sic him, Pete! Sic him!"

Phoenix heard the dogs fighting, and heard the man running and throwing sticks. She even heard a gunshot. But she was slowly bending forward by that time, further and further forward, the lids stretched down over her eyes, as if she were doing this in her sleep. Her chin was lowered almost to her knees. The yellow palm of her hand came out from the fold of her apron. Her fingers slid down and along the ground under the piece of money with the grace and care they would have in lifting an egg from under a setting hen. Then she slowly straightened up, she stood erect, and the nickel was in her apron pocket. A bird flew by. Her lips moved. "God watching me the whole time. I come to stealing."

The man came back, and his own dog panted about them. "Well, I scared him off that time," he said, and then he laughed and lifted his gun and pointed it at Phoenix.

She stood straight and faced him.

"Doesn't the gun scare you?" he said, still pointing it.

"No, sir, I seen plenty go off closer by, in my day, and for less than what I done," she said, holding utterly still.

He smiled, and shouldered the gun. "Well, Granny," he said, "you must be a hundred years old, and scared of nothing. I'd give you a dime if I had any money with me. But you take my advice and stay home, and nothing will happen to you."

"I bound to go on my way, mister," said Phoenix. She inclined her head in the red rag. Then they went in different directions, but she could hear the gun shooting again and again over the hill.

She walked on. The shadows hung from the oak trees to the road like curtains. Then she smelled wood-smoke, and smelled the river, and she saw a steeple and the cabins on their steep steps. Dozens of little black children whirled around her. There ahead was Natchez shining. Bells were ringing. She walked on.

In the paved city it was Christmas time. There were red and green electric lights strung and crisscrossed everywhere, and all turned on in the daytime. Old Phoenix would have been lost if she had not distrusted her eyesight and depended on her feet to know where to take her.

She paused quietly on the sidewalk where people were passing by. A lady came along in the crowd, carrying an armful of red-, green- and silver-wrapped presents; she gave off perfume like the red roses in hot summer, and Phoenix stopped her.

"Please, missy, will you lace up my shoe?" She held up her foot.

"What do you want, Grandma?"

"See my shoe," said Phoenix. "Do all right for out in the country, but wouldn't look right to go in a big building."

"Stand still then, Grandma," said the lady. She put her packages down on the sidewalk beside her and laced and tied both shoes tightly.

"Can't lace 'em with a cane," said Phoenix. "Thank you, missy. I doesn't mind asking a nice lady to tie up my shoe, when I gets out on the street."

Moving slowly and from side to side, she went into the big building, and into a tower of steps, where she walked up and around and around until her feet knew to stop.

She entered a door, and there she saw nailed up on the wall the document that had been stamped with the gold seal and framed in the gold frame, which matched the dream that was hung up in her head.

"Here I be," she said. There was a fixed and ceremonial stiffness over her body.

"A charity case, I suppose," said an attendant who sat at the desk before her.

But Phoenix only looked above her head. There was sweat on her face, the wrinkles in her skin shone like a bright net.

"Speak up, Grandma," the woman said. "What's your name? We must have your history, you know. Have you been here before? What seems to be the trouble with you?"

Old Phoenix only gave a twitch to her face as if a fly were bothering her.

"Are you deaf?" cried the attendant.

But just then the nurse came in.

"Oh, that's just old Aunt Phoenix," she said. "She doesn't come for herself—she has a little grandson. She makes these trips just as regular as clockwork. She lives away back off the Old Natchez Trace." She bent down. "Well, Aunt Phoenix, why don't you just take a seat? We won't keep you standing after your long trip." She pointed.

The old woman sat down, bolt upright in the chair.

"Now, how is the boy?" asked the nurse.

Old Phoenix did not speak.

"I said, how is the boy?"

But Phoenix only waited and stared straight ahead, her face very solemn and withdrawn into rigidity.

"Is his throat any better?" asked the nurse. "Aunt Phoenix, don't you hear me? Is your grandson's throat any better since the last time you came for the medicine?"

With her hands on her knees, the old woman waited, silent, erect and motionless, just as if she were in armor.

"You mustn't take up our time this way, Aunt Phoenix," the nurse said. "Tell us quickly about your grandson, and get it over. He isn't dead, is he?"

At last there came a flicker and then a flame of comprehension across her face, and she spoke.

"My grandson. It was my memory had left me. There I sat and forgot why I made my long trip."

"Forgot?" The nurse frowned. "After you came so far?"

Then Phoenix was like an old woman begging a dignified forgiveness for waking up frightened in the night. "I never did go to school, I was too old at the Surrender," she said in a soft voice. "I'm an old woman without an education. It was my memory fail me. My little grandson, he is just the same, and I forgot it in the coming."

"Throat never heals, does it?" said the nurse, speaking in a loud, sure voice to old Phoenix. By now she had a card with something written on it, a little list. "Yes. Swallowed lye. When was it?—January—two-three years ago—"

Phoenix spoke unasked now. "No, missy, he not dead, he just the same. Every little while his throat begin to close up again, and he not able to swallow. He not get his breath. He not able to help himself. So the time come around, and I go on another trip for the soothing medicine."

"All right. The doctor said as long as you came to get it, you could have it," said the nurse. "But it's an obstinate case."

"My little grandson, he sit up there in the house all wrapped up, waiting by himself," Phoenix went on. "We is the only two left in the world. He suffer and it don't seem to put him back at all. He got a sweet look. He going to last. He wear a little patch quilt and peep out holding his mouth open like a little bird. I remembers so plain now. I not going to forget him again, no, the whole enduring time. I could tell him from all the others in creation."

"All right." The nurse was trying to hush her now. She brought her a bottle of medicine. "Charity," she said, making a check mark in a book.

Old Phoenix held the bottle close to her eyes, and then carefully put it into her pocket.

"I thank you," she said.

"It's Christmas time, Grandma," said the attendant. "Could I give you a few pennies out of my purse?"

"Five pennies is a nickel," said Phoenix stiffly.

"Here's a nickel," said the attendant.

Phoenix rose carefully and held out her hand. She received the nickel and then fished the other nickel out of her pocket and laid it beside the new one. She stared at her palm closely, with her head on one side.

Then she gave a tap with her cane on the floor.

"This is what come to me to do," she said. "I going to the store and buy my child a little windmill they sells, made out of paper. He going to find it hard to believe there such a thing in the world. I'll march myself back where he waiting, holding it straight up in this hand."

She lifted her free hand, gave a little nod, turned around, and walked out of the doctor's office. Then her slow step began on the stairs, going down.

# BIFF
## Carson McCullers

On a black, sultry night in early summer Biff Brannon stood behind the
cash register of the New York Café. It was twelve o'clock. Outside the
street lights had already been turned off, so that the light from the café
made a sharp, yellow rectangle on the sidewalk. The street was deserted,
but inside the café there were half a dozen customers drinking beer or
Santa Lucia wine or whiskey. Biff waited stolidly, his elbow resting on the
counter and his thumb mashing the tip of his long nose. His eyes were
intent. He watched especially a short, squat man in overalls who had
become drunk and boisterous. Now and then his gaze passed on to the
mute who sat by himself at one of the middle tables, or to others of the
customers before the counter. But he always turned back to the drunk in
overalls. The hour grew later and Biff continued to wait silently behind the
counter. Then at last he gave the restaurant a final survey and went toward
the door at the back which led upstairs.

Quietly he entered the room at the top of the stairs. It was dark inside
and he walked with caution. After he had gone a few paces his toe struck
something hard and he reached down and felt for the handle of a suitcase
on the floor. He had only been in the room a few seconds and was about
to leave when the light was turned on.

Alice sat up in the rumpled bed and looked at him. "What you doing
with that suitcase?" she asked. "Can't you get rid of that lunatic without
giving him back what he's already drunk up?"

"Wake up and go down yourself. Call the cop and let him get soused on
the chain gang with cornbread and peas. Go to it, Misses Brannon."

"I will all right if he's down there tomorrow. But you leave that bag
alone. It don't belong to that sponger any more."

"I know spongers, and Blount's not one," Biff said. "Myself—I don't
know so well. But I'm not that kind of a thief."

Calmly Biff put down the suitcase on the steps outside. The air was not
so stale and sultry in the room as it was downstairs. He decided to stay for a
short while and douse his face with cold water before going back.

"I told you already what I'll do if you don't get rid of that fellow for good
tonight. In the daytime he takes them naps at the back, and then at night
you feed him dinners and beer. For a week now he hasn't paid one cent.
And all his wild talking and carrying-on will ruin any decent trade."

"You don't know people and you don't know real business," Biff said.
"The fellow in question first came in here twelve days ago and he was a
stranger in the town. The first week he gave us twenty dollars' worth of
trade. Twenty at the minimum."

"And since then on credit," Alice said. "Five days on credit, and so drunk it's a disgrace to the business. And besides, he's nothing but a bum and a freak."

"I like freaks," Biff said.

"I reckon you do! I just reckon you certainly ought to, Mister Brannon—being as you're one yourself."

He rubbed his bluish chin and paid her no attention. For the first fifteen years of their married life they had called each other just plain Biff and Alice. Then in one of their quarrels they had begun calling each other Mister and Misses, and since then they had never made it up enough to change it.

"I'm just warning you he'd better not be there when I come down tomorrow."

Biff went into the bathroom, and after he had bathed his face he decided that he would have time for a shave. His beard was black and heavy as though it had grown for three days. He stood before the mirror and rubbed his cheek meditatively. He was sorry he had talked to Alice. With her, silence was better. Being around that woman always made him different from his real self. It made him tough and small and common as she was. Biff's eyes were cold and staring, half-concealed by the cynical droop of his eyelids. On the fifth finger of his calloused hand there was a woman's wedding ring. The door was open behind him, and in the mirror he could see Alice lying in the bed.

"Listen," he said. "The trouble with you is that you don't have any real kindness. Not but one woman I've ever known had this real kindness I'm talking about."

"Well, I've known you to do things no man in this world would be proud of, I've known you to —"

"Or maybe it's curiosity I mean. You don't ever see or notice anything important that goes on. You never watch and think and try to figure anything out. Maybe that's the biggest difference between you and me, after all."

Alice was almost asleep again, and through the mirror he watched her with detachment. There was no distinctive point about her on which he could fasten his attention, and his gaze glided from her pale brown hair to the stumpy outline of her feet beneath the cover. The soft curves of her face led to the roundness of her hips and thighs. When he was away from her there was no one feature that stood out in his mind and he remembered her as a complete, unbroken figure.

"The enjoyment of a spectacle is something you have never known," he said.

Her voice was tired. "That fellow downstairs is a spectacle, all right, and a circus too. But I'm through putting up with him."

"Hell, the man don't mean anything to me. He's no relative or buddy of mine. But you don't know what it is to store up a whole lot of details and then come upon something real." He turned on the hot water and quickly began to shave.

. . .

He stood behind the cash register, and his face contracted and hardened as he tried to recall the things that had happened during the night. He had the feeling that he wanted to explain something to himself. He recalled the incidents in tedious detail and was still puzzled.

The door opened and closed several times as a sudden spurt of customers began to come in. The night was over. Willie stacked some of the chairs up on the tables and mopped at the floor. He was ready to go home and was singing. Willie was lazy. In the kitchen he was always stopping to play for a while on the harmonica he carried around with him. Now he mopped the floor with the sleepy strokes and hummed his lonesome Negro music steadily.

The place was still not crowded—it was the hour when men who have been up all night meet those who are freshly wakened and ready to start a new day. The sleepy waitress was serving both beer and coffee. There was no noise or conversation, for each person seemed to be alone. The mutual distrust between the men who were just awakened and those who were ending a long night gave everyone a feeling of estrangement.

The bank building across the street was very pale in the dawn. Then gradually its white brick walls grew more distinct. When at last the first shafts of the rising sun began to brighten the street, Biff gave the place one last survey and went upstairs.

Noisily he rattled the doorknob as he entered so that Alice would be disturbed. "Motherogod!" he said. "What a night!"

Alice awoke with caution. She lay on the rumpled bed like a sulky cat and stretched herself. The room was drab in the fresh, hot morning sun, and a pair of silk stockings hung limp and withered from the cord of the window-shade.

"Is that drunk fool still hanging around downstairs?" she demanded.

Biff took off his shirt and examined the collar to see if it were clean enough to be worn again. "Go down and see for yourself. I told you nobody will hinder you from kicking him out."

Sleepily Alice reached down and picked up a Bible, the blank side of a menu, and a Sunday-School book from the floor beside the bed. She rustled through the tissue pages of the Bible until she reached a certain passage and began reading, pronouncing the words aloud with painful concentration. It was Sunday, and she was preparing the weekly lesson for her class of boys in the Junior Department of her church. "Now as he walked by the sea of Galilee, he saw Simon and Andrew his brother casting a net into the sea: for they were fishers. And Jesus said unto them, 'Come ye after me, and I will make you to become fishers of men.' And straightway they forsook their nets, and followed him."

Biff went into the bathroom to wash himself. The silky murmuring continued as Alice studied aloud. He listened. ". . . and in the morning, rising up a great while before day, He went out, and departed into a solitary place, and there prayed. And Simon and they that were with Him followed after Him. And when they had found Him, they said unto Him, 'All men seek for Thee.' "

She had finished. Biff let the words revolve again gently inside him. He tried to separate the actual words from the sound of Alice's voice as she had spoken them. He wanted to remember the passage as his mother used to read it when he was a boy. With nostalgia he glanced down at the wedding ring on his fifth finger that had once been hers. He wondered again how she would have felt about his giving up church and religion.

"The lesson for today is about the gathering of the disciples," Alice said to herself in preparation. "And the text is, 'All men seek for Thee.' "

Abruptly Biff roused himself from meditation and turned on the water spigot at full force. He stripped off his undervest and began to wash himself. Always he was scrupulously clean from the belt upward. Every morning he soaped his chest and arms and neck and feet—and about twice during the season he got into the bathtub and cleaned all of his parts.

Biff stood by the bed, waiting impatiently for Alice to get up. From the window he saw that the day would be windless and burning hot. Alice had finished reading the lesson. She still lay lazily across the bed, although she knew that he was waiting. A calm, sullen anger rose in him. He chuckled ironically. Then he said with bitterness: "If you like I can sit and read the paper awhile. But I wish you would let me sleep now."

Alice began dressing herself and Biff made up the bed. Deftly he reversed the sheets in all possible ways, putting the top one on the bottom, and turning them over and upside down. When the bed was smoothly made he waited until Alice had left the room before he slipped off his trousers and crawled inside. His feet jutted out from beneath the cover and his wiry-haired chest was very dark against the pillow. He was glad he had not told Alice about what had happened to the drunk. He had wanted to talk to somebody about it, because maybe if he told all the facts out loud he could put his finger on the thing that puzzled him. The poor son-of-a-bitch talking and talking and not ever getting anybody to understand what he meant. Not knowing himself, most likely. And the way he gravitated around the deaf-mute and picked him out and tried to make him a free present of everything in him.

Why?

Because in some men it is in them to give up everything personal at some time, before it ferments and poisons—throw it to some human being or some human idea. They have to. In some men it is in them—The text is "All men seek for Thee." Maybe that was why—maybe—He was a Chinaman, the fellow had said. And a nigger and a wop and a Jew. And if he believed it hard enough maybe it was so. Every person and every thing he said he was—

Biff stretched both of his arms outward and crossed his naked feet. His face was older in the morning light, with the closed, shrunken eyelids and the heavy, iron-like beard on his cheeks and jaw. Gradually his mouth softened and relaxed. The hard, yellow rays of the sun came in through the window so that the room was hot and bright. Biff turned wearily and covered his eyes with his hands. And he was nobody but— Bartholomew—old Biff with two fists and a quick tongue—Mister Brannon—by himself.

.  .  .

Biff sat by her bed at the hospital in stunned reflection. He had been present when she died. Her eyes had been drugged and misty from the ether and then they hardened like glass. The nurse and the doctor withdrew from the room. He continued to look into her face. Except for the bluish pallor there was little difference. He noted each detail about her as though he had not watched her every day for twenty-one years. Then gradually as he sat there his thoughts turned to a picture that had long been stored inside him.

The cold green ocean and a hot gold strip of sand. The little children playing on the edge of the silky line of foam. The sturdy brown baby girl, the thin little naked boys, the half-grown children running and calling out to each other with sweet, shrill voices. Children were here whom he knew, Mick and his niece, Baby, and there were also strange young faces no one had ever seen before. Biff bowed his head.

After a long while he got up from his chair and stood in the middle of the room. He could hear his sister-in-law, Lucile, walking up and down the hall outside. A fat bee crawled across the top of the dresser, and adroitly Biff caught it in his hand and put it out the open window. He glanced at the dead face one more time, and then with widowed sedateness he opened the door that led out into the hospital corridor.

Late the next morning he sat sewing in the room upstairs. Why? Why was it that in cases of real love the one who is left does not more often follow the beloved by suicide? Only because the living must bury the dead? Because of the measured rites that must be fulfilled after a death? Because it is as though the one who is left steps for a time upon a stage and each second swells to an unlimited amount of time and he is watched by many eyes? Because there is a function he must carry out? Or perhaps, when there is love, the widowed must stay for the resurrection of the beloved—so that the one who has gone is not really dead, but grows and is created for a second time in the soul of the living? Why?

Biff bent close over his sewing and meditated on many things. He sewed skillfully, and the calluses on the tips of his fingers were so hard that he pushed the needle through the cloth without a thimble. Already the mourning bands had been sewn around the arms of two gray suits, and now he was on the last.

The day was bright and hot, and the first dead leaves of the new autumn scraped on the sidewalks. He had gone out early. Each minute was very long. Before him there was infinite leisure. He had locked the door of the restaurant and hung on the outside a white wreath of lilies. To the funeral home he went first and looked carefully at the selection of caskets. He touched the materials of the linings and tested the strength of the frames.

"What is the name of the crêpe of this one—Georgette?"

The undertaker answered his questions in an oily, unctuous voice.

"And what is the percentage of cremations in your business?"

Out on the street again Biff walked with measured formality. From the west there was a warm wind and the sun was very bright. His watch had stopped, so he turned down toward the street where Wilbur Kelly had recently put out his sign as watchmaker. Kelly was sitting at his bench in a patched bathrobe. His shop was also a bedroom, and the baby Mick pulled around with her in a wagon sat quietly on a pallet on the floor. Each minute was so long that in it there was ample time for contemplation and enquiry. He asked Kelly to explain the exact use of jewels in a watch. He noted the distorted look of Kelly's right eye as it appeared through his watchmaker's loupe. They talked for a while about Chamberlain and Munich. Then as the time was still early he decided to go up to the mute's room.

Singer was dressing for work. Last night there had come from him a letter of condolence. He was to be a pallbearer at the funeral. Biff sat on the bed and they smoked a cigarette together. Singer looked at him now and then with his green observant eyes. He offered him a drink of coffee. Biff did not talk, and once the mute stopped to pat him on the shoulder and look for a second into his face. When Singer was dressed they went out together.

Biff bought the black ribbon at the store and saw the preacher of Alice's church. When all was arranged he came back home. To put things in order—that was the thought in his mind. He bundled up Alice's clothes and personal possessions to give to Lucile. He thoroughly cleaned and straightened the bureau drawers. He even rearranged the shelves of the kitchen downstairs and removed the gaily colored crêpe streamers from the electric fans. Then when this was done he sat in the tub and bathed himself all over. And the morning was done.

Biff bit the thread and smoothed the black band on the sleeve of his coat. By now Lucile would be waiting for him. He and she and Baby would ride in the funeral car together. He put away the work basket and fitted the coat with the mourning band very carefully on his shoulders. He glanced swiftly around the room to see that all was well before going out again.

. . .

Why?

The question flowed through Biff always, unnoticed, like the blood in his veins. He thought of people and of objects and of ideas and the question was in him. Midnight, the dark morning, noon. Hitler and the rumors of war. The price of loin of pork and the tax on beer. Especially he meditated on the puzzle of the mute. Why, for instance, did Singer go away on the train and, when he was asked where he had been, pretend that he did not understand the question? And why did everyone persist in thinking the mute was exactly as they wanted him to be—when most likely it was all a very queer mistake? Singer sat at the middle table three times a day. He ate what was put before him—except cabbage and oysters. In the battling tumult of voices he alone was silent. He liked best little green soft butter beans and he stacked them in a neat pile on the prongs of his fork. And sopped their gravy with his biscuits.

Biff thought also of death. A curious incident occurred. One day while rummaging through the bathroom closet he found a bottle of Agua Florida that he had overlooked when taking Lucile the rest of Alice's cosmetics. Meditatively he held the bottle of perfume in his hands. It was four months now since her death—and each month seemed as long and full of leisure as a year. He seldom thought of her.

Biff uncorked the bottle. He stood shirtless before the mirror and dabbled some of the perfume on his dark, hairy armpits. The scent made him stiffen. He exchanged a deadly secret glance with himself in the mirror and stood motionless. He was stunned by the memories brought to him with the perfume, not because of their clarity, but because they gathered together the whole long span of years and were complete. Biff rubbed his nose and looked sideways at himself. The boundary of death. He felt in him each minute that he had lived with her. And now their life together was whole as only the past can be whole. Abruptly Biff turned away.

The bedroom was done over. His entirely now. Before it had been tacky and flossy and drab. There were always stockings and pink rayon knickers with holes in them hung on a string across the room to dry. The iron bed had been flaked and rusty, decked with soiled lace boudoir pillows. A bony mouser from downstairs would arch its back and rub mournfully against the slop jar.

All of this he had changed. He traded the iron bed for a studio couch.

There was a thick red rug on the floor, and he had bought a beautiful cloth of Chinese blue to hang on the side of the wall where the cracks were worst. He had unsealed the fireplace and kept it laid with pine logs. Over the mantel was a small photograph of Baby and a colored picture of a little boy in velvet holding a ball in his hands. A glassed case in the corner held the curios he had collected—specimens of butterflies, a rare arrowhead, a curious rock shaped like a human profile. Blue-silk cushions were on the studio couch, and he had borrowed Lucile's sewing-machine to make deep red curtains for the windows. He loved the room. It was both luxurious and sedate. On the table there was a little Japanese pagoda with glass pendants that tinkled with strange musical tones in a draught.

In this room nothing reminded him of her. But often he would uncork the bottle of Agua Florida and touch the stopper to the lobes of his ears or to his wrists. The smell mingled with his slow ruminations. The sense of the past grew in him. Memories built themselves with almost architectural order. In a box where he stored souvenirs he came across old pictures taken before their marriage. Alice sitting in a field of daisies. Alice with him in a canoe on the river. Also among the souvenirs there was a large bone hairpin that had belonged to his mother. As a little boy he had loved to watch her comb and knot her long black hair. He had thought that hairpins were curved as they were to copy the shape of a lady and he would sometimes play with them like dolls. At that time he had a cigar box full of scraps. He loved the feel and colors of beautiful cloth and he would sit with his scraps for hours under the kitchen table. But when he was six his mother took the scraps away from him. She was a tall, strong woman with a sense of duty like a man. She had loved him best. Even now he sometimes dreamed of her. And her worn gold wedding ring stayed on his finger always.

Along with the Agua Florida he found in the closet a bottle of lemon rinse Alice had always used for her hair. One day he tried it on himself. The lemon made his dark white-streaked hair seem fluffy and thick. He liked it. He discarded the oil he had used to guard against baldness and rinsed with the lemon preparation regularly. Certain whims that he had ridiculed in Alice were now his own. Why?

Every morning Louis, the colored boy downstairs, brought him a cup of coffee to drink in bed. Often he sat propped on the pillows for an hour before he got up and dressed. He smoked a cigar and watched the patterns the sunlight made on the wall. Deep in meditation he ran his forefinger between his long, crooked toes. He remembered.

Then from noon until five in the morning he worked downstairs. And all day Sunday. The business was losing money. There were many slack hours. Still at meal-times the place was usually full and he saw hundreds of acquaintances every day as he stood guard behind the cash register.

"What do you stand and think about all the time?" Jake Blount asked him. "You look like a Jew in Germany."

"I am an eighth part Jew," Biff said. "My Mother's grandfather was a Jew from Amsterdam. But all the rest of my folks that I know about were Scotch-Irish."

. . .

Biff shut himself in his room downstairs. This was the place where he kept his files. The room had only one small window that looked out on the side alley, and the air was musty and cold. Huge stacks of newspapers rose up to the ceiling. A home-made filing case covered one wall. Near the door there was an old-fashioned rocking-chair and a small table laid with a pair of shears, a dictionary, and a mandolin. Because of the piles of newspaper it was impossible to take more than two steps in any direction. Biff rocked himself in the chair and languidly plucked the strings of the mandolin. His eyes closed and he began to sing in a doleful voice:

I went to the animal fair.
The birds and the beasts were there.
And the old baboon by the light of the moon
Was combing his auburn hair.

He finished with a chord from the strings and the last sounds shivered to silence in the cold air.

To adopt a couple of little children. A boy and a girl. About three or four years old so they would always feel like he was their own father. Their Dad. Our Father. The little girl like Mick (or Baby?) at that age. Round cheeks and gray eyes and flaxen hair. And the clothes he would make for her— pink crêpe de Chine frocks with dainty smocking at the yoke and sleeves. Silk socks and white buckskin shoes. And a little red-velvet coat and cap and muff for winter. The boy was dark and black-haired. The little boy walked behind him and copied the things he did. In the summer the three of them would go to a cottage on the Gulf and he would dress the children in their sun suits and guide them carefully into the green, shallow, waves. And then they would bloom as he grew old. Our Father. And they would come to him with questions and he would answer them.

Why not?

Biff took up his mandolin again. "*Tum*-ti-*tim*-ti-*tee*, ti-*tee*, the *wedd*-ing of the painted *doll.*" The mandolin mocked the refrain. He sang through all the verses and wagged his foot to the time. Then he played "K-K-K-Katie," and "Love's Old Sweet Song." These pieces were like the Agua Florida in the way they made him remember. Everything. Through the first year when he was happy and when she seemed happy even too. And when the bed came down with them twice in three months. And he didn't know that all the time her brain was busy with how she could save a nickel or squeeze out an extra dime. And then him with Rio and the girls at her place, Gyp and Madeline and Lou. And then later when suddenly he lost it. When he could lie with a woman no longer. Motherogod! So that at first it seemed everything was gone.

Lucile always understood the whole set-up. She knew the kind of woman Alice was. Maybe she knew about him, too. Lucile would urge them to get a divorce. And she did all a person could to try to straighten out their messes.

Biff winced suddenly. He jerked his hands from the strings of the mandolin so that a phrase of music was chopped off. He sat tense in his chair. Then suddenly he laughed quietly to himself. What had made him come across this? Ah, Lordy Lordy Lord! It was the day of his twenty-ninth birthday, and Lucile had asked him to drop by her apartment when he finished with an appointment at the dentist's. He expected from this some little remembrance—a plate of cherry tarts or a good shirt. She met him at the door and blindfolded his eyes before he entered. Then she said she would be back in a second. In the silent room he listened to her footsteps and when she had reached the kitchen he broke wind. He stood in the room with his eyes blindfolded and pooted. Then all at once he knew with horror he was not alone. There was a titter and soon great rolling whoops of laughter deafened him. At that minute Lucile came back and undid his eyes. She held a caramel cake on a platter. The room was full of people. Leroy and that bunch and Alice, of course. He wanted to crawl up the wall. He stood there with his bare face hanging out, burning hot all over. They kidded him and the next hour was almost as bad as the death of his mother—the way he took it. Later that night he drank a quart of whiskey. And for weeks after—Motherogod!

. . .

## Night

All was serene. As Biff dried his face and hands a breeze tinkled the glass pendants of the little Japanese pagoda on the table. He had just awakened from a nap and had smoked his night cigar. He thought of Blount and wondered if by now he had traveled far. A bottle of Agua Florida was on the bathroom shelf and he touched the stopper to his temples. He whistled an old song, and as he descended the narrow stairs the tune left a broken echo behind him.

Louis was supposed to be on duty behind the counter. But he had soldiered on the job and the place was deserted. The front door stood open to the empty street. The clock on the wall pointed to seventeen minutes before midnight. The radio was on and there was talk about the crisis Hitler had cooked up over Danzig. He went back to the kitchen and found Louis asleep in a chair. The boy had taken off his shoes and unbuttoned his trousers. His head drooped on his chest. A long wet spot on his shirt showed that he had been sleeping a good while. His arms hung straight down at his sides and the wonder was that he did not fall forward on his face. He slept soundly and there was no use to wake him. The night would be a quiet one.

Biff tiptoed across the kitchen to a shelf which held a basket of tea olive and two water pitchers full of zinnias. He carried the flowers up to the front of the restaurant and removed the cellophane-wrapped platters of the last special from the display window. He was sick of food. A window of fresh summer flowers—that would be good. His eyes were closed as he imagined how it could be arranged. A foundation of the tea olive strewn over the bottom, cool and green. The red pottery tub filled with the brilliant zinnias. Nothing more. He began to arrange the window carefully. Among the flowers there was a freak plant, a zinnia with six bronze petals and two red. He examined this curio and laid it aside to save. Then the window was finished and he stood in the street to regard his handiwork. The awkward stems of the flowers had been bent to just the right degree of restful looseness. The electric lights detracted, but when the sun rose the display would show at its best advantage. Downright artistic.

The black, starlit sky seemed close to the earth. He strolled along the sidewalk, pausing once to knock an orange peel into the gutter with the side of his foot. At the far end of the next block two men, small from the distance and motionless, stood arm in arm together. No one else could be seen. His place was the only store on all the street with an open door and lights inside.

And why? What was the reason for keeping the place open all through the night when every other café in the town was closed? He was often asked that question and could never speak the answer out in words. Not money. Sometimes a party would come for beer and scrambled eggs and spend five or ten dollars. But that was rare. Mostly they came one at a time and ordered little and stayed long. And on some nights, between the hours of twelve and five o'clock, not a customer would enter. There was no profit in it—that was plain.

But he would never close up for the night—not as long as he stayed in the business. Night was the time. There were those he would never have seen otherwise. A few came regularly several times a week. Others had come into the place only once, had drunk a Coca-Cola, and never returned.

Biff folded his arms across his chest and walked more slowly. Inside the arc of the street light his shadow showed angular and black. The peaceful silence of the night settled in him. These were the hours for rest and meditation. Maybe that was why he stayed downstairs and did not sleep. With a last quick glance he scanned the empty street and went inside.

The crisis voice still talked on the radio. The fans on the ceiling made a soothing whirl. From the kitchen came the sound of Louis snoring. He thought suddenly of poor Willie and decided to send him a quart of whiskey sometime soon. He turned to the crossword puzzle in the newspaper. There was a picture of a woman to identify in the center. He recognized her and wrote the name—Mona Lisa—across the first spaces. Number one down was a word for beggar, beginning with *m* and nine letters long. Mendicant. Two horizontal was some word meaning to remove afar off. A six-letter word beginning with *e*. Elapse? He sounded trial combinations of letters aloud. Eloign. But he had lost interest. There were puzzles enough without this kind. He folded and put away the paper. He would come back to it later.

He examined the zinnia he had intended to save. As he held it in the palm of his hand to the light the flower was not such a curious specimen after all. Not worth saving. He plucked the soft, bright petals and the last one came out on love. But who? Who would he be loving now? No one person. Anybody decent who came in out of the street to sit for an hour and have a drink. But no one person. He had known his loves and they were over. Alice. Madeline and Gyp. Finished. Leaving him either better or worse. Which? However you looked at it.

And Mick. The one who in the last months had lived so strangely in his heart. Was that love done with too? Yes. It was finished. Early in the evenings Mick came in for a cold drink or a sundae. She had grown older. Her rough and childish ways were almost gone. And instead there was something ladylike and delicate about her that was hard to point out. The earrings, the dangle of her bracelets, and the new way she crossed her legs and pulled the hem of her skirt down past her knees. He watched her and felt only a sort of gentleness. In him the old feeling was gone. For a year this love had blossomed strangely. He had questioned it a hundred times and found no answer. And now, as a summer flower shatters in September, it was finished. There was no one.

Biff tapped his nose with his forefinger. A foreign voice was now speaking over the radio. He could not decide for certain whether the voice was German, French, or Spanish. But it sounded like doom. It gave him the jitters to listen to it. When he turned it off the silence was deep and unbroken. He felt the night outside. Loneliness gripped him so that his breath quickened. It was far too late to call Lucile on the telephone and speak to Baby. Nor could he expect a customer to enter at this hour. He went to the door and looked up and down the street. All was empty and dark.

"Louis!" he called. "Are you awake, Louis?"

No answer. He put his elbow on the counter and held his head in his hands. He moved his dark bearded jaw from side to side and slowly his forehead lowered in a frown.

The riddle. The question that had taken root in him and would not let him rest. The puzzle of Singer and the rest of them. More than a year had gone by since it had started. More than a year since Blount had hung around the place on his first long drunk and seen the mute for the first time. Since Mick had begun to follow him in and out. And now for a month Singer had been dead and buried. And the riddle was still in him, so that he could not be tranquil. There was something not natural about it all— something like an ugly joke. When he thought of it he felt uneasy and in some unknown way afraid.

He had managed about the funeral. They had left all that to him. Singer's affairs were in a mess. There were installments due on everything he owned and the beneficiary of his life insurance was deceased. There was just enough to bury him. The funeral was at noon. The sun burned down on them with savage heat as they stood around the open dank grave. The flowers curled and turned brown in the sun. Mick cried so hard that she choked herself and her father had to beat her on the back. Blount scowled down at the grave with his fist to his mouth. The town's Negro doctor, who was somehow related to poor Willie, stood on the edge of the crowd and moaned to himself. And there were strangers nobody had ever seen or heard of before. God knows where they came from or why they were there.

The silence in the room was deep as the night itself. Biff stood transfixed, lost in his meditations. Then suddenly he felt a quickening in him. His heart turned and he leaned his back against the counter for support. For in a swift radiance of illumination he saw a glimpse of human struggle and of valor. Of the endless fluid passage of humanity through endless time. And of those who labor and of those who—one word—love. His soul expanded. But for a moment only. For in him he felt a warning, a shaft of terror. Between the two worlds he was suspended. He saw that he was looking at his own face in the counter glass before him. Sweat glistened on his temples and his face was contorted. One eye was opened wider than the other. The left eye delved narrowly into the past while the right gazed wide and affrighted into a future of blackness, error, and ruin. And he was suspended between radiance and darkness. Between bitter irony and faith. Sharply he turned away.

"Louis!" he called. "Louis! Louis!"

Again there was no answer. But, motherogod, was he a sensible man or was he not? And how could this terror throttle him like this when he didn't even know what caused it? And would he just stand here like a jittery ninny or would he pull himself together and be reasonable? For after all *was* he a sensible man or was he not? Biff wet his handkerchief beneath the water tap and patted his drawn, tense face. Somehow he remembered that the awning had not yet been raised. As he went to the door his walk gained steadiness. And when at last he was inside again he composed himself soberly to await the morning sun.

# A WOMEN'S COMMUNITY

Monique Wittig

When it rains the women stay in the summer-house. They hear the water beating on the tiles and streaming down the slopes of the roof. Fringes of rain surround the summer-house, the water that runs down at its angles flows more strongly, it is as if springs hollow out the pebbles at the places where it reaches the ground. At last someone says it is like the sound of micturition, that she cannot wait any longer, and squats down. Then some of them form a circle around her to watch the labia expel the urine.

The women frighten each other by hiding behind the trees. One or other of them asks for grace. Then they chase each other in the darkness, ill-wishing the one who is caught. Or else they search gropingly, scenting the one whose perfume is to be honoured. Amomum aniseed betel cinnamon cubeb mint liquorice musk ginger clove nutmeg pepper saffron sage vanilla receive homage in turn. Then the wearers of these perfumes are chased in the dark as in blindman's-buff. Cries laughter sounds of falling are heard.

By the lakeside there is an echo. As they stand there with an open book the chosen passages are re-uttered from the other side by a voice that becomes distant and repeats itself. Lucie Maure cries to the double echo the phrase of Phénarète, I say that that which is is. I say that that which is not also is. When she repeats the phrase several times the double, then triple, voice endlessly superimposes that which is and that which is not. The shadows of brooding over the lake shift and begin to shiver because of the vibrations of the voice.

The women are seen to have in their hands small books which they say are feminaries. These are either multiple copies of the same original or else there are several kinds. In one of them someone has written an inscription which they whisper in each other's ears and which provokes them to full-throated laughter. When it is leafed through the feminary presents numerous blank pages in which they write from time to time. Essentially, it consists of pages with words printed in a varying number of capital letters. There may be only one or the pages may be full of them. Usually they are isolated at the centre of the page, well spaced black on a white background or else white on a black background.

The women say that they expose their genitals so that the sun may be reflected therein as in a mirror. They say that they retain its brilliance. They say that the pubic hair is like a spider's web that captures the rays. They are seen running with great strides. They are all illuminated at their centre, starting from the pubes the hooded clitoris the folded double labia. The glare they shed when they stand still and turn to face one makes the eye turn elsewhere unable to stand the sight.

Daniela Nervi, while digging foundations, has unearthed a painting representing a young girl. She is all flat and white lying on one side. She has no clothes. Her breasts are barely visible on her torso. One of her legs, crossed over the other, raises her thigh, so concealing the pubis and vulva. Her long hair hides part of her shoulders. She is smiling. Her eyes are closed. She half leans on one elbow. The other arm is crooked over her head, the hand holding a bunch of black grapes to her mouth. The women laugh at this. They say that Daniela Nervi has not yet dug up the knife without a blade that lacks a handle.

The women say that the feminary amuses the little girls. For instance three kinds of labia minora are mentioned there. The dwarf labia are triangular. Side by side, they form two narrow folds. They are almost invisible because the labia majora cover them. The moderate-sized labia minora resemble the flower of a lily. They are half-moon shaped or triangular. They can be seen in their entirety taut supple seething. The large labia spread out resemble a butterfly's wings. They are tall triangular or rectangular, very prominent.

They say that as possessors of vulvas they are familiar with their characteristics. They are familiar with the mons pubis the clitoris the labia minora the body and bulbs of the vagina. They say that they take a proper pride in that which has for long been regarded as the emblem of fecundity and the reproductive force in nature.

They say that they have found inscriptions on plaster walls where vulvas have been drawn as children draw suns with multiple divergent rays. They say that it has been written that vulvas are traps vices pincers. They say that the clitoris has been compared to the prow of a boat to its stem to the comb of a shellfish. They say that vulvas have been compared to apricots pomegranates figs roses pinks peonies marguerites. They say these comparisons may be recited like a litany.

As regards the feminaries the women say for instance that they have forgotten the meaning of one of their ritual jokes. It has to do with the phrase, The bird of Venus takes flight towards evening. It is written that the lips of the vulva have been compared to the wings of a bird, hence the name of bird of Venus that has been given them. The vulva has been compared to all kinds of birds, for instance to doves, starlings, bengalis, nightingales, finches, swallows. They say that they have unearthed an old text in which the author, comparing vulvas to swallows, says that he does not know which of them moves better or has the faster wing. However, The bird of Venus takes flight towards evening, they say they do not know what this means.

The golden fleece is one of the designations that have been given to the hairs that cover the pubis. As for the quests for the golden fleece to which certain ancient myths allude, the women say they know little of these. They say that the horseshoe which is a representation of the vulva has long been considered a lucky charm. They say that the most ancient figures depicting the vulva resemble horseshoes. They say that in fact it is in such a shape that they are represented on the walls of palaeolithic grottos.

The women say that the feminaries give pride of place to the symbols of the circle, the circumference, the ring, the O, the zero, the sphere. They say that this series of symbols has provided them with a guideline to decipher a collection of legends they have found in the library and which they have called the cycle of the Grail. These are to do with the quests to recover the Grail undertaken by a number of personages. They say it is impossible to mistake the symbolism of the Round Table that dominated their meetings. They say that, at the period when the texts were compiled, the quests for the Grail were singular unique attempts to describe the zero the circle the ring the spherical cup containing the blood. They say that, to judge by what they know about their subsequent history, the quests for the Grail were not successful, that they remained of the nature of a legend.

There are also legends in which young women having stolen fire carry it in their vulvas. There is the story of her who fell asleep for a hundred years from having wounded her finger with her spindle, the spindle being cited as the symbol of the clitoris. In connection with this story the women make many jokes about the awkwardness of the one who lacked the priceless guidance of a feminary. They say laughing that she must have been the freak spoken of elsewhere, she who, in place of a little pleasure-greedy tongue, had a poisonous sting. They say they do not understand why she was called the sleeping beauty.

Snow-White runs through the forest. Her feet catch in the roots of the trees, which make her trip repeatedly. The women say that the little girls know this story by heart. Rose-Red follows behind her, impelled to cry out while running. Snow-White says she is frightened. Snow-White running says, O my ancestors, I cast myself at your holy knees. Rose-Red laughs. She laughs so much that she falls, that she finally becomes angry. Shrieking with rage, Rose-Red pursues Snow-White with a stick, threatening to knock her down if she does not stop. Snow-White whiter than the silk of her tunic drops down at the foot of a tree. Then Rose-Red red as a peony or else red as a red rose marches furiously to and fro before her, striking the ground with her stick shouting, You haven't got any, you haven't got any, until eventually Snow-White asks, What is it that I have not got? the effect of which is to immobilize Rose-Red saying, Sacred ancestors, you haven't got any. Snow-White says that she has had enough, especially as she is no longer at all frightened and seizing hold of the stick she begins to run in all directions, she is seen striking out with all her might against the tree-trunks, lashing the yielding shrubs, striking the mossy roots. At a certain point she gives a great blow with the stick to Rose-Red asleep at the foot of an oak and resembling a stout root, pink as a pink rose.

The women say that they perceive their bodies in their entirety. They say that they do not favour any of its parts on the grounds that it was formerly a forbidden object. They say that they do not want to become prisoners of their own ideology. They say that they did not garner and develop the symbols that were necessary to them at an earlier period to demonstrate their strength.

Sometimes the women may chance to talk together about the latest fable that has been told them. For example Diane Èbèle tells Aimée Dionis the fable of Koue Feï which is about a young girl who pursues the sun. She is constantly on the point of catching it. To escape her, the sun plunges into the sea. Koue Feï then starts to swim after it. Thus she traverses the entire ocean. She comes up to it just when it is leaving the water, about to escape her again. Hastily Koue Feï jumps into the sun and instals herself within it. She makes it sway from side to side in its course, several stars fall because of this. But Koue Feï has managed to sit inside the sun. Now she controls its path. She can make it follow its orbit faster or slower as she wishes. That is why, in order to have good weather when they leave for the fishing, the two little girls address themselves to Koue Feï, mistress of the sun, so that she may pause for a while above the sea.

In speaking of their genitals the women do not employ hyperboles metaphors, they do not proceed sequentially or by gradation. They do not recite long litanies, whose refrain is an unending imprecation. They do not strive to multiply the intervals so that in sum they signify a deliberate lapse. They say that all these forms denote an outworn language. They say everything must begin over again. They say that a great wind is sweeping the earth. They say that the sun is about to rise.

To Hippolyta was sent the lion of the triple night. They say that it took three nights to engender a monster with a human face capable of overcoming the queen of the Amazons. The stern fight she had using bow and arrows, his desperate resistance when she dragged it far into the mountains so as not to jeopardize the life of her kin, they say they know nothing of these, that the story has not been written. They say that until that day the women had always been defeated.

The game consists of posing a series of questions, for example, Who says, I wish it, I order it, my will must take the place of reason? Or, Who must never act according to their will? Or else, Who is only an animal the colour of flowers? There are plenty of others such as, Who must observe the three obediences and whose destiny is written in their anatomy? The answer to all the questions is the same. Then they begin to laugh ferociously slapping each other on the shoulders. Some of the women, lips parted, spit blood.

To sleep they enter the white cells. These are hollowed out in the rock-face by hundreds of thousands. Their concentric openings are tangential. The women travel there rapidly, at full speed in fact. Naked, their hair covering their shoulders, they choose their places as they climb. It is possible to lie down in the cell, which resembles an egg, a sarcophagus, an O in view of the shape of its aperture. Several can stay there together gesticulating, singing, sleeping. It is a place of privileged sanctuary though not sealed off. The isolation of one cell from another is such that, even if one bangs with all one's might against the ovoid wall, the sound of the blows is not perceived in the adjacent cell. When one is lying down in the cell it is impossible to discern the occupants of the other cells. Before the general retirement for the night confused murmurs of voices are heard, then, distinctly, the phrase, This order must be changed, forcefully repeated by thousands of voices.

The women say that men put all their pride in their tail. They mock them, they say that the men would like a long tail but that they would run away whining as soon as they stepped on it. The women guffaw and begin to imitate some ridiculous animal that has difficulty in getting about. When they have a prisoner they strip him and make him run through the streets crying, it is your rod/cane/staff/wand/peg/skewer/staff of lead. Sometimes the subject has a fine body broadened at the hips with honeyed skin and muscles not showing. Then they take him by the hand and caress him to make him forget all their bad treatment.

The women say, you are really a slave if ever there was one. Men have made what differentiates them from you the sign of domination and possession. They say, you will never be numerous enough to spit on their phallus, you will never be sufficiently determined to stop speaking their language, to burn their currency their effigies their works of art their symbols. They say, men have foreseen everything, they have christened your revolt in advance a slave revolt, a revolt against nature, they call it revolt when you want to appropriate what is theirs, the phallus. The women say, I refuse henceforward to speak this language, I refuse to mumble after them the words lack of penis lack of money lack of insignia lack of name. I refuse to pronounce the names of possession and nonpossession. They say, If I take over the world, let it be to dispossess myself of it immediately, let it be to forge new links between myself and the world.

The women say, unhappy one, men have expelled you from the world of symbols and yet they have given you names, they have called you slave, you unhappy slave. Masters, they have exercised their rights as masters. They write, of their authority to accord names, that it goes back so far that the origin of language itself may be considered an act of authority emanating from those who dominate. Thus they say that they have said, this is such or such a thing, they have attached a particular word to an object or a fact and thereby consider themselves to have appropriated it. The women say, so doing the men have bawled shouted with all their might to reduce you to silence. The women say, the language you speak poisons your glottis tongue palate lips. They say, the language you speak is made up of words that are killing you. They say, the language you speak is made up of signs that rightly speaking designate what men have appropriated. Whatever they have not laid hands on, whatever they have not pounced on like many-eyed birds of prey, does not appear in the language you speak. This is apparent precisely in the intervals that your masters have not been able to fill with their words of proprietors and possessors, this can be found in the gaps, in all that which is not a continuation of their discourse, in the zero, the O, the perfect circle that you invent to imprison them and to overthrow them.

The women address the young men in these terms, now you understand that we have been fighting as much for you as for ourselves. In this war, which was also yours, you have taken part. Today, together, let us repeat as our slogan that all trace of violence must disappear from this earth, then the sun will be honey-coloured and music good to hear. The young men applaud and shout with all their might. They have brought their arms. The women bury them at the same time as their own saying, let there be erased from human memory the longest most murderous war it has ever known, the last possible war in history. They wish the survivors, both male and female, love strength youth, so that they may form a lasting alliance that no future dispute can compromise. One of the women begins to sing, Like unto ourselves/men who open their mouths to speak/a thousand thanks to those who have understood our language/and not having found it excessive/have joined with us to transform the world.

# GARP

## John Irving

He spent his day writing (or trying to write), running, and cooking. He got up early and fixed breakfast for himself and the children; nobody was home for lunch and Garp never ate that meal; he fixed dinner for his family every night. It was a ritual he loved, but the ambition of his cooking was controlled by how good a day he'd had writing, and how good a run he'd had. If the writing went poorly, he took it out on himself with a long, hard run; or, sometimes, a bad day with his writing would exhaust him so much that he could barely run a mile; then he tried to save the day with a splendid meal.

Helen could never tell what sort of day Garp had experienced by what he cooked for them; something special might mean a celebration, or it might mean that the food was the *only* thing that had gone well, that the cooking was the only labor keeping Garp from despair. "If you are careful," Garp wrote, "if you use good ingredients, and you don't take any shortcuts, then you can usually cook something very good. Sometimes it is the only worthwhile product you can salvage from a day: what you make to eat. With writing, I find, you can have all the right ingredients, give plenty of time and care, and still get nothing. Also true of love. Cooking, therefore, can keep a person who tries hard sane."

He went into the house and looked for a pair of shoes. About the only shoes he owned were running shoes—many pairs. They were in different phases of being broken in. Garp and his children wore clean but rumpled clothes; Helen was a smart dresser, and although Garp did her laundry, he refused to iron anything. Helen did her own ironing, and an occasional shirt for Garp; ironing was the only task of conventional housewifery that Garp rejected. The cooking, the kids, the basic laundry, the cleaning up—he did them. The cooking, expertly; the cleaning up, a little compulsively. He swore at errant clothes, dishes, and toys, but he left nothing lie; he was a maniac for picking things up. Some mornings, before he sat down to write, he raced over the house with a vacuum cleaner, or he cleaned the oven. The house never looked untidy, was never dirty, but there was always a certain haste to the neatness of it. Garp threw a lot of things away and the house was always missing things. For months at a time he would allow most of the light bulbs to burn out, unreplaced, until Helen would realize that they were living in almost total darkness, huddled around the two lamps that worked. Or when he remembered the lights, he forgot the soap and the toothpaste.

Helen brought certain touches to the house, too, but Garp took no responsibilities for these: plants, for example; either Helen remembered them, or they died. When Garp saw that one appeared to be drooping, or was the slightest bit pale, he would whisk it out of the house and into the trash. Days later, Helen might ask, "Where is the red arronzo?"

"That foul thing," Garp would remark. "It had some disease. I saw worms on it. I caught it dropping its little spines all over the floor."

Thus Garp functioned at housekeeping.

In the house Garp found his yellow running shoes and put them on. He put the phone book away in a cabinet where he kept the heavy cooking gear (he stashed phone books all over the house—then would tear the house down to find the one he wanted). He put some olive oil in a cast-iron skillet; he chopped an onion while he waited for the oil to get hot. It was late to be starting supper; he hadn't even gone shopping. A standard tomato sauce, a little pasta, a fresh green salad, a loaf of his good bread. That way he could go to the market after he started the sauce and he'd only need to shop for greens. He hurried the chopping (now some fresh basil) but it was important not to throw anything into the skillet until the oil was just right, very hot but not smoking. There are some things about cooking, like writing, that you don't hurry, Garp knew, and he never hurried them.

. . .

Garp drove a wooden spoon deep into his tomato sauce. He flinched as some fool took the corner by the house with a roaring downshift and a squeal of tires that cut through Garp with the sound of a struck cat. He looked instinctively for Walt, who was right there—safe in the kitchen.

Helen said, "Where's Duncan?" She moved to the door but Garp cut in front of her.

"Duncan went to Ralph's," he said; he was not worried, *this* time, that the speeding car meant Duncan had been hit, but it was Garp's habit to chase down speeding cars. He had properly bullied every fast driver in the neighborhood. The streets around Garp's house were cut in squares bordered every block by stop signs; Garp could usually catch up to a car, on foot, provided that the car obeyed the stop signs.

He raced down the street after the sound of the car. Sometimes, if the car was going really fast, Garp would need three or four stop signs to catch up to it. Once he sprinted five blocks and was so out of breath when he caught up to the offending car that the driver was sure there'd been a murder in the neighborhood and Garp was either trying to report it or had done it himself.

Most drivers were impressed with Garp, and even if they swore about him later, they were polite and apologetic to his face, assuring him they would not speed in the neighborhood again. It was clear to them that Garp was in good physical shape. Most of them were high school kids who were easily embarrassed—caught hot-rodding around with their girl friends or leaving little smoking rubber stains in front of their girl friends' houses. Garp was not such a fool as to imagine that he changed their ways; all he hoped to do was make them speed somewhere else.

. . .

When Walt caught colds, Garp slept badly. It was as if he were trying to breathe for the boy, and for himself. Garp would get up in the night to kiss and nuzzle the child; anyone seeing Garp would have thought that he could make Walt's cold go away by catching it himself.

"Oh, God," Helen said. "It's just a cold. Duncan had colds all winter when he was five." Nearing eleven, Duncan seemed to have outgrown colds; but Walt, at five, was fully in the throes of cold after cold—or it was one long cold that went away and came back. By the March mud season, Walt's resistance struck Garp as altogether gone; the child hacked himself and Garp awake each night with a wet, wrenching cough. Garp sometimes fell asleep listening to Walt's chest, and he would wake up, frightened, when he could no longer hear the thump of the boy's heart; but the child had merely pushed his father's heavy head off his chest so that he could roll over and sleep more comfortably.

Both the doctor and Helen told Garp, "It's just a cough."

. . .

In the house he gave Walt a hot bath, slipping into the tub with him—an excuse, which he often took, to wrestle with that little body. Duncan was too big for Garp to fit in the tub with him anymore.

"What's for supper?" Duncan called upstairs.

Garp realized he had forgotten supper.

"I forgot supper," Garp called.

"You *forgot?*" Walt asked him, but Garp dunked Walt in the tub, and tickled him, and Walt fought back and forgot about the issue.

"You forgot *supper?*" Duncan hollered from downstairs.

Garp decided he was not going to get out of the tub. He kept adding more hot water; the steam was good for Walt's lungs, he believed. He would try to keep the child in the tub with him as long as Walt was content to play.

They were still in the bath together when Helen got home.

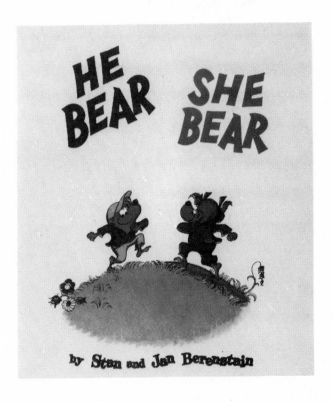

I see her.
She sees me.

We see that we
are he and she.

Every single
bear we see
has lots of things
to do and be.

Every single
bear we see
is a he bear
or a she.

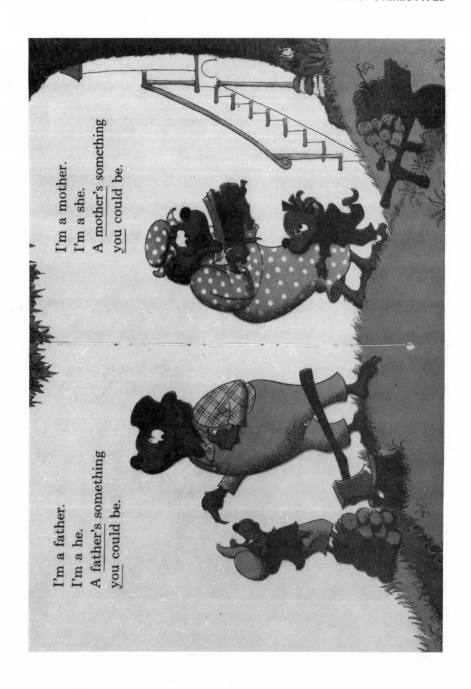

But there are
other things to be.
Come on, He Bear,
follow me!

Dad's a he.
Mom's a she.

Those are things
that we could be
just because
we're he and she.

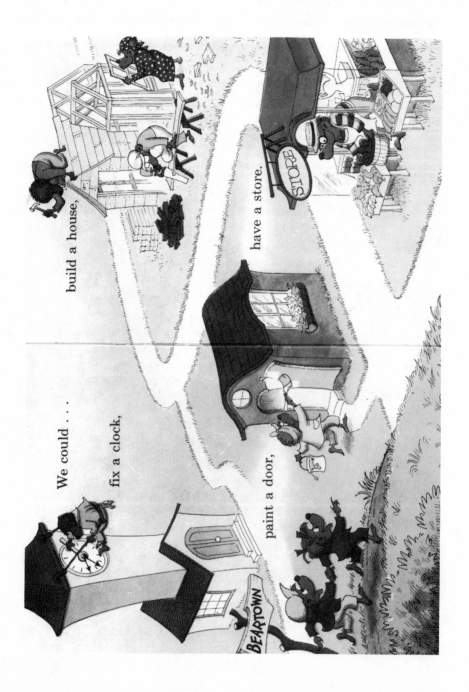

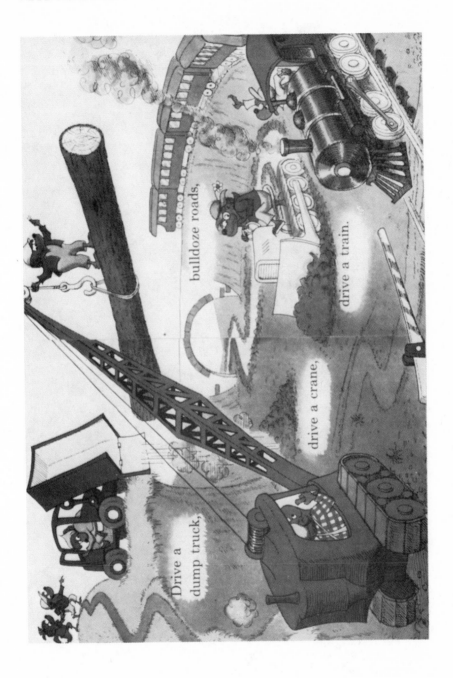

Drive a
dump truck,

drive a crane,

bulldoze roads,

drive a train.

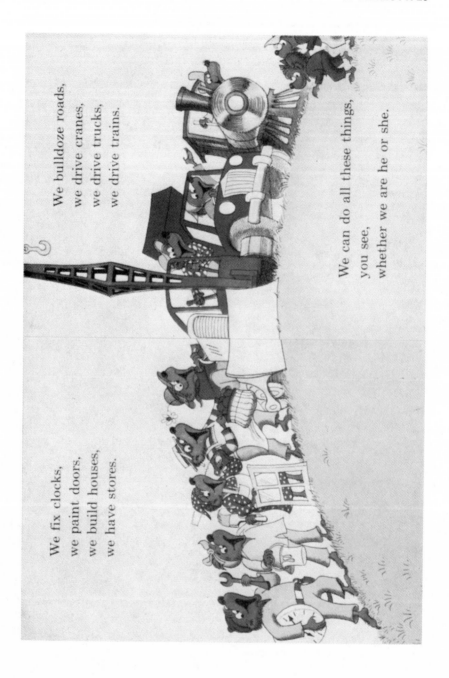

We fix clocks,
we paint doors,
we build houses,
we have stores.

We bulldoze roads,
we drive cranes,
we drive trucks,
we drive trains.

We can do all these things,
you see,
whether we are he or she.

We climb ladders
to put out fires.

That's Officer Marguerite.
She tells us when
to cross the street.

We climb ladders
to fix the wires.

You could . . .

Be a doctor—
make folks well.

Teach kids how
to add and spell.

Knit a sock,

sew a dress,

paint a picture—

what a mess!

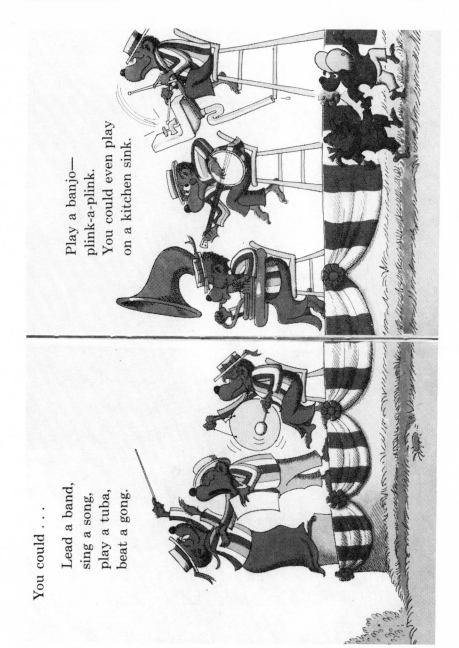

You could . . .

Lead a band,
sing a song,
play a tuba,
beat a gong.

Play a banjo—
plink-a-plink.
You could even play
on a kitchen sink.

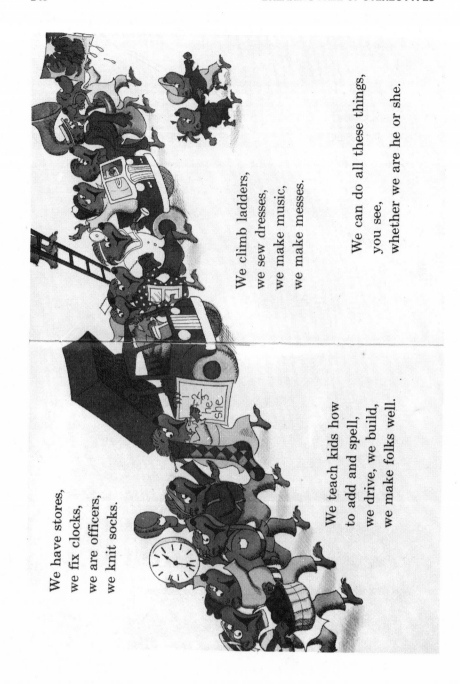

We climb ladders,
we sew dresses,
we make music,
we make messes.

We can do all these things,
you see,
whether we are he or she.

We have stores,
we fix clocks,
we are officers,
we knit socks.

We teach kids how
to add and spell,
we drive, we build,
we make folks well.

I may build bridges,

I may climb poles,

I may race cars,

I may dig holes.

What will we do,
you and I?

I'll tell you what
I'm going to try . . .

I could study the fish who live in the sea.

I could be a magician,

I could go on TV,

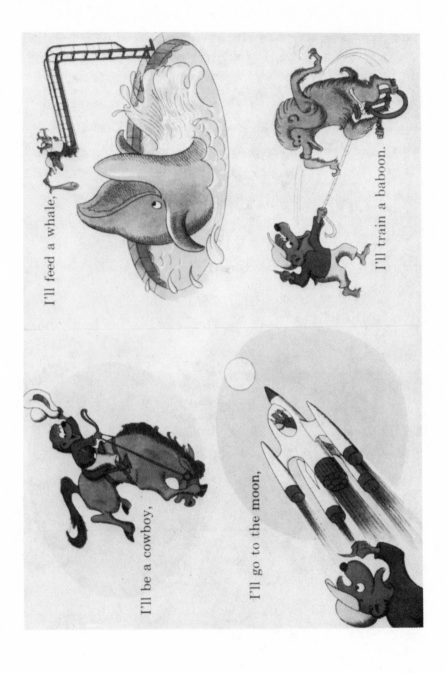

I'll feed a whale,

I'll train a baboon.

I'll be a cowboy,

I'll go to the moon,

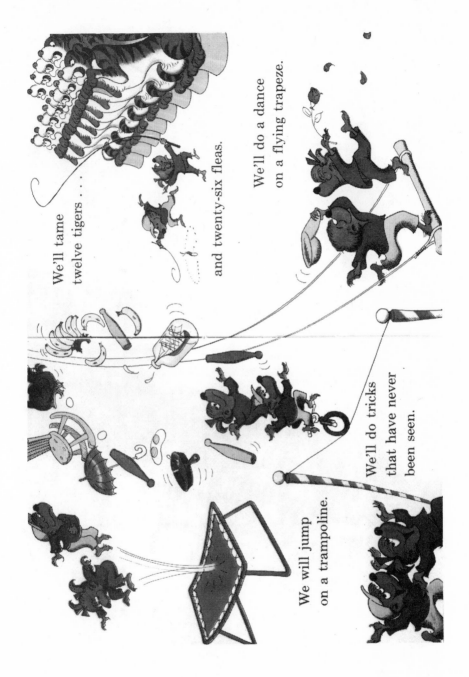

We'll tame twelve tigers . . .

and twenty-six fleas.

We'll do a dance on a flying trapeze.

We'll do tricks that have never been seen.

We will jump on a trampoline.

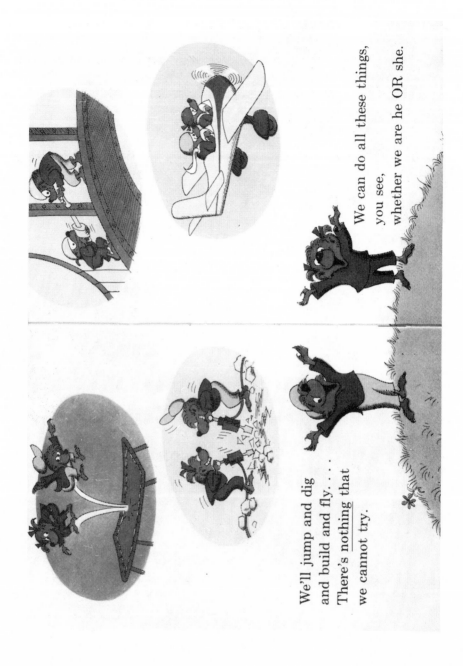

We can do all these things,
you see,
whether we are he OR she.

We'll jump and dig
and build and fly. . . .
There's nothing that
we cannot try.

So many things
to be and do,
He Bear, She Bear,
me . . . and you.

# ATALANTA

## Edith Hamilton

Sometimes there are said to have been two heroines of that name. Certainly two men, Iasus and Schoenius, are each called the father of Atalanta, but then it often happens in old stories that different names are given to unimportant persons. If there were two Atalantas it is certainly remarkable that both wanted to sail on the *Argo*, both took part in the Calydonian boar hunt, both married a man who beat them in a foot race, and both were ultimately changed into lionesses. Since the story of each is practically the same as that of the other it is simpler to take it for granted that there was only one. Indeed it would seem passing the bounds of the probable even in mythological stories to suppose that there were two maidens living at the same time who loved adventure as much as the most dauntless hero, and who could outshoot and outrun and outwrestle, too, the men of one of the two great ages of heroism.

Atalanta's father, whatever his name was, when a daughter and not a son was born to him, was, of course, bitterly disappointed. He decided that she was not worth bringing up and had the tiny creature left on a wild mountainside to die of cold and hunger. But, as so often happens in stories, animals proved kinder than humans. A she-bear took charge of her, nursed her and kept her warm, and the baby grew up thus into an active, daring little girl. Kind hunters then found her and took her to live with them. She became in the end more than their equal in all the arduous feats of a hunter's life. Once two Centaurs, swifter and stronger by far than any mortal, caught sight of her when she was alone and pursued her. She did not run from them; that would have been folly. She stood still and fitted an arrow to her bow and shot. A second arrow followed. Both Centaurs fell, mortally wounded.

Then came the famous hunt of the Calydonian boar. This was a terrible creature sent to ravage the country of Calydon by Artemis in order to punish the King, Oeneus, because he forgot her when he was sacrificing the first fruits to the gods at the harvest-time. The brute devastated the land, destroyed the cattle, killed the men who tried to kill it. Finally Oeneus called for help upon the bravest men of Greece, and a splendid band of young heroes assembled, many of whom sailed later on the *Argo*. With them came as a matter of course Atalanta, "the pride of the woods of Arcady." We have a description of how she looked when she walked in on that masculine gathering: "A shining buckle clasped her robe at the neck; her hair was simply dressed, caught up in a knot behind. An ivory quiver hung upon her left shoulder and in her hand was a bow. Thus was she attired. As for her face, it seemed too maidenly to be that of a boy, and too boyish to be that of a maiden." To one man there, however, she looked lovelier and more desirable than any maiden he had ever seen. Oeneus' son, Meleager, fell in love with her at first sight. But, we may be sure, Atalanta treated him as a good comrade, not as a possible lover. She had no liking for men except as companions in the hunt and she was determined never to marry.

Some of the heroes resented her presence and felt it beneath them to go hunting with a woman, but Meleager insisted and they finally gave in to him. It proved well for them that they did, because when they surrounded the boar, the brute rushed upon them so swiftly that it killed two men before the others could come to their help, and, what was equally ominous, a third man fell pierced by a misdirected javelin. In this confusion of dying men and wildly flying weapons Atalanta kept her head and wounded the boar. Her arrow was the first to strike it. Meleager then rushed on the wounded creature and stabbed it to the heart. Technically speaking it was he who killed it, but the honors of the hunt went to Atalanta and Meleager insisted that they should give her the skin.

Strangely enough this was the cause of his own death. When he was just a week old the Fates had appeared to his mother, Althea, and thrown a log of wood into the fire burning in her chamber. Then spinning as they ever did, twirling the distaff and twisting the thread of destiny, they sang,

> *To you, O new-born child, we grant a gift,*
> *To live until this wood turns into ash.*

Althea snatched the brand from the fire, quenched the flame, and hid it in a chest. Her brothers were among those who went to hunt the boar. They felt themselves insulted and were furiously angry at having the prize go to a girl—as, no doubt, was the case with others, but they were Meleager's uncles and did not need to stand on any ceremony with him. They declared that Atalanta should not have the skin and told Meleager he had no more right to give it away than anyone else had. Whereupon Meleager killed them both, taking them completely off their guard.

This news was brought to Althea. Her beloved brothers had been slain by her son because he had made a fool of himself over a shameless hussy who went hunting with men. A passion of rage took possession of her. She rushed to the chest for the brand and threw it into the fire. As it blazed up, Meleager fell to the ground dying, and by the time it was consumed his spirit had slipped away from his body. It is said that Althea, horror-stricken at what she had done, hanged herself. So the Calydonian boar hunt ended in tragedy.

To Atalanta, however, it was only the beginning of her adventures. Some say that she sailed with the Argonauts; others that Jason persuaded her not to do so. She is never mentioned in the story of their exploits and she was certainly not one to hold back when deeds of daring were to be done, so that it seems probable that she did not go. The next time we hear of her is after the Argonauts returned, when Medea had killed Jason's uncle Pelias under the pretext of restoring him to youth. At the funeral games held in his honor Atalanta appeared among the contestants, and in the wrestling match conquered the young man who was to be the father of Achilles, the great hero Peleus.

It was after this achievement that she discovered who her parents were and went to live with them, her father apparently being reconciled to having a daughter who really seemed almost if not quite as good as a son. It seems odd that a number of men wanted to marry her because she could hunt and shoot and wrestle, but it was so; she had a great many suitors. As a way of disposing of them easily and agreeably she declared that she would marry whoever could beat her in a foot race, knowing well that there was no such man alive. She had a delightful time. Fleet-footed young men were always arriving to race with her and she always outran them.

But at last one came who used his head as well as his heels. He knew he was not as good a runner as she, but he had a plan. By the favor of Aphrodite, always on the lookout to subdue wild young maidens who despised love, this ingenious young man, whose name was either Mela-nion (Milanion) or Hippomenes, got possession of three wondrous apples, all of pure gold, beautiful as those that grew in the garden of the Hes-perides. No one alive could see them and not want them.

On the race course as Atalanta—poised for the starting signal, and a hundredfold more lovely disrobed than with her garments on—looked fiercely around her, wonder at her beauty took hold of all who saw her, but most of all the man who was waiting to run against her. He kept his head, however, and held fast to his golden apples. They started, she flying swift as an arrow, her hair tossed back over her white shoulders, a rosy flush tinging her fair body. She was outstripping him when he rolled one of the apples directly in front of her. It needed but a moment for her to stoop and pick the lovely thing up, but that brief pause brought him abreast of her. A moment more and he threw the second, this time a little to the side. She had to swerve to reach it and he got ahead of her. Almost at once, however, she had caught up with him and the goal was now very near. But then the third golden sphere flashed across her path and rolled far into the grass beside the course. She saw the gleam through the green, she could not resist it. As she picked the apple up, her lover panting and almost winded touched the goal. She was his. Her free days alone in the forest and her athletic victories were over.

The two are said to have been turned into lions because of some affront offered either to Zeus or to Aphrodite. But before that Atalanta had borne a son, Parthenopaeus, who was one of the Seven against Thebes.

# ATALANTA

Betty Miles

Once upon a time, not long ago, there lived a princess named Atalanta, who could run as fast as the wind.

She was so bright, and so clever, and could build things and fix things so wonderfully, that many young men wished to marry her.

"What shall I do?" said Atalanta's father, who was a powerful king. "So many young men want to marry you, and I don't know how to choose."

"You don't have to choose, Father," Atalanta said. "I will choose. And I'm not sure that I will choose to marry anyone at all."

"Of course you will," said the king. "Everybody gets married. It is what people do."

"But," Atalanta told him, with a toss of her head, "I intend to go out and see the world. When I come home, perhaps I will marry and perhaps I will not."

The king did not like this at all. He was a very ordinary king; that is, he was powerful and used to having his own way. So he did not answer Atalanta, but simply told her, "I have decided how to choose the young man you will marry. I will hold a great race and the winner—the swiftest, fleetest young man of all—will win the right to marry you."

Now Atalanta was a clever girl as well as a swift runner. She saw that she might win both the argument and the race—provided that she herself could run in the race, too. "Very well," she said. "But you must let me race along with the others. If I am not the winner, I will accept the wishes of the young man who is."

The king agreed to this. He was pleased; he would have his way, marry off his daughter, and enjoy a fine day of racing as well. So he directed his messengers to travel throughout the kingdom announcing the race with its wonderful prize: the chance to marry the bright Atalanta.

As the day of the race drew near, flags were raised in the streets of the town, and banners were hung near the grassy field where the race would be run. Baskets of ripe plums and peaches, wheels of cheese, ropes of sausages and onions, and loaves of crusty bread were gathered for the crowds.

Meanwhile, Atalanta herself was preparing for the race. Each day at dawn, dressed in soft green trousers and a shirt of yellow silk, she went to the field in secret and ran across it—slowly at first, then faster and faster, until she could run the course more quickly than anyone had ever run it before.

As the day of the race grew nearer, young men began to crowd into the town. Each was sure he could win the prize, except for one; that was Young

John, who lived in the town. He saw Atalanta day by day as she bought nails and wood to make a pigeon house, or chose parts for her telescope, or laughed with her friends. Young John saw the princess only from a distance, but near enough to know how bright and clever she was. He wished very much to race with her, to win, and to earn the right to talk with her and become her friend.

"For surely," he said to himself, "it is not right for Atalanta's father to give her away to the winner of the race. Atalanta herself must choose the person she wants to marry, or whether she wishes to marry at all. Still, if I could only win the race, I would be free to speak to her, and to ask for her friendship."

Each evening, after his studies of the stars and the seas, Young John went to the field in secret and practiced running across it. Night after night, he ran fast as the wind across the twilight field, until he could cross it more quickly than anyone had ever crossed it before.

At last, the day of the race arrived.

Trumpets sounded in the early morning, and the young men gathered at the edge of the field, along with Atalanta herself, the prize they sought. The king and his friends sat in soft chairs, and the townspeople stood along the course.

The king arose to address them all. "Good day," he said to the crowds. "Good luck," he said to the young men. To Atalanta he said, "Good-bye. I must tell you farewell, for tomorrow you will be married."

"I am not so sure of that, Father," Atalanta answered. She was dressed for the race in trousers of crimson and a shirt of silk as blue as the sky, and she laughed as she looked up and down the line of young men.

"Not one of them," she said to herself, "can win the race, for I will run fast as the wind and leave them all behind."

And now a bugle sounded, a flag was dropped, and the runners were off!

The crowds cheered as the young men and Atalanta began to race the field. At first they ran as a group, but Atalanta soon pulled ahead, with three of the young men close after her. As they neared the halfway point, one young man put on a great burst of speed and seemed to pull ahead for an instant, but then he gasped and fell back. Atalanta shot on.

Soon another young man, tense with the effort, drew near to Atalanta. He reached out as though to touch her sleeve, stumbled for an instant, and lost speed. Atalanta smiled as she ran on. I have almost won, she thought.

But then another young man came near. This was Young John, running like the wind, as steadily and as swiftly as Atalanta herself. Atalanta felt his closeness, and in a sudden burst she dashed ahead.

Young John might have given up at this, but he never stopped running. Nothing at all, thought he, will keep me from winning the chance to speak with Atalanta. And on he ran, swift as the wind, until he ran as her equal, side by side with her, toward the golden ribbon that marked the race's end. Atalanta raced even faster to pull ahead, but Young John was a strong match for her. Smiling with the pleasure of the race, Atalanta and Young John reached the finish line together, and together they broke through the golden ribbon.

Trumpets blew. The crowd shouted and leaped about. The king rose. "Who is that young man?" he asked.

"It is Young John from the town," the people told him.

"Very well. Young John," said the king, as John and Atalanta stood before him, exhausted and jubilant from their efforts. "You have not won the race, but you have come closer to winning than any man here. And so I give you the prize that was promised—the right to marry my daughter."

Young John smiled at Atalanta, and she smiled back. "Thank you, sir," said John to the king, "but I could not possibly marry your daughter unless she wished to marry me. I have run this race for the chance to talk with Atalanta, and, if she is willing, I am ready to claim my prize."

Atalanta laughed with pleasure. "And I," she said to John, "could not possibly marry before I have seen the world. But I would like nothing better than to spend the afternoon with you."

Then the two of them sat and talked on the grassy field, as the crowds went away. They ate bread and cheese and purple plums. Atalanta told John about her telescopes and her pigeons, and John told Atalanta about his globes and his studies of geography. At the end of the day, they were friends.

On the next day, John sailed off to discover new lands. And Atalanta set off to visit the great cities.

By this time, each of them has had wonderful adventures, and seen marvelous sights. Perhaps some day they will be married, and perhaps they will not. In any case, they are friends. And it is certain that they are both living happily ever after.

# MODESTY SAVES WILLIE

Peter O'Donnell

Fraser adjusted his spectacles to the angle which he knew would produce the effect of prim stupidity he favored most. Running a finger down his nose, he stared obtusely at the open dossier in his hands.

"I would suppose, sir," he said cautiously, "that Modesty Blaise might be a person awfully difficult for us—er—actually to get." He blinked towards the big, grey-haired man who stood by the window, looking down at the night traffic hurrying along Whitehall.

"For a moment," Tarrant said, turning from the window, "I hoped you might split that infinitive, Fraser."

"I'm sorry, Sir Gerald." Fraser registered contrition. "Another time, perhaps."

Tarrant moved to the big desk across one corner of the room. Settling in his chair, he opened a polished wooden box, took out a cigar, and addressed himself to lighting it.

"A remarkable woman, Fraser," he said, watching the heavy smoke coiling up in the warm fluorescent light. "If you had been a child, on your own, in a Middle East D.P. camp in '45, do you think you could have managed to retire at twenty-six with well over half a million sterling? A small female child, of course."

Fraser quickly reviewed his selection of expressions, and chose the slightly offended one with pursed lips. Tarrant studied the look, then nodded his approval.

"The point is," he went on, "that we're hardly likely to get her for money. Not on the Civil Service scale of two thousand a year, anyway."

Fraser lifted a hand with middle finger delicately bent, and scratched minutely at the scalp beneath his thinning hair. "Some of our people have a vocation for the work," he said diffidently.

"Yes. She seems to have a feeling for this country." Tarrant frowned at his cigar. "After all, she chose to settle here. But I don't feel that a clarion call to service is the way to get her, either."

"Blackmail?" Fraser tried to combine furtiveness, daring and distaste in one expression. He fell short, and received a sympathetic wag of the head from Tarrant.

"No . . . not blackmail. I don't think we really have the levers for it, Fraser. And we need much more than reluctant cooperation."

"I wonder if . . . ?" Fraser let the sentence hang while he carefully selected a buff half-sheet from the dossier and peered at it unnecessarily for several seconds. "I wonder if this might do?"

Tarrant took the slip and read the short message through twice. "The hesitant but hopeful look," he thought, and looked up at Fraser to find that he was right.

Briefly he wondered why a man with Jack Fraser's field record should take such pains to project himself as an ineffectual dolt, now that he was safely behind a desk. Sheer habit, probably. The pose had served him handsomely in the past and might be hard to put aside now. Tarrant had no objection to the game. The two men were old friends and Fraser could speak with earthy bluntness on the brief occasions when he laid the pose aside. In any case it was a harmless game, sometimes useful and frequently amusing.

"The message only came up from Cipher an hour ago," Fraser said with a vague, apologetic gesture. "They wouldn't attach any importance to it, of course. Just part of a general routine report. But it did occur to me that perhaps . . . ?"

"I think it might do very well indeed." Tarrant passed the half-sheet back and glanced at his watch. "Ten o'clock. Do you think she might see us tonight?"

"No time like the present." Fraser rolled the phrase sententiously, not quite able to hide his delight at the opportunity. "Shall I try her number, sir?"

There was a pleasant warmth in the night air as Fraser drove his old Bentley down Constitution Hill and swung with bland belligerence through the traffic at Hyde Park Corner. Rightly drawing an outraged cry from a taxi-driver, he responded with an apologetic simper, immediately followed by a bellow of such horrific imagination that Tarrant was hard put to conceal his admiration.

"Your conversation with Modesty Blaise was very brief," Tarrant said as they drove through the park. "Did she ask no questions?"

"None, Sir Gerald." Fraser hunched over the wheel and blinked worriedly through the windscreen. "When I asked if you might call she just said: 'Yes. Now if you wish.' She seemed to know your name."

"She does. On two occasions she sent Willie Garvin over from Tangier to sell me rather valuable items of information. Some Nasser stuff, and a very useful thing on the Russian organisation in The Lebanon."

"What impression did you have of Garvin, sir?"

"A rough diamond, but remarkably well polished in parts. His speech is Bethnal Green—though I believe his French and Arabic are very good. His manners are impeccable; I lunched him at Rand's Club to over-awe him, but he might have been born to it. His bargaining was cheerful but ruthless. And he had the relaxed superiority of . . . well, of a plenipotentiary sent by a reigning empress."

"Not of a consort?" Fraser asked diffidently.

"Definitely not that. As courtier to a queen. No more."

"A pity, really." Fraser sighed, and shouldered an Austin Mini aside. "If that *had* been the relationship, it might have made your position stronger. I mean, now that Garvin's in trouble."

"Yes. But on the other hand . . . ?" Tarrant made it a question inviting completion.

"That's true." Fraser nodded solemnly several times. "With a consort relationship, Garvin probably wouldn't be in trouble. And you'd have no position at all, sir."

The tall block looking over the park had been designed by a disciple of Le Corbusier and completed little more than a year ago, a triumph of simple elegance. Below ground-level lay a private swimming-pool, squash courts and a gymnasium, for use of the residents and their guests. The facade was of rubbed stone, the roof-line broken by receding planes with balconies. At the summit, the penthouse faced south and was bounded on two sides by a covered terrace of concrete flags with grass-grown joints.

The penthouse had sold for seventy thousand pounds.

At the desk in the large foyer a uniformed commissionaire inclined his head politely in response to Tarrant's enquiry.

"Yes, sir. Miss Blaise rang down that she was expecting you."

Beyond a field of soft maroon carpeting stood the solid doors of a private lift. The commissionaire touched a button and they slid quietly open.

"Yes, here we are. She's sent the lift down for you. If you gentlemen would step in, please? It'll take you direct to the top—doesn't serve any other floors."

"Thank you." Tarrant pressed the button and the doors slid shut. The lift started with slow courtesy, then accelerated smoothly. At the top, the doors slid back and the two men stepped out.

They were in a broad open foyer floored with ceramic tiles in charcoal-grey. Beyond lay a large room extending some fifty feet to the far wall, where a floor-to-ceiling window looked out over the park. The room was contiguous with the foyer but on a lower level, three steps down from a slender wrought-iron balustrade which edged the foyer across the width of the room.

Throughout there was the imprint of a strong personality, and the immediate impression was of warmth and simplicity. But then the eye began to find strange enigmas in that simplicity, a curious mingling of styles which should have clashed but astonishingly blended.

The foyer was furnished with two chairs, Louis XVI bergère, and a drum table. To one side was an alcove for coats, behind a maize velvet curtain. The floor of the room proper was set with plain octagonal tiles, dull ivory in colour. On it were scattered seven or eight rugs of varying size, glowing with the rich colours of Isfahan.

The middle of one wall was broken by a run of masonry in natural stone, with a hole-in-the-wall fireplace. The remaining walls were of golden cedar strip. They bore half a dozen pictures and a François Boucher tapestry. Of the pictures, Tarrant recognised a Miro, a Braque still life, and a Modigliani. The others were unknown to him.

All doors leading from the room, and the two leading off from the foyer, were of teak veneer. They extended from floor to ceiling, and were sliding doors.

In one corner of the room, broad curving shelves held a scattering of ornaments—a porcelain-mounted lion clock after Caffieri, backed by a pair of Sèvres plates; a jade dragon bowl of the Chia Ch'ing period, and a silver vinaigrette; three superb ivories, a Clodion statuette, and an antique mahogany knife-urn.

The lighting was superb, and the larger pieces of furniture were in plain colours against the rich patterns of the rugs. Tarrant noted the deep-buttoned chesterfield in black hide, the two Barcelona chairs in mellow tan, and a long, low table tiled in white and gold.

Built-in shelves along part of one wall held books and records, with the satisfactory, slightly untidy look of usage. There was a hi-fi towards the end of the shelves, partly hidden by a Coromandel screen.

But it was to the rugs that Tarrant's eyes kept returning. They touched him with the same pleasurable melancholy as certain music, *Les Préludes* of Liszt, perhaps.

Beside him he heard a long, reverent sigh from his companion.

"Hannibal's piles," breathed Fraser, who found relief from emotion in coarseness. "What a bloody cracker."

Together they moved to the steps dividing the low wrought-iron balustrade. Fraser, himself again now, hugged his briefcase awkwardly and darted suspicious glances about him. From an open doorway on the right of the room there came the faint greenish glow of daylight fluorescent, and the soft hum of a small machine.

Tarrant put down his bowler hat and umbrella on a chair.

"I think you'd better cough, Fraser," he suggested.

"Don't trouble yourself, Mr. Fraser." The voice held a mellow timbre with a slight foreign inflexion. The intonation was cool but not unfriendly. She stood in the open doorway with the fluorescent light behind her. The face was smooth and calm, with high cheekbones under dark, contemplative eyes. She would be five foot six, Tarrant thought, but with the black hair drawn up into a chignon on the crown of her head she appeared taller.

Her skin held a soft, matt tan that would have made a fortune for any man who could get it into a bottle. Her mouth baffled Tarrant. Studied in isolation it was a touch too wide, but in the totality of her features a smaller mouth would have been wrong. Her neck, he decided, though magnificent, was definitely too long . . . but then again that wonderful poise of the head would have been marred by a shorter neck. Her legs—

No, dammit, they weren't too long. He wasn't going to fall into the same trap again. This girl was made to be looked at as a whole—and as often as possible, for preference. He was surprised to find that he had an urgent wish to see her smile.

She wore a cling sweater in winter-white with a polo neck. The sleeves were pushed carelessly back almost to her elbows. It was tucked into a wine-red skirt of fine tweed, with pleats at each side and pocket flaps. The skirt was held by a broad black leather belt with a double ring, and fell just to the middle of the knee. Her legs, of that same matt tan, were bare. She wore dull gold open sandals with set-back heels, and the touch of coral red on her toenails matched her lips.

"Miss Blaise. . . ." Tarrant moved down the steps, extending his hand. "I'm Tarrant. And may I introduce my colleague, John Fraser."

Her hand was cool, and he felt the play of wiry sinews in the long fingers. She turned a little to greet Fraser, and Tarrant saw her eyes strip the man of his obtuseness, label him "not-to-be-underestimated," and file him away in her mind.

"Forgive us for calling so late, Miss Blaise." Tarrant let no more than a hint of apology colour his words. "Are we disturbing you?"

"Not very much. I'm interested to see you." The directness of the answer disposed of formality. "But there's something I'd like to get finished. It will only take three or four minutes—please come in."

She turned back into the room, and they followed. Tarrant had been in a lapidary's workshop before, but had never seen one as tidy as this. There were three separate benches, each with a tall stool. One bench held a bed of three horizontal wheels connected to a motor at the end. The lead wheel was some distance from the other two, and behind it stood a jar of carborundum. There was a tin of finest emery flour behind the wooden wheel, and a small jar of putty powder behind the felt wheel.

On the second bench stood a small, watchmaker's lathe fitted with a slitting-saw—a four-inch vertical disc of phosphor-bronze, its edge impregnated with diamond dust.

Modesty Blaise seated herself at the third bench, and gestured for the men to take the other two stools. She picked up a dopstick with a sapphire cemented on its broad head. At a long glance, Tarrant estimated the gem at forty carats. It had been cut en cabochon, and now she was working on it with a point carver. She switched on, and the running spindle began to turn.

Her face grew absorbed. Holding the dopstick in two hands, the butts of her palms resting on the angle plate, she slid the gem towards the cutting bit.

Tarrant looked about him. A large wall-safe stood open. Several drawers of varying sizes had been taken from a rack in the safe and lay on the bench at his elbow. One drawer was filled with a dozen or more gems in the rough—diamonds and rubies, emeralds and sapphires. Another held smaller gems, cut, faceted and polished.

Then, in a larger drawer, he saw the carved semi-precious stones, and caught his breath. There were tiny jars and bottles carved from jade and agate, a satanic head in gold sheen obsidian, and a rose in pink alabaster. He saw an eight-armed goddess in white chalcedony, and a huge flat oval of intricately chased jet.

For three minutes there was no sound in the room except for the whine of the motor. Fraser, his mask forgotten, watched intently.

Modesty Blaise switched off the motor and stood up. She screwed a jeweller's glass into one eye and studied the sapphire for ten seconds, then lifted her head, allowing the glass to drop into her hand.

"May I see it, please?" Tarrant asked with a hint of genuine diffidence.

"Of course. There's still some polishing to be done." She passed him the glass and the dopstick.

The head of a girl was cameo-sculpted on the sapphire in semi-profile, long hair drawn back, shoulders bare. Incredibly, the tiny face was alive. Tarrant tried to see how it had been achieved by those simple outlines and hollows, but it was beyond analysis. In silence he passed the dopstick and glass to Fraser, then looked at Modesty Blaise.

"This is your hobby, carving gemstones?" he asked.

"Yes." She met his eyes. "I don't handle them professionally any more." Her face was suddenly illumined by a surge of silent laughter. Here was the smile he had wanted to see. It was rich with delight, completely without restraint, and holding a gamine touch of mischief. Tarrant found himself grinning back at her.

"Not professionally," he said, and inclined his head in agreement. "We know you're retired, Miss Blaise. And naturally you need a hobby to occupy you."

Her smile had gone now, leaving only a memory of it in the eyes. With Tarrant's last words the memory vanished and she looked at him thoughtfully.

"Of course." Her voice was neutral. "Now, what will you drink?"

They followed her into the big room, and she moved to a small bar, jutting from an alcove, which held shelves of bottles and glass.

"Please sit down. Sir Gerald?"

"A small brandy, please."

"And you, Mr. Fraser?"

"Oh—er . . ." Fraser drew a finger down his nose. "A large one, please," he said with nervous bravado, then shrank back into his chair.

Fumbling busily, he took two folders from his briefcase and rested them on his lap.

Tarrant watched with approval the economy of movement she brought to the business of fixing drinks. The brandies were placed on a small table between the two men. She poured a glass of red wine for herself, a vin ordinaire he noticed, then settled at one end of the chesterfield and drew her feet up.

"It's interesting to meet you, Sir Gerald," she said, lifting the glass slightly in acknowledgment. "I used to have a dossier on you before I retired."

"Oh, I'm a dull old stick, Miss Blaise." He sipped the brandy, and felt the Midas touch that turned the throat to gold. "You have a much more fascinating biography."

"How much do you know of it?"

"Ah. Fraser would be terribly upset if I claimed that we *knew* anything. Most of it is a series of guesses and deductions."

"May I hear them?"

"Of course."

Tarrant nodded to Fraser, who opened a folder and frowned at the typescript within.

"Well—er—briefly, Miss Blaise," he said uneasily, "we first have you on record at *about* the age of seventeen. We believe you came from a D.P. camp in the Middle East, and there was no way to check your exact age."

"I can't help you there, Mr. Fraser," she said gravely. "I've never been able to check it myself."

"I see. Well, to summarise, you were a stateless person, and at this approximate age of seventeen we have you working in a small gambling establishment in Tangier. It was controlled by the Louche group—Henri Louche being a man who headed a small criminal organisation. On his death at the hands of rivals one year later, you took control and there followed a remarkable expansion."

Fraser looked up from the dossier owlishly.

"I am not," he said, "at this stage differentiating between items of fact and items of supposition, you understand?"

"That's very wise, Mr. Fraser." She rose, picked up a silver cigarette box and offered it to Fraser. The cigarettes were Perfecto Finos. When he declined, she took one herself and set a humidor of cigars at Tarrant's elbow.

"I wasn't expecting you," she said. "I'm afraid there's only a choice of Burma cheroots and Petit Coronas."

"I shall enjoy a Petit Corona, thank you. But what if you had been expecting me, Miss Blaise?"

"You smoke a Punch-Punch claro, I believe."

"I do." He rolled the cigar gently between his fingers, watching her as she returned to her seat. "Willie Garvin has an eye for detail. Your dossier on me must be quite exhaustive."

"It was. But it wasn't dull. Please go on, Mr. Fraser."

"The group," said Fraser, turning a page, "under the—ah—new management, became known in due course as The Network and operated on an international scale. The crimes included art and jewel thefts; smuggling; currency and gold manipulations; and an espionage service."

"My own information," she said, exhaling a feather of smoke, "is that The Network at no time traded in secrets belonging to Her Majesty's Government."

"We have wondered about that," Tarrant said reflectively. "Can you suggest a reason?"

"It might be that the responsible person wanted to settle here eventually, and had no wish to be considered undesirable."

"Why here?"

"That could be a long story. I don't think it's important."

"We also note," Fraser said dubiously, "that The Network abstained completely from two profitable fields of crime—drugs and vice. On two occasions it gave valuable help to the United States Bureau of Narcotics."

She nodded. "So I believe. I suppose if one takes a point of view one must act positively when opportunity offers."

"In 1962," said Fraser, "we have as a fact that you married and divorced a derelict Englishman in Beirut. We believe this was a purely financial arrangement for gaining British nationality."

"Yes. Very purely." Again the sudden smile briefly lit her face. Fraser cleared his throat, looked embarrassed, and stared down at the typescript.

"So," he went on, "we now go back to the time two or three years after you started The Network, when you were joined by William Garvin. We have his personal dossier as an appendix here." He fluttered some pages. "He was in an approved school in England, and later served two short prison sentences before disappearing abroad. There, for a number of years, he was in many kinds of trouble in different parts of the world. I will omit what details we have, but we believe you found him in Saigon, soon after he was discharged from the Foreign Legion. From that point on, we—ah—move into the field of speculation again."

Fraser paused and drank some brandy. Fraser was a brandy man, and Tarrant watched with interest his struggle to suppress a look of astonished pleasure. Bravely, after a frozen moment, Fraser put down the glass and wrinkled his nose noncommittally.

"It would seem," he said, returning to the dossier, "that Garvin was a close associate of yours for six or seven years, Miss Blaise—until last year, in fact, when The Network was split up among its various—er—branch-managers in different countries."

He closed the folder and looked up archly. "We know that you both came to this country eleven months ago, Miss Blaise, and we know that Garvin bought a public house called *The Treadmill,* on the river. We also know that you are both extremely wealthy, which may explain why there has been no hint," he paused and gave a furtive leer, "of any—um—illegal activities since that time."

"Very good," said Tarrant. "Beautifully articulated, Fraser. You have delightful vowels." He received the expected simper of demurral, and glanced across at Modesty Blaise enquiringly.

"It's interesting," she said slowly, "but as you say, mainly speculation. I don't feel you can use it for any drastic move."

"I've no thought of using it." Tarrant paused, and there was silence. One good thing about this girl was that silence didn't worry her. She allowed time to think, without rushing to fill the gaps.

Tarrant was thinking now, and he was conscious of disappointment. This girl fascinated him. She was beautiful and stimulating. Her serenity, against the strange dark background of her life, was enormously exciting. But so far there was something missing—a quality he had learned to sense in his agents as he could sense the quality of a fine cigar before smoking it.

This was a thing hard to define. More of a potential than a quality, perhaps. The potential for cold ferocity joined to an inflexible will. Good God, she must have had it once. Could she have lost it now? So far he had caught no hint of it in Modesty Blaise. She was perfectly relaxed, perfectly controlled, and that was right. But he could detect nothing of the vital potential to turn tiger. Was the core of steel rusted and the flame of will dead?

"Far from using our suspicions against you in any way," he said amiably, "we rather hoped you might be useful to us."

She drank from the glass of red wine, not taking her eyes from him.

"Nobody uses me, Sir Gerald," she answered very quietly. "Nobody. I made up my mind about that long ago—before that dossier begins."

"I understand. But I hoped to persuade you."

"How?" She looked at him curiously. Tarrant studied the tip of his cigar and glanced casually across at Fraser, who sat with one hand resting on his knee. The fingers and thumb were straight, and close together; the hand was palm down. Fraser's opinion was that this should be played straight. Tarrant agreed.

"We realize it would be pointless to offer you money, Miss Blaise," he said. "But we can offer you Willie Garvin."

"Willie?" The dark eyebrows arched upwards.

"Yes. Have you been in touch with him recently?"

"Not for about six weeks. Then he was in town for a couple of nights and spent them here. We went back to *The Treadmill* together for the weekend to try his new speedboat. After that I spent a month with some friends in Capri, and got back a week ago. I haven't been in touch again yet."

"You won't find him at *The Treadmill*."

"That doesn't surprise me. Willie's dream of running his own little pub has palled rather quickly. He moves around quite a lot—and he has a wonderfully varied list of girl-friends. From *premier cru* to honest *vin du pays*."

"Garvin isn't indulging his romantic palate. He's a very long way away, on the other side of the world. And he's in prison, Miss Blaise. Not under his own name, I may say. But I suppose it hardly matters what name a man is hanged under."

Then it came, and Tarrant savoured it with infinite joy. Modesty Blaise had not changed her expression or posture by a hair's-breadth. She still sat with legs drawn up at one end of the couch, the glass of wine in her hand. Nothing had altered. Yet suddenly the whole room seemed charged with the crackling emanation of force from that still figure.

To Tarrant it came as the briny scent of a storm, when the static potential builds up to breaking point before discharging to earth in a savage explosion of energy.

"Hanged?" Her voice was still mellow. As mellow, thought Tarrant, as the martial call of Roland's horn.

"Or shot," he answered with a slight gesture. "It's not exactly imminent because the situation in . . . in the place where Garvin finds himself is still a little confused. I feel there might just be time for somebody to do something—if they managed it within the next eight or nine days."

Modesty Blaise crushed out the half-smoked Perfecto Fino and drew a jar of Sèvres porcelain towards her. From it she took thick black tobacco and a yellow paper. Absently, with practised ease, she spread tobacco along the paper, rolled and lit it.

"This is all a little cryptic, Sir Gerald," she said.

"Yes. Intentionally so, of course."

"You want to use me for—?"

"For one operation," he broke in quickly. "One special job, my dear. That's all. It's something you're uniquely fitted for, and it may prove to be no more than a watching brief."

"In return, you'll tell me where Willie Garvin is now?"

Her question hung on the air. Tarrant drank and put down his glass. Fraser's hand, still resting on his knee, had turned and was loosely curled. Opinion—put the screw on hard. Tarrant reviewed the advice and rejected it.

"No," he said, rising. "We'll make it a gift, Miss Blaise. And we'll go now, since I'm sure you'll have a lot to arrange in a very short time. Fraser, pass Miss Blaise the copy of that message, please."

For an instant Fraser's eyes widened in genuine surprise, then he re-
covered and ducked his head obsequiously, fumbling in his briefcase. She
took the buff half-sheet from him and paced slowly across to the huge
window, reading it, the cigarette clipped between her fingers.

"Thank you." She returned to where the two men stood waiting, and
handed the slip to Fraser, her eyes on Tarrant. "I take it this job of yours
isn't too immediate, Sir Gerald. I shall be out of the country for the next ten
days or so."

"If I might talk to you when you return, it would be very satisfactory."
He took her hand. "Goodbye, and I hope your trip goes well."

"Thank you again." She walked with them to the raised foyer and the
lift. The doors slid back as she pressed two buttons on the control-panel.

"You're a clever man, Sir Gerald." She looked at him with frank interest. "How did you know?"

"I'm sorry. Know what?"

"That I hate blackmail. But that I'm a compulsive payer of debts. I'm
sure that isn't in my dossier."

"No." Tarrant picked up his hat and umbrella. "But I've met your Willie
Garvin."

"He wouldn't have discussed me."

"Indeed not. But he's not an enigma—I found him easy to read. And I
felt he must reflect you. After all, you created him."

Fraser seized the opening.

"Like master, like man," he said portentously and with hidden delight.

When the two men had gone she stood by the window looking out
across the dark park while she finished her cigarette. Once she half smiled
and shook her head.

"Should have seen it coming," she murmured. "Hard to blame you,
Willie. My God, I know just how you felt."

She stubbed out the cigarette and went to the telephone. For the next
hour she was busy making several calls, one to a startled man eight
thousand miles away. When this was done she went through into her
bedroom, of pale green, ivory and silver-grey. The wall was panelled, and
the panel to the right of the big double bed was of painted steel. It opened
by the setting of the dressing-table drawers in a particular order and position, and it moved on soundless bearings.

Beyond lay a tall cubby-hole, six feet square, originally intended as a
walk-in wardrobe. For a moment she stood looking at the three heavy
trunks which stood on the floor, and at the variety of smaller boxes on the
side-shelves. There was a glint of amused resignation in her eyes.

"I wonder why we kept all our gear, Willie love?" she said aloud.

Bending, she began to open one of the trunks.

In the parked car, Fraser sat behind the wheel and spoke with the pinched approval of the loser congratulating the winner.

"I feel you handled that with great success, Sir Gerald, if I may say so. I didn't dare to hope that putting her in debt would be effective."

"You may say so, Fraser. You may. But I take it you realise that putting her in our debt was almost irrelevant?"

"I beg your pardon?"

"She's lived on a dangerous tight-rope for the best part of twenty-six years. How easy do you think it is to stop?"

"But she has achieved her ambition, sir. Half a million or so, and a life to match."

"Meaningless. Or tragic, perhaps. Danger can be a drug, and she's hooked by it. Dammit man, you were still hooked by it yourself at nearly twice her age. I had to *drag* you behind a desk. This girl doesn't show it, of course. She's totally controlled. But the withdrawal pains must be there." His voice grew dry. "They didn't show with Willie Garvin until now."

"I'm sorry." Faser swallowed miserably and shot him a hunted look. "I haven't taken your point yet, sir. You seem to be saying that putting her in debt over Garvin isn't the *real* reason that we were able to get her."

"It's the excuse," Tarrant said softly. "She needed an excuse, whether she knows it or not. I wasn't looking for a way to force her. I was looking for the right way to *let* her do this job for us, Jack."

The use of the first name called a halt to the game Fraser loved, and signalled that for the time being play was suspended. Fraser relaxed and rested his arms on the wheel, a slow grin spreading over his face.

"Well stuff me standing load," he said admiringly. "You bloody old fox."

## Two

Modesty Blaise stood with her flank against the trunk of a palm, some ten feet from the thinning fringe of trees. Night had long since fallen. The bellbirds and parrots were silent, and from behind her there came only the rustle and murmur of the living forest. From a star-splashed sky a waning moon glinted down upon the metalled road which wound between the forest and the savanna.

The prison stood in a half-circle of beaten earth where the ground had been cleared in a wide curve reaching back from the road. It was a temporary prison, converted from a barracks, a long single-storied building of adobe, shaped like a letter T. The cross of the T faced the road, the upright jutted back towards the trees, with a wide door at its base. Immediately beyond the door lay the guard-room.

Modesty had stood there, motionless, for two hours now. Every ten minutes a ragged sentry with a slung Garand rifle passed within thirty feet of her on his beat. A useless sentry, she thought. You could hear him coming and going, catch the clink of rifle on bandolier, and see the red glow of his cigarette a hundred yards away.

Six weeks ago he had been a rebel. Now he and the rest of his friends were Government troops. The ex-Government troops were now the rebels, but not for much longer. General Kalzaro's coup had succeeded beyond the point of reverse, beyond the point where he needed to be prudent about disposing of those who had fought on the losing side.

Six days had passed since her meeting with Tarrant, and she knew now that his assessment of the situation had been a shrewd one. Santos, in Buenos Aires, had confirmed that assessment only forty-eight hours ago. If Willie Garvin was to be brought out alive it would have to be very soon.

She wore black denim slacks, loose enough in the leg for free movement, the bottoms tucked into thick-soled combat boots. A thin black polo-neck sweater covered her body, neck and arms. Her hands and face were dark with camouflage cream. The high chignon of her hair was now a short, tightly-bound club hanging at the nape of her neck.

She watched a ramshackle truck pull away from the prison and out on to the road. Its grass-stuffed tyres squealed as it jolted away round the bend, carrying the day-guards who supervised working-parties of prisoners repairing the road two miles north. Fifteen minutes later the sentry patrolling this rear beat of the unfenced perimeter was relieved.

Soon now she could begin. The tingling warmth within her spread in a glow of curious happiness through every part of her being. She resented it, tried to quell it, then yielded in the wry knowledge of wasted energy.

You couldn't make yourself over again at twenty-six. She had learned that lesson over the past twelve months. Willie must have learned it too, and studiously hidden it from her as she had hidden it from him.

In the dark years long gone, almost from the first dawnings of memory, each night and each day had held fear and danger for the lone child moving like some small wild creature through the war-turmoil of the Balkans and the Levant. But later, with puberty, there came a time when fear was transmuted into stimulus, and the moments of danger which had once brought terror now brought only a keener sense of being alive.

It was a pity. There were so many better ways of living fully. But it was too late now, and she had long ago learned not to cry for the unattainable.

The new sentry was starting his return beat from the west. Modesty flexed her fingers round the little object in her right hand. It was a kongo, or yawara-stick, a thing of hard smooth wood, shaped like an elongated dumb-bell so that the shaft fitted into the palm with the mushroom-shaped ends protruding from the clenched fist.

Placing her feet carefully, she moved forward. There was no sound, for the ground was covered with a thick moist carpet of rotting leaves.

The sentry was thinking about women, specifically about a girl in the village they had taken a week ago. That had been a night. He grinned at the memory, his blood stirring.

She was about eighteen, and completely new to it, but obedient as a cowed bitch once Sergeant Alvarez had explained how it would be for her otherwise. It was Alvarez, too, who had produced the amusing idea of offering a bottle of whisky to whichever of the six men could devise the most imaginative position.

Ricco had won, of course. The sentry chuckled admiringly at the memory. It was a miracle the old sod hadn't pulled a leg muscle, or suffocated the girl—

Something white lay on the ground ahead and to one side, near the bole of a tree. He moved forward, peering. It was a square piece of paper, but with something resting on it. He bent closer. A coin. A *gold* coin . . .

Modesty moved out behind the bent form. One hand darted out to grip him by the hair, the other came down like a hammer, the lower butt of the kongo striking precisely below the ear.

He slumped bonelessly, and she caught the rifle, lowering it with him. From the small pocket on her left thigh she took a slender metal tube and uncapped it. Into her palm she tipped two little white cylinders of compressed cotton-wool, about the size of cigarette-tips. She sniffed them warily, catching the faint, sickly-sweet smell, then knelt and slid them into the man's nostrils.

Her feet made no sound as she moved swiftly across the open stretch of beaten earth towards the pool of light which spread from the lamp above the open door. Here, to one side of the door, a man leaned against the wall looking at a tattered girlie magazine, his rifle propped beside him. She circled a little to approach him from the side, edging along the wall, her back flat against it.

When she was six feet away he lifted his head. Even as shock widened his eyes she took one long pace and twisted to bring her leg swinging in an arc. The booted foot took him full in the groin. For an instant the unconscious body was rigid with paralysis, then it melted slowly to the ground. No need for the anaesthetic nose-plugs.

She stepped over him and went throught the doorway. Now the kongo was in her left hand, and in her right was the little MAB Brevete automatic, drawn from the soft leather holster belted beneath her sweater. The gun was no stopper, unless you were very accurate. Modesty Blaise was very accurate. And the advantage lay in the gun's comparative quietness.

Ahead of her was a long, broad corridor with steel-barred cell doors on either side. From it came the stench of unwashed humanity, the wailing of a man broken by fear, and the shrill, gasping cries of one in a nightmare.

On her right, the heavy door of the guard-room stood half open. Within, a radio was blaring martial music interspersed by news bulletins gabbled at a high pitch of excitement.

Modesty spent two seconds reviewing alternatives. She would have liked to push on, but had learned the hard way that nothing was more vital than to secure the line of retreat. There was a white bullet-scar on her flank, just below the buttock, to remind her of the penalty for neglect.

She slipped the kongo into its squeeze-pouch in the ribbing at the bottom of her sweater. From the stretch-pocket on the front of her right thigh she drew out a curious object consisting of a nose-clip and a mouthpiece, with a small drum, one inch deep, connecting the two. A miniature gas-mask.

For a moment she hesitated over whether to use The Nailer. This meant taking off her sweater and bra, and going into the room stripped to the waist. She felt no reticence about the idea, for it was a highly practical one, first improvised on a life-and-death occasion with Willie Garvin in Agrigento five years ago, and she had proved it twice since. The technique was guaranteed to nail a roomful of men, holding them frozen for at least two or three vital seconds.

She decided that it was unnecessary here. With the guards relaxed and unsuspecting, The Nailer was superfluous. Quickly she fixed the gas-mask on, the clip gripping her nose, her lips holding the rubbery mouthpiece firmly against her gums.

She pushed open the door and moved in, eyes sweeping the whole room on the instant of entry. Four soldiers sat round an upturned crate playing cards. The window beyond them was shuttered. Good. The men were grouped in a limited target. Better still. They sat frozen, eight eyes staring towards her, a hand rigid in the act of gathering scattered cards for the deal.

The man facing her was burly and wore sergeant's stripes on his grubby jacket. He was the first to recover, and as she kicked the door shut behind her she tabbed him as the danger-man. A slow grin began to spread across the stubbly face as his eyes moved from the strangely obscured features to the thrust of her breasts and curves of her body.

She moved the gun slightly, drawing his eyes so that he stared straight at the round black eye of the automatic, as steady as if held in a clamp. The grin faded and the eyes narrowed watchfully.

From the other thigh-pocket she drew out a black, domed metal cylinder. It was like a pepper-pot. She moved forward and reached out to place it on the crate. For that moment her gun hand was no more than a foot from the shoulder of one of the men. She sensed the inward tensing of his muscles for sudden movement, but she kept the gun aimed unwaveringly at the middle of the sergeant's face. A bead of sweat trickled down his brow, and he rapped out a savage whisper of command in Spanish. *"Don't move, you son of a pig!"*

The man hesitated. She put down the squat pepper-pot and heard the faint click of the mechanism at its base as she stepped back two paces. A soft hissing came from the pepper-pot, barely audible under the blaring radio.

The sergeant stared, sniffed in renewed alarm, then looked at her with vicious eyes. His left hand still lay splayed on the crate, over some cards. His right began to creep slowly round his belt to the holstered revolver there.

For an instant she altered her aim, and the gun yapped sharply. A bullet drilled into the crate between two of his spread fingers, throwing up a little crater of splinters. The olive face grew grey, and he sat like a statue, eyes fixed on the hissing cylinder like the eyes of a hypnotised rabbit.

One man lurched sideways and crumpled to the floor. The sergeant and, another fell only five seconds later. With an inward wave of laughter she saw that the fourth man was holding his breath. His face was growing darker and his eyes bulged in hopeless desperation.

There came an explosive huff of exhaled air and the long sighing sob of helplessly indrawn breath. Still glaring stonily, the eyes closed and he keeled over.

Modesty turned to the two things she had marked on the wall in that first photographic survey of the room—a bunch of large keys on a ring, hanging on a hook; and beneath them, on the same hook, a curious harness of black elasticised webbing, a chest harness. Attached to it were two slim black sheaths of hard leather, each bearing a flat, black-handled throwing knife.

Later, when danger was past and she could unblock her mind to feeling again, this moment would bring a strange mixture of emotions. There was the warmth of happening upon a souvenir of times past. There was the sadness of seeing a symbol that marked a vain pipe-dream, never to be realised. And there was the touch of something like fear in seeing this thing alone, separate from the man of whom it was a part.

She took down the keys and the harness, moved quickly out of the room, and closed the door. Quietly she began to move down the broad corridor between the cells, taking the gas-mask off as she went.

Willie Garvin lay on the splintered boards of a narrow bunk, hands behind his head, staring dully at a lizard on the cracked ceiling of the cell. A wedge of light from the passage threw the bars of the door in broad black shadows across the stone floor.

He was a big man, an inch or two over six feet, thirty-four years old, with tousled fair hair and blue eyes set in a face made up of small flat planes. His hand were large, with square-tipped fingers, and his body was hard and well-muscled, particularly the powerful deltoids running from neck to shoulder.

On the back of his right hand was a big scar, shaped like an uncompleted S. It had been made with a red-hot knife-blade, wielded carefully by a man called Suleiman, and it was uncompleted because Modesty Blaise had come into that room beneath the warehouse and killed Suleiman by breaking his neck, using the man's own considerable weight to do it.

Alone in the tiny cell, Willie Garvin lay with a grey lethargy blanketing his mind. It was like the old days, the grimy, pointless and hated days, which stretched back from a time seven years ago through the whole of his life; the days before Modesty Blaise, who had suddenly and magically turned his world upside down and made everything All Right.

But now the light that had been turned on in his head throughout those seven years was no longer there. The old groping obscurity was back.

Willie Garvin knew that he should be doing something. A crummy load of ragged-arsed soldiers had caught him and put him in gaol and were going to shoot him soon. If this had been a couple of years back, and on a caper for The Princess, it would have been a dawdle. His mind would have been buzzing with ideas. Given two hours he could have figured six different capers for walking out of this stinking hole.

But a couple of years back he would never have got himself into this anyway—not against such half-hard opposition.

He felt sickened by himself, but there was nothing to be done now because the light had gone out and the wheels in his head had stopped turning. After seven years in which he had walked like a man ten feet tall, he was back in the void again, without anchor or purpose or hope. And soon he would be dead.

"Christ, she'll be mad at me when she hears," Willie thought vaguely.

Something clinked gently against the bars of the door. He turned his head and saw the black figure half-crouched in the wedge of light.

There was no instant of delay in recognition. Willie Garvin sat up unhurriedly, swung his feet to the ground, and walked quietly to the door. In that time, smoothly and quite undramatically, the light in his head was there again and the wheels were turning. The recent past fell away like a fading dream.

She looked at him carefully, gave a little nod, then passed the knife-harness through the bars and began methodically to try the six keys. Willie stripped off his grimy shirt, slipped the harness in place, with the hilts of the knives lying snugly in echelon against his left breast, and put on the shirt again, leaving it unbuttoned from the top to a few inches above the waist.

A key turned and the door swung open. Across the flagged corridor a huddle of four gaunt prisoners in a small cell stared with dull, incurious eyes. Modesty put the keys down on the floor, a bare arm's-reach from them, and saw hope spark in their faces. She nodded to Willie. A knife was in his hand now, held by the point between two fingers and thumb.

They walked side by side along the middle of the corridor at an unhurried pace, and turned at the T-junction along the shorter stretch which led to the guardroom at the end.

Modesty felt the comforting glow of familiarity expanding within her, and sensed the same in Willie. She was moving half-turned to watch the rear and left, so she could not look at him, but she knew that his eyes would be scanning front and right, calmly alert for the first hint of trouble. There was no point in telling him to use minimum force. He would know.

They were ten yards from the open doorway when there came a startled exclamation from outside, and she knew the unconscious soldier there had been found. A man appeared in the doorway, hurriedly bringing his rifle round from the slung position. They moved on without change of pace under his shaken stare.

The rifle came to bear, and they split to either side of the broad corridor, offering separate targets. The soldier swung his rifle uncertainly from one to the other as he fumbled with the bolt.

Modesty lifted her automatic, and like a magnet drew the rifle-barrel towards her as the bolt snicked back.

Willie's move.

He dived, somersaulting, and the rifle swung frantically back to cover him. But one foot hooked behind the soldier's ankle, the other drove for his knee, and the man went down flat on his back as if drawn by a coiled spring attached to the back of his neck. As the breath exploded from his lungs Modesty's boot swung with controlled force to the side of his head.

Willie was on his feet, coming up with that flickering shoulder-spring— the one move she had never been able to learn for all his patient teaching.

They moved on, easing warily round the stone uprights of the doorway, and facing opposite ways.

All clear. Modesty turned and nodded. Together they ran hard for the trees.

As the thick layer of decaying vegetation sank underfoot there came an outbreak of shouting from the prison. Scattered shots began to sound from the road which formed the front of the perimeter. Some of the prisoners were out, and confusion was beginning.

Modesty slowed to a steady pace. They ran on through vine-hung trees and small clearings. Dappled moonlight touched them as it filtered through the trees. Every fifty yards a scrap of white paper pinned to a tree-trunk charted their route. After half a mile they emerged on to a narrow dirt road.

The car, a black Chrysler, was parked behind a clump of shoulder-high grass. Willie held the door open for Modesty to take the wheel, then ran round to the passenger seat. With dipped headlights the car lifted from the bumpy verge and on to the road. Modesty held the speed at fifty in third until they reached the junction with the metalled road, then slipped into top and pressed the accelerator hard down.

There was a long silence, broken only by the smooth purr of the engine and the drumming of tyres. She was aware that Willie, beside her, was no longer at ease as he had been throughout the action. He sat very upright, tense and awkward. A quick glance at the mirror showed her the sheepish apprehension on his brown face.

Hesitantly he felt in the glove-compartment, found cigarettes, and lit two of them, passing one to her. She took it and inhaled, keeping her eyes on the dark road.

"Over the border in half-an-hour," she said quietly. "No problem there. I spread a gold carpet on the way in."

"I'm sorry, Princess." Willie Garvin shifted uneasily. "You didn't ought to 've come."

"No?" She snapped a glance at him. "They were all set to top you, Willie, you damn fool. And I wouldn't even have known if Tarrant hadn't told me."

"Tarrant?"

"The same one."

"That was decent of 'im." He frowned. "But there'll be a pay-off?"

She made no answer, letting him sweat. This was the first time in many years that she had needed to jolt Willie, but he had asked for it and he knew it.

"How d'you get here, Princess?" he asked after a while.

"I heard about you from Tarrant a week ago, booked a flight, and rang Santos in B.A. Asked him to set up a quick in-and-out job for me—the layout, the bribes, everything."

"You *asked* 'im?" There was a touch of indignation in Willie's voice.

"I couldn't tell him. Santos doesn't work for me any longer. Remember?"

"But he played ball, anyway?"

"He knew I'd break his arms if he didn't." Her tone sharpened. "What the hell got into you, Willie? We quit, didn't we? No more crime. We made our pile, split up the organization, and quit."

"I wasn't going bent again, Princess—"

"Be quiet and listen, Willie love." She felt the swift relief in him at her use of the old familiar term. "You've got a bankful of money and a nice little pub on the river. All you ever wanted. So why come out here and get tangled up as a mercenary in a banana-state revolution?"

Willie sighed. "My manager runs the pub better'n I could," he said with a touch of bitterness. "I was going bonkers, Princess, honest. Up the wall. I 'ad to 'ave a break."

"Did you have to get caught? And my God, *stay* caught? Willie, it's humiliating. You've gone solo for me often enough before."

"Yes—for you. It's always been easy when you told me to go an' do it." He ran a hand through his hair. "I just couldn't get me 'eart into this lot, Princess. Being on me tod, everything just seemed to shut down. I was scared it might . . . but I 'ad to do *something*." He inhaled broodingly on his cigarette. "It's no good. Retirement don't suit me some'ow. I dunno 'ow you stick it," he ended respectfully.

Modesty swung the car off the main road and on to another track, following Santos's careful instructions to the letter.

"Neither do I," she said in a neutral voice. "This is the first time I've come alive in a year."

Willie sat up straight and turned to stare at her.

"Well, then," he said softly. "Look, suppose we went back on the old caper, Princess? Start fresh and build up a new Network—?"

"It wouldn't have any point now. We've got all we wanted. And without a point, we'd soon lose out."

He nodded bleakly. The light was full and clear in his head now, the wheels meshing smoothly, and he knew that her words were true.

"Then what we going to do?" he asked helplessly. "I mean, just for a break now an' then! *You* know how it is, Princess. The bits between capers are good, but only because they're in between. Without the capers it's all just . . . just stale beer."

"Tarrant's pay-off," she said slowly. "It's a job he wants done. But I don't know anything about it yet."

"Us working under Tarrant?" There was mingled hope and annoyance in Willie's voice.

"Not under. For him. On a particular job. And he didn't pressure me, Willie. But I don't know about 'us.' This latest effort of yours won't have impressed him."

"Ah, look Princess! That's different. You can tell Tarrant. I mean, I never laid an egg like this before, all the time I worked for you, did I?"

"No. But that's over now, Willie. I can't bring you in just because I might need help. It means you taking orders from me again. And you're a big boy now. I want you to be your own man."

"I don't." He spoke with flat desperation. "If you don't take me back, I'm a goner."

"Oh, Willie . . . I don't know." She was troubled. "Look, we'll see what Tarrant brings. But I hate taking you for granted, and I won't have Tarrant do it, either. Just leave it with me and keep your nose clean. I don't want you in any more trouble."

"Don't worry, Princess. I've been a right burk. I'm sorry."

"I won't worry." The lights of the small border-post showed ahead, and she lifted her foot, turning to look full at him for a moment. Willie saw the rare smile that suddenly lit her face, the smile worth waiting a week for. "All I'm worrying about now is flight schedules, Willie. I've got a date at Covent Garden on Tuesday."

# STUDY QUESTIONS

1. Eudora Welty's "A Worn Path" depicts a woman imprisoned by poverty. Nevertheless, in what way is she free?

2. Because he combines strength and emotional expressiveness, Biff Brannon in Carson McCullers' "Biff" is a rarity in American literature. Write an essay in which you explain why this may be so, or describe a male character in another work who is similarly portrayed.

3. Select a myth from our own culture that stereotypes one or both sexes. Revise it in the way Monique Wittig does in "A Women's Community" to portray a more balanced view of sex roles.

4. What kind of a person is Garp in John Irving's story? Are you comfortable with the kind of fathering he does?

5. Do you think there are any activities or occupations that only one sex should perform, or do you agree with views expressed in "He Bear She Bear"? Defend your idea.

6. How has Betty Miles changed the traditional Atalanta myth in her version of it? Why has each alteration been made?

7. Many have compared Modesty Blaise to Ian Fleming's James Bond. How are they alike and in what important ways are they different?

# Bibliography

## Part I: Development of Sex-Role Attitudes

*Fiction*

BROOKS, GWENDOLYN. *Maud Martha*. New York: AMS Press, 1974.

McCARTHY, MARY. *Memories of a Catholic Girlhood*. New York: Harcourt Brace Jovanovich, 1972.

McCULLERS, CARSON. "Wunderkind." In *The Ballad of the Sad Cafe: The Novels and Stories of Carson McCullers*. New York: Houghton Mifflin, 1955.

PORTER, KATHERINE ANNE. "The Grave." In *The Collected Stories of Katherine Anne Porter*. New York: Harcourt Brace and World, 1930.

ROTH, PHILIP. *Portnoy's Complaint*. New York: Bantam, 1972.

STAFFORD, JEAN. "Cops and Robbers." In *The Collected Stories of Jean Stafford*. New York: Farrar Straus & Giroux, 1953.

*Research and Popular Culture*

DARROW, WHITNEY, JR. *I'm Glad I'm A Boy! I'm Glad I'm A Girl!* New York: Windmill Books, n.d.

MACCOBY, ELEANOR EMMONS, and CAROL NAGY JACKLIN. "On the Origins of Psychological Sex Differences." In *The Psychology of Sex Differences*. Stanford, Calif.: Stanford University Press, 1974.

PETRAS, JOHN W. *Sex: Male/Gender: Masculine.* Port Washington, N.Y.: Alfred Publishing, 1975.

SERBIN, LISA A., and DANIEL K. O'LEARY. "How Nursery Schools Teach Girls to Shut Up." *Psychology Today*, December 1975.

TUCHMAN, GAYE; ARLENE KAPLAN DANIELS; and JAMES BINET, eds. *Hearth and Home: Images of Women in the Mass Media*. New York: Oxford University Press, 1978.

## Part II: Examining Sex-Role Stereotypes

*Fiction*

FAULKNER, WILLIAM. "A Rose for Emily." In *Collected Stories of William Faulkner*. New York: Random House, 1977.

JOHNSON, DOROTHY M. *A Man Called Horse*. New York: Ballantine, 1973.